Dealing with an International Clientele:
Communications, Diplomacy and Etiquette

Information Services Management Series

Series Editor: *Guy St Clair*

Meri Meredith

Dealing with an International Clientele:
Communications, Diplomacy and Etiquette

K· G· Saur München 2005

Bibliographic information published by Die Deutsche Bibliothek
Die Deutsche Bibliothek lists this publication in the Deutsche Nationalbibliografie;
detailed bibliographic data is available in the internet at http://dnb.ddb.de.

Printed on acid-free paper

Typesetting by Florence Production Ltd., Stoodleigh, Devon, Great Britain.
Printed and bound by Strauss GmbH, Mörlenbach, Germany.
ISBN 3-598-24370-7

About the author

Meri Meredith is an Assistant Professor at the Ohio State University. She is also the Reference Librarian there in the Business Library. She has over twenty years of experience working with people from around the world, first as the head of the Business Library for Cummins Engine Company, a Fortune 500 company and a multinational corporation with locations throughout the world. She has published numerous articles in the international arena.

Dedication:
I dedicate this book to my heavenly Father
who was with me in every step of this journey.

Introduction to the series

A Broader Management Perspective for Information Services

Since the early 1990s, when the development of *The Information Services Management Series* was first thought about, particular effort has been given to bringing general management theory and practice to the work of those with information delivery responsibility. For several years – decades, it seemed – librarians and other information professionals (and particularly those with oversight responsibility for information workers) lamented the fact that there was not enough emphasis on management in their education and training. These practitioners did of course learn their subjects, and librarians especially connected very early on in their training to the concepts of service and the organization of information. But management skills were – and, sadly, in some cases still are – neglected or given minimal attention. Many of these practitioners (who we now generally refer to as 'knowledge services professionals') find themselves working in the corporate environment, in research and technology organizations, in government information units, in community/public administration organizations, and in similar situations where management skills are required. They discover, to their sorrow, that they are simply not prepared to take on management responsibility. Of course many of these people get what they need from on-the-job training and experience, and other approaches, such as continuing education programs, are utilized by those who have the initiative to recognize that they must do something to educate themselves to be managers.

Some of it works and some of it does not.

The Information Services Management Series, for which I serve as Series Editor, seeks to address this need. The series was conceived as a specific and conscientious effort to bring a management focus to information services, and in making this effort, the publishers, editors, and authors took special pains to ensure that this message, this linking of

organizational management to service delivery, was broadcast far and
wide. Special attention was given to presenting management concepts
that would serve librarianship but, at that same time, would appeal
beyond that specific information delivery environment. Looking back, this
effort has been notably successful, for the books in the series have been
consistently well received. And if – as we generally suppose – imitation
is the sincerest form of flattery, success has certainly been achieved, for
considerable attention is now given in the literature to the marriage of
organizational management and information delivery, and readers seeking
further knowledge in these areas now have much to choose from.

Such success should not be surprising, though, since the authors of
these books have carefully sought to address this need for bringing
management and information delivery together. When the series began,
the audience for the books, the information services community, was
intentionally defined very broadly. The time had come to recognize that
the various constituent units of our society concerned with information
have many of the same goals and objectives, and, not surprisingly, many
of the same concerns. The practice of management was, and is, one of
these concerns, and for our purposes it does not matter if the reader is
employed as an information manager, information provider, information
specialist, or indeed, as an information counsellor (as these information
workers have been described by one business leader). In fact, it does
not matter whether the reader of these books is employed in information technology, telecommunications, traditional librarianship, specialized
librarianship, records management, corporate or organization archives, the
information brokerage field, publishing, consulting, or any of the myriad
branches of information services (including service to the information
community and the many vendors who make up that branch of the
profession). These new titles on the management of information services
have been chosen specifically for their value to all who are part of this
community of information workers.

In fact, at this point in time, and particularly with the publication of
the current volume of the series, it is entirely appropriate to acknowledge
that perceptions are changing, both in society at large and, specifically,
within the general management field. Naturally the nomenclature of
service delivery in what we formerly referred to as 'information services'
is changing as well. We have now seen a shift from thinking about information – and the management of information – as a cultural entity in and
of itself to something else, altogether different. Indeed, it is now being
acknowledged that, for most of us, information is only of value when it
is used to produce knowledge. While this relationship between information and knowledge has existed throughout history, as a society we've
not previously put it together in exactly this way before. Now, as this
acknowledgement is being made, and especially during the last decade
or so, the whole notion of information management as a discipline and,

indeed, of information services as an operational function, has been turned upside down. Now information customers openly and frankly identify their quest with what they are going to do with the information, with how they are going to turn the information into knowledge for some particular purpose and use. As a consequence of this change in customers' requirements and expectations, those with information delivery responsibility must now provide information customized to how it will be used. Thus new disciplines have been added to those described above (with others being added every day!), and that community of information workers is now a community of knowledge services workers, a community that includes knowledge management professionals and training and learning professionals as well as information management professionals.

Although much work is being done in the various professions, disciplines, and types of work that make up this community of knowledge services workers, not much of it concentrates on management, and that work which is done generally concentrates on one or another of the specific subgroups of knowledge services. This series seeks to unite management concepts throughout knowledge services, and whereas some of the titles will be directed to a specific group, most will be broad-based and will attempt to address issues of concern to all information services employees. For example, one book in the series deals with entrepreneurial librarianship, which would seem limited to the library profession but in fact offers information and guidance to anyone working in knowledge services who is willing to incorporate entrepreneurial thinking into his or her work. Another book in the series looks at the information audit as a management tool, and the audit concept presented in the book can be applied to any service delivery activity, whether it has to do with information management, knowledge management, or learning. Yet a third book looks at how information leaders are developed and how the talents of the younger generation of information employees can be directed toward professional leadership. While the book ostensibly describes techniques for the information management profession, in fact these techniques can be generously and successfully applied to any younger employee working in any of the professions, disciplines, or types of work that make up knowledge services.

As we attempt to bring general management practices into the realm of knowledge services, it will be pointed out that the practice of management is addressed within the organizations, enterprises, and communities that employ knowledge workers. This is true, and certainly within the for-profit sector (and, arguably, in the nonprofit and not-for-profit communities as well) there are plenty of occasions for knowledge workers to participate in management training as provided in-house. There is nothing wrong with that approach and in many organizations it works very well, but the training does not proceed from a knowledge services point of view. Thus the knowledge services professional is forced to adapt, as best he or she can, the management practices of the organization to the management practices needed for the best provision of information, knowledge, and learning delivery. The books of *The Information Services Management Series* will enable the knowledge services worker to relate *knowledge services* management to *organizational* management, thus putting the knowledge workers (especially those with executive responsibility for such functions) in a position of considerable strength in the enterprise, organization, or community where they are employed. By understanding management principles (admittedly, as frequently 'borrowed' from the general practice of management) and relating them to the way knowledge services as an organizational management function is practised in the parent organization, not only does the knowledge worker position himself or herself for better service delivery, but the entire knowledge services function is positioned as a respectable participant in organizational or community operations.

This last point perhaps needs some elaboration, for it should be made clear that the books in the series are not intended exclusively for the corporate or specialized knowledge services field. It is our intention to provide useful management criteria for all kinds of knowledge services operations. Our basic thesis is that quality management leads to quality service delivery, regardless of the environment or organization with which a knowledge services function is affiliated. Writing for this series are and will be authors who, I am sure, will challenge some of the usual barriers to effective management practices in this or that type of information management, knowledge management, or learning operation. And certainly there will be librarians, records managers, archivists, content and knowledge professionals, and others who will be able to relate some of their management practices in such a way that CIOs, CKOs, and CLOs will benefit from the telling. In other words, our attempt here is to clear away the usual preconceptions about management within the various branches of information management, knowledge management, and training and learning, to do away with the concept of 'well-that-might-work-for-you-but-it-won't-work-for-me' kind of thinking. We can no longer afford to fight turf battles about whether or not management is 'appropriate' in one or another of the various sub-units of knowledge services. What we must do, and what *The Information Services Management Series* expects to do, is to bring together the best of all of us, and to share our management expertise so that we all benefit.

Guy St. Clair
Series Editor

Contents

Acknowledgments

Certainly no book is ever written without help from many people. First and foremost I would like to thank Guy St. Clair for giving me the opportunity to write this book. Secondly, I would like to thank Geraldine Turpie, my editor, for her patience and all her suggestions. Thirdly, I would like to thank Pierce Butler and his company, Indexing Services, for his expert indexing help. I would also like to thank Amanda Clark, a co-worker, Courtney Jones, a student who helped proof read, Hussein Kahn, from Saudi Arabia, Chang Hun Lee, from South Korea, Pat Petersen, a co-worker, Arvind Rajandren, from Singapore, Professor Edward A. Riedinger, Latin American Studies Librarian at the Ohio State University, Dr. R. V. S. Rao, a visiting scholar from India, Andrew Rosselli, my neighbor, Dr. Oded Shenkar, from Israel, and Leslie Smith, my editor on this side of the ocean, Professor Walter Zinn, from the Fisher College of Business, for their helpful input on various countries and their editing help. I would like to thank Claudia Heyer of K. G. Saur for her meticulous editing help in completing this book. My hope is that this book will be very helpful to librarians who must interact with people from other countries, especially those new to the field and reference librarians in public libraries who are seeing a dramatic change in the ethnic composition of their communities. Did you know when you smile, you use 14 muscles in your face?

Introduction

Today, we are all working in a global environment; our clientele reflect the cultural diversity of the world. According to Census Bureau Projections, the United States population will rise 49 percent to 420 million by 2050. In 1950 the white non-Hispanic population comprised 90 percent of the population. By 2050 that percentage will have decreased to 50 percent. In 2002 the Hispanic population in the United States was 38.8 million people or 13 percent of the total, surpassing blacks as the largest minority group. By 2050 their population is projected to almost double at 24 percent of the population numbering 103 million people. The number of African Americans will rise 71 percent to 61.4 million. Their share of the total population will rise from 13 percent to 15 percent of the total. Asian Americans' share will double at 8 percent of the total. By 2030 20 percent of Americans will be 65 or older and ready for retirement. (El Nasser P 1A).

In 1976 the Asian enrollment in higher educational institutions in the United States was 97,000 students and in 1997 that enrollment had increased to 291,000 students. (Statistical Abstract of the United States 1998 p. 190). European student enrollment has increased from 14,000 to 68,000 for the same period and Latin American students had increased from 30,000 to 50,000 for the same period (Ibid p. 190).

Clearly we are operating in a multi cultural environment. The international students informational needs span a range from truly simple to extremely complex subject matter and often they cannot differentiate which is which. What they think is a simple request may involve hours of research and what they think is a complex request may turn out to be quite simple. The process of answering a request may involve teaching the workings of databases, explaining information packaging, or translating a data set into the vocabulary of the particular database. We often acts as translators when connecting the international client to the needed information. In this book I will discuss attributes needed to provide excellent reference service to international clients.

This consideration leads, naturally enough, to the role of the librarian/ information provider, wherever he or she may be employed. It is not my intention to write a book that is 'U.S.-centric' but of course I am writing as an American. My purpose here, though, is *not* "U.S.-specific" but to present concepts, ideas, situations, case studies, and the like which will stimulate *any* librarian/information provider to review his or her service skills, regardless of the country or culture in which he or she is employed. Obviously all of the examples and situations presented here are not universally applicable but surely – if we are willing to 'think out of the box' we can apply these concepts behind these situations and turn them around so that they apply in whatever country or culture the reader is in.

As is becoming more obvious all the time, we Americans are not the only service providers who are dealing, on a daily basis, with clients and users and colleagues who come to us for the services we provide from different cultures and environments. My purpose in this book is to get *all* readers to become aware of the need to adjust one's thinking from the *local* to the *global* as one provides library and information services in today's global, international research environment.

In January 1977 a statement was published entitled *Public Libraries in a Multi-cultural Britain*. Its message 27 years ago is at the core of this book; not just for Britain, but for all librarians/information providers around the globe. "It could reasonably be said that the responsibility of all public librarians is to ensure that everybody living in this country has the opportunity of learning something of the social, cultural, and historical background of the various minorities which now form a part of our multi-cultural society. Of course, it is of greater importance to provide such unbiased material in depth to a community that has people from these minorities as the need for understanding by the indigenous population becomes more sharply focused. Even more important is the need to supply information to the people who are in these minority groups and to do so within an integrated service. The sense of social and cultural deprivation they feel should concern us all and librarians have a particular responsibility to help overcome it (Jackson p. 453).

As for my methodology, I sent out a survey to academic reference librarians asking where they saw a need concerning interactions with people from around the world. The overwhelming response was tell us about the cultures of the world. When studying cultures it is important to keep in mind there a two different sets of philosophy. The first is individualistic to which the United States, Canada, and France adhere and the second is group-oriented or collectivist to which many Asian, Latin American and some European countries adhere. The way we interact with these cultures is crucial to a successful encounter. If a patron bows to the reference librarian before posing a question, the librarian should bow back and in the same manner. By this I mean if it is a slight bow, the librarian's bow should be slight. Seldom would one be asked to make a deep bow in this country but abroad this may well be the case. In a country like Japan the extent of the bow signifies the rank of the persons exchanging the greeting. It should also be noted that in many countries age brings with it much respect and admiration. This is seldom the case in the United States.

I wonder how many times I have offended people from other countries just with my ignorance. One of the major issues in dealing with people from other cultures is that of being gentle and soft spoken. It is rare to hear someone from an Asian country speaking really loudly. Most of the time I cannot even hear them on their cell phones. I was raised to give a firm handshake, it shows directness and honesty; a "fish" handshake is a sign the person is weak and very shy. A firm handshake is very offensive to an Asian. Their eyes do not meet for very long and their handshake is very soft.

First impressions are very important especially in the reference environment. One needs to dress professionally and conservatively. One needs to exude expertise in one's field, giving the patron the confidence that you really know what you are doing. They are in need of help. Since I am in an educational environment I try to approach the question in a teaching manner. I am the old wise one and they are the students, who in certain cultures, will then in turn become my teachers.

Dress and appearance are important to many people from other countries as it can convey religious beliefs. Be conscious that revealing clothing is very much frowned upon by some peoples. It can send the wrong message. The other day I was observing a young lady and I asked myself if she had any idea how her attire would offend many a foreigner. She had on a sleeveless tight turtle neck, a short mini-skirt and very high heels. To me she looked like a hooker, but I really doubt that she was. Brittany Spears was actually offended to learned that people thought of her as a sex object. Someone needs to open her eyes. Actions speak louder than words.

For Americans a smile means happiness, kindness, and welcome. For the Asian peoples it can also mean covering up embarrassment, hiding pain or shame. It can also appear to be saying "yes" when in fact just the opposite is being said,"no". Their communication is much less direct and takes much more time. This is also true in many Latin American countries where the collective mind-set is more important than that of the individual. In our working environment today we must create a new frame work for understanding the world. People from all over the world are attending our schools, doing our jobs, and developing communities within communities. The Latino and Chicano populations have exploded in our country over the last decade. America has always been a melting pot, but mostly composed of Western Europeans. Now we are seeing more and more Asians. Some of these students are first generation Americans – Chinese Americans, Arab Americans, Japanese Americans and so on. We have American born Indians whose parents immigrated here from India. This young generation has been schooled here, raised here, and speak perfect American. They have developed with two entirely different cultures, one of which they may be ashamed. The same is true of people from Latin America, Ireland and Poland. How does one understand from whence comes these people.

Every Spring the Fisher College of Business plays host to a group of French students from Nantes. On their first day of orientation we give them a tour of the library. Now keep in mind they just got off the airplane the day before, are probably suffering from jet lag, and do not speak very much English. The technology in the schools in France is not nearly as sophisticated as ours although they seem to be quickly catching up. During the course of the tour I encourage the students to ask questions, but they seldom do. Then one year one of the students did ask a question. He wanted to know how many questions he was allowed to ask the reference librarian. Of course I replied as many as you want and asked why had he asked that question. He replied that where he comes from in France, students are only allowed to ask the reference librarian **two** questions during the course of a semester! I assured him we have no rule like that in this country.

On numerous occasions I have observed a patron walk up to the circulation desk with a question or needing help which they did not receive. This is a result of the person on the other side of the desk being ignorant, lazy, naive or just lack of caring enough. They do not want to go out of their way to help solve the problem or worse they do not think they can be of any help. They are standing watch at the desk and simply cannot leave their watch. They do not think out of the box or use any problem solving skills at all. Part of the problem is their training or lack thereof and a total lack of knowledge of customer service. It is my hope that the reader will learn some tips and techniques on how to better serve and support the customer base whether it be in a public library environment, an Academic library environment or a special library environment.

So much of the time we simply react to the situation. Today, people are so accustomed to instant gratification that if you cannot answer the question "Now", they cannot wait. One tactic is to throw as many resources as you can at them in the space of a few minutes. This makes them sit back, listen and think about what they really want. Often they decide they will have to come back when they have more time. This is good because it gives them time to think about their project.

Chapter One discusses the problem that librarians need to become more proactive and customer driven. Librarians have always been territorial and "keepers of the keys." They need to reach out to their customers and put themselves in the place of the user. Chapter Two discusses how to make a client feel comfortable and how to relieve his fears about the reference experience. Some initial introductions are presented to allow a better understanding of people from other countries. Chapter Three might be the most important chapter in the book. It talks about the objectives of the book and how one learns to show respect to every single client who walks in the door. The important thing about respect is to smile, make a friendly yet keen observation of the client, and take the request seriously. Chapter Four talks about the real give and take in an international encounter. It is important not to rush this encounter, but to allow enough time for a full understanding of the situation at hand. Chapter Five discusses the many levels of communications especially active listening and body language. When do you show versus explaining, when do you use different statements to get your point across, how do you encourage the patron to explain the information need more fully. Chapter Six discusses certain aspects of etiquette in the United States as well as Asian etiquette and Latin American etiquette. Although etiquette is mentioned throughout the book and especially in the section on cultures, it seems to me to be a "dying breed", if you will, and I would like to see it make a substantial comeback. Chapter Seven discusses social protocol, the rules of the American library and how it differs from libraries in other countries. Chapter Eight talks about ways to be pro-active and interactive with the client. It discusses steps to take that extra mile in performing your job one hundred and twenty percent of the time. Finally Chapters Nine and Ten discusses briefly the cultures of various countries for a better understanding of the people you meet and are trying to help. It is hoped that by the end of the book you will be better educated on the twenty-first century client, his/her needs and expectations.

Chapter One

The Problem

Territoriality Versus Shared Space

There is a problem in the way our reference services are offered in our libraries, whether it be in an academic or public setting. The problem is the reference librarian's attitude. There is also a ten to one odds that the next sentence on the reader's mind will sound something like this, "What's wrong with my attitude?" or there will be complete denial, "There is nothing wrong with my attitude." There is something wrong or at least not pro-active about the way our reference services are offered. Librarians have been ingrained in Territoriality – protecting our turf. No one can be a reference librarian without a Master's in Library Science from an accredited institution. One has to have taken reference courses, be an expert in a subject field and know everything there is to know about public services. Well guess what. There has been a slow transition over the last twenty years. Staff are doubling as reference librarians, students are helping other students with reference questions, and reference librarians are working part time. Listen to the voice of experience and concern.

Since the rest of the world is going global it is time for us to engage in educated pro-active reference service. The real challenge is for us to put ourselves in the user's shoes, to gain an understanding of the person on the other side of the desk. This is no small feat since more or more of the people on the other side of the desk are from countries all over the world and I am talking about patrons of small rural libraries as well as those in large cities. It is hoped that this work will help all of us gain a better understanding of other cultures as well as our own, how they differ, how they are similar, and how we can communicate in a way to obtain a greater respect for each other. It is my sincere hope that those who pick up this book will do so with open minds, willing to see through different eyes, keeping our own values in tack, and learning to accept those of others as long as they are embedded in love and peace like ours.

The following are the five major points of the problem:

1. Need to Move from Behind the desk
2. Put Yourself in Their Place
3. Be Patient and Take Your Time
4. Ask What They Have Done up to this Point
5. Show respect by Genuine Caring

Need to Move from Behind the Reference Desk

Here is a typical encounter of a librarian by a customer. So many times I have walked into the reference section of a library and not even been given a greeting by the people behind the desk. They are busy reading their newspaper or magazine with an air about them that says "Please Do Not Disturb." It is as if their feet are glued to the reference desk floor and their eyes are glued to the newspaper. When asked a question, they just point in the direction of where the source resides as if I am supposed to know the call number much less how to find it. Please I have never been in this library. Another thing, they dare not smile. The patron may take this as an invitation to approach. The last thing that slays me is the demand to Whisper as if we might disturb someone. This is the reference section. It is by necessity noisy. People are asking questions, people are doing reference interviews, people are explaining how the library works, what resources answer which questions, etc. The most likely culprit resides in training techniques, and before we can even begin to address the problem, some understanding must be reached with management for building customer service into the reference employee's orientation.

According to Garcia Marco on LIS education in the 21 century, he writes: "If we accept that information work is a user-oriented one we have to include in our curricula and in the practical development of our training, personal, group and public relations concepts, attitudes and techniques, and these subjects are rarely found in LIS training pro-grammes. ... Today the whole services sector–and also the industrial world–is looking for new organisational structures, more flattened and adaptive, which rely on a more educated work force and the intensive use of computers, networks and new technologies. These processes are irreversibly impacting the organisation of the library and information unit. At least in Spain, the educational system has yet to respond to such a challenge." (Garcia Marco p. 152).

True, many students today know more than the reference librarians about where to find certain kinds of general information in such places as "yahoo.com/finance", but I am reminded of a time when looking for other kinds of information the librarian probably won hands down. Chances are a google search will not find a quality "SWOT" analysis on a company for you, but your librarian can. A goggle search probably will not yield the consumer price index table for twenty years. Some data sets are more accessible in reference works. Students are more sophisticated in many ways today. They certainly know more about the Internet than I do. I know there is a lot of wrong information on the Internet and often students cannot ascertain the validity of the information. Often students will come to me when they have exhausted their own sources of resources. They will say they have searched a certain database and found nothing. The result may be the technique they used to search the database. They may be fast, quick witted, and computer savvy, but they do not spend much time thinking or being flexible in the way they think. This issue might best be addressed by creating a flowchart indicating steps one, two, three, etc. The ability to read between the lines and come to a conclusion on the mission statement of a company is beyond their scope.

A Typical Introduction to Today's Business Library

Electronic Media has rewritten the rules of how a library functions in today's world. In some countries like Brazil, citizens have access to the Internet from their homes which is fast replacing the need to go to the library building. In one of the lesser developed Asian countries, they went straight to the cell phone and never developed land lines. A premium has been placed on gathering time sensitive information in its electronic format. This capability is not only expected, it is demanded. And when customers receive excellent service, they will provide repeat business.

A case in point is Dan Oglevee, a finance professor, who has been coming to me for help since 1995 because he gets the help he needs. Of course professionalism of the reference librarian varies from situation to situation.

Many libraries around the world today are very complex establishments, with various databases requiring complex search strategies, not like your old library that had a card catalog, books, magazines, and microfiche. Today one has access to the electronic catalog of one library, access to the catalogs of a consortium of libraries, many databases, some exclusive to one library, others accessible through a local area network, magazines and journals available in paper format, but also available full text electronically, microfilm, microfiche, ready reference shelves, reference shelves, special collections housed in special rooms, new book shelves, compact shelving, and the list goes on. It is almost impossible to find one's way around the library today and of course one needs to know how the library is set up in order to find one's way around it. There are also closed reserve collections and course specific closed reserves, and electronic closed reserves. I just spent one and a half hours with a new patron this morning explaining our system, how it works, what she could expect to find, how to check out a book, how to check her record in case a book has been recalled, how to get to the home page from her office, and finding some experts in her field here at the university. She thanked me very much for all the time I had spent with her and said she would be coming back frequently. I had to keep going back to the basics of how to function in my library such as reading a call number, properly searching the catalog, finding articles written by an expert in her field, getting her properly set up in the system. She did not just waltz into the library, she called ahead and made an appointment. That is what it takes in today's complex world.

A New Changing World

Not only are libraries around the world becoming more complex, but so is the user base. Wolfgang Ratzek in his article entitled "Core Competencies of Front-Line Employees: The German Contribution to a New Service Culture" explains the situation in Germany. He writes about the changes in the psycho-/socio demographic structure of library users. "The tremendous cultural change in the last two decades in the European countries has also changed the make-up of library customers. After the fall of the Berlin Wall in 1989, a stream of people from Poland, the former Soviet Union, former Yugoslavia, Africa, and Vietnam wanted to live in Germany. In addition to the new citizens, the German culture is strongly characterized by the Italians, Spanish, and the biggest ethnic group- the Turkish. When we speak of policy in public libraries' new target groups, their need for literature and access to information about their homeplaces becomes relevant. Another critical and logical result of the psycho-/socio-demographic structure of library users is holliganism and drug dealing . . . librarians undergo special training sessions to help them cope with these real social situations."

He goes on to say. "The new librarians are multi-skilled persons with competencies in EDP, psychology, cultural communication, and business administration. Post-modern librarians are customer oriented. They need consultative skills. We have to keep in mind that especially in mixed cultures, politically correct communication methods and behavior are of importance for a librarian with customer contact. Learning from America what political correctness implies, we Germans have made a cult of it." (Ratzek p. 284) We not only have to have "IT" savvy, but we need to be able to span the gap between the "real world" and the "virtual reality" of cyberspace by instructing customers in how to use electronic sources and developing sophisticated search strategies.

A anonymous student said to me one day, "I have never set foot in the library in the five years I have been here." A plausible response to him might be, "Maybe you would have only needed to be here four years if you had made a trip to the library." When I said get out from behind the desk, I meant it. Treat the patron as if he is your guest and is visiting your facility for the very first time. We should make no assumptions about the patron. Many are intimidated by the library and need a helping hand to just get started on their research. They may have many other issues on their mind, such as coping with the English language, saving face, not appearing stupid, scared beyond belief, or feeling threatened by other students or their environment. They may just need a quiet, safe haven to study. We need to reassure them that they are in a safe haven and you are there to help and protect them.

During the 69th International Federation of Library Associations and Institutions (IFLA) in Berlin, Germany on August 1–9, 2003, the then president of the American Libraries Association (ALA), Carla Hayden stated that, "it became clear rather quickly that many of the concerns that libraries and librarians face in the United States are shared by our colleagues all over the world." (Hayden p. 5). The three major issues literacy, lifelong learning, and equitable access. "From a global perspective three challenges to equal access were identified. The first is directly related to the theme of lifelong learning: People need to achieve not only basic print literacy skills in order to access and use library resources effectively, but also information, oral, and cultural literacies as well. The second addresses the need for increased professional development in our graduate programs to ensure inclusion of equity access in curricula. The third challenge is the need for more than adequate funding for libraries of all types, including strategic partnerships and increased advocacy efforts. It was heartening to hear librarians from Botswana to Norway discuss the challenge of achieving equitable access for all . . . there are changing populations throughout the world that need flexible and creative library services." (Ibid p. 5) I might add that librarians need to become more involved in outreach and distance learning programs. We may need to go to the user instead of the user coming to us.

Put Yourself in Their Place

To quote Les Brown, "You only get one chance to make a first impression." Moving into a new culture can be daunting. A Saudi diplomat's wife states, *It was my first evening in the United States. I was so tired, unpacking my suitcases in our new apartment. Then the doorbell rang. When I opened the door, I saw monsters with bloody teeth and terrible faces! They shouted something I didn't understand, and I screamed and slammed the door. A few minutes later, the bell rang again. I looked through the peephole. There were more horrible demons at my door, different ones! I phoned my husband at the embassy; I was ready to go back to Saudi Arabia that minute. But he just started laughing, and then he explained to me about a holiday called Halloween . . . (Expat p. 57).*

A typical reaction to this passage may include a range from anger to blame to even rage. Where was the husband, he should have warned her about Halloween. Men, they only think about themselves. He was busy doing his job. Yes, someone should have warned her, probably the person helping her relocate. The point is that the situation was totally alien to her and frightened her out of her wits. She is immediately confronted with evil in this country. What a way to start a visit. She was not greeted with a smile or a word of welcome, she was confronted with monsters demanding something from her and she did not even understand what it was they were demanding. The noise alone must have unnerved her. When I moved to France one of the upmost concerns I had was that someone would cheat me out of my money or take advantage of me. This never happened. I met very honest people and I think that was because I was honest with them.

One of the best ways we can begin to put ourselves in another's place is to develop listening skills so that we can understand what they have to say. Within ten minutes they will tell you were they are coming from, what is important to them, how their day is going. The minute I walk in the door someone is ready to pounce. Remember the exam I was telling you about, well I talked to the professor and he changed my grade so I will be getting a B+ or an A–. This student was elated with his news. He is an science student and they see the world a little differently. I have to keep reminding myself that what is important to me as an American is not as important to people from other countries. Here at the university, one of the most important issues for students is comprehension, the second is grades. One cannot get a good grade without understanding the material studied. Power point handouts have become very popular because they give the student, especially international students, class materials they can take with them and study over and over again.

Argentina is rapidly becoming a consumer of sophisticated information products. The theme of the 32nd Congress of the Argentine Library Association was "The Library in the Global Village." Some of the goals of the libraries should be to increase literacy, assure equity of access to information, and work cooperatively in this new world of global information networks. Librarians should be agents of change in order to affect how information is delivered. Of particular importance during this congress was the celebration of the first meeting of the working groups of the Commission of Professional Entities of Mercosur, a trade partnership between Argentina, Brazil, Paraguay, and Uruguay (Griego p. 40).

A Digital Divide

According to Edward A. Riedinger, head of the Latin American Library Collection at Ohio State University, high school and college students in Latin America are not accustomed to reliable or plentiful library resources and services. Academic and public libraries do not have regular acquisitions budgets, and the existence of a professionally organized library within an educational institution is not a standard assumption. Recognizing the budgetary and professional limitations under which they operate, libraries in the region increasingly seek recourse through digitization of books, manuscripts, newspapers, periodicals, pictorial material, and recordings. However, at most, only major national libraries (such as Argentina, Chile, Brazil, Cuba, Mexico) and limited private (Catholic) or public (state and federal) university libraries with established budgets and trained staff can develop such resources. The availability of such materials has limited effectiveness, depending on the ability of users to know about and access them.

Among the middle and upper classes, the rapidly developing current framework of expectations for finding information is not through libraries but the Internet. Laptops or home and office computers are the means by which the upper stratum of students finds information or does research–although writing term papers is rarely a course requirement. Personal computer resources as a means of finding information are a steadily emerging phenomenon worldwide, as apparent in Latin America as in Europe or Asia. Whether such users also assume that a library environment offers similar electronic access is a major variable. Most do not expect such availability, except in rare circumstances at major metropolitan public or academic libraries in Britain, France, or Germany; Hong Kong, Singapore, or Australia.

Riedinger is the author of *Where in the World to Learn* (Greenwood, 1995), a guide to applications of information management to international educational advising, and the former coordinator of US advising services in Brazil and South America. He believes that the most significant challenge to American libraries in orienting the current generation of foreign students coming to the US is to demonstrate to them that libraries offer not only as much as their computers but abundantly more both in terms of a wide array of resources and extensive professional services. In many respects this challenge dovetails with the objectives libraries have vis-a-vis American students. Within this contest, therefore, the most significant variables regarding public policy for foreign students become addressing the general communications dilemmas and cultural bewilderment of such students to American academic life overall. In so far as universities offer orientation for incoming foreign students, such programs must include emphasis on library use, based on presentations given by librarians sensitive to the special library needs of foreign students.

Every year we host students from Nantes, France. We have been doing this for twenty years. Until recently, these students had great difficulty with our technologically advanced computer system. They did not have computers in their school back home. However, in the last couple of years, there has been a noticeable improvement in both their English and their computer savvy. I was told a few years ago that the French students were allowed to ask only two questions of the reference librarian. Today when I ask them about such limitations, they tell me there are no limitations. Our students from Hong Kong and Singapore are quite computer and Internet savvy.

Case Study

One technique I use to put myself in the shoes of the student is to ask to see their assignment. I need to read the assignment in context. This informs me about the class level of the assignment and the expectations of the teacher. When the assignment specifically states that five different sources should be consulted, I understand that the teacher is looking for sources other than the Internet. If the assignment is a two page paper, this request is entirely different from a 15 page paper. When a student came to me with a request to find information on the labor movements in Taiwan, we looked in normal databases to no avail. We then looked at some other databases with which I was not entirely familiar. Still no luck. Then she told me that the assignment was for a social behavioral class. I then asked her if she could read Chinese. She said yes she could. I then called the East Asian Studies librarian only to find out he was in East Asia and would be back at the end of the month. Seize the moment! I explained that I thought the student would need to search some of our Chinese databases in order to do the assignment. I asked the person on the other end of the line if maybe she could help me with this patron's request. Her response was that someone was helping another student at that very moment with the same assignment. I asked her if it would be possible for me to send my student over to her. She gave me her name and office location and said she would be glad to help the student. I sent her to the East Asian studies area because we could not find sufficient information in my databases. Unfortunately I got very busy and did not follow up on this request.

From a slow start in the middle of the 20th century Australia vaulted into now being one of the most accessible and heavily used public library networks in the world. This is due to state and local funding. The pouring of funds into the public library system was greatly stimulated by the 1935 Munn-Pitt report funded by the Carnegie Corporation and sponsored by the Australian Council for Educational Research which criticized that Australia was better provided with local libraries in the 1880s than it is today.

Australia now has a public library system for which aggregated performance and statistics are substantial. It is by far the most heavily used and valued investment by local and state government. The return on investment is at least $2.50 for every $1, higher than the Dow Jones industrial average. The libraries are the most heavily trafficked public buildings in Australia. There are 534 services, with 1597 access points, 52 million books and other items, and increasing electronic resources. There are 90 million visits each year with 154 million loans. Ninety nine percent of Australians have some form of access to the public library. The libraries host 4000 public internet terminals – the number one access point for people without computers. All states now have in place programs to facilitate fast access to the internet by public libraries and their users. (Bundy p. 39)

Today's students lack the kind of confidence we had when we were growing up. They hate to ask questions even if something is new to them. They are afraid of being different or standing out. They also do not seem to have the ability to stay the course. They seem to be saying what if I cannot carry this load, what if I fail? I did not understand what it meant to fail until I was a Sophomore in college and almost flunked out because I had been playing more than I had been studying. It was a hard lesson to learn, but it woke me up for the next two years. Some students today study from 8 in the morning until midnight every day. That is dedication and most of these students are international ones who truly value the education they are getting here which they cannot get in their home country because it is too difficult to get accepted in their very limited number of universities. These students do not take up your time with what they consider to be menial questions. However, there is no menial question. I tell my students in all my workshops that there is no such thing as a stupid or silly question. They are in a learning mode and they cannot learn without asking questions.

Now more than any other time I can remember, the grade has become extremely significant. For many students all that matters is the grade. One just needs to memorize the material and get a good grade. They do not care if they comprehend the material. There is such great competition, both here and abroad, to getting accepted into the university that the grade has taken on a new level of importance. A person who is on the honor roll in a school in a rural area may not have the same academic qualities as someone on the honor roll in a suburban area. One student came to me irate that she received a 19 out of a possible 20. I looked at her assignment. She clearly had not followed the directions. In the Asian countries, parents push students very hard to do well. This even increases their lack of confidence. Japan has a very high rate of suicide among young children because if they do not get into the right schools their whole life is ruined. Librarians can build self confidence in the children they serve if they take a special interest in them, listening to them, addressing their fears, and pointing out ways to be successful. Developing literacy skills is one of the surest ways to increase self confidence. In this country, teachers work with students as individuals with individual personalities. In many other countries, the students are seen as a group without personalities so the rules and regulations are very rigid.

Be Patient and Take Your Time

Everyone is in such a rush at least according to the movies, television and big city life. Women are not respected in other countries like they are in the United States. I was surprised to learn from my friend from South Korea that women are treated as second rate citizens over there if they are lucky. In some countries their only worth is producing male babies and nothing more. So in this country they are very surprised to learn that they matter and what they think matters. This respect must be conveyed to all female students regardless of their country of origin. When someone approaches the librarian for help with a paper due the next day, usually the librarian has no sympathy for the patron and really feels it is their own fault that they have left such a task until the last moment. This is not for us to judge. It may not always be the case. They may have had to study really hard for their exams and a paper is the least important thing on their agenda.

I know some people who will not step foot in the library. May I ask why? One major reason for some older patrons is the computer. They do not feel comfortable using it. They find it intimidating. Another is again, the librarian's attitude. They look at you as if you are stupid. "What do you mean you do not know how to use a computer. My two year old can use a computer." Instead of coming away from the desk and going to the patron, they will just sit there and use their computer to do a search. Then they will give you the information and expect you to be happy and run along. A better scenario would be for the librarian to take the patron over to the computer, sit down with them and show them how to use the computer to find what they need. The next time the patron will know how to do it on his own. Rarely does it cross the librarian's mind that this might be the very first time you have used their library and you may function well in other libraries, but not this particular one. Some librarians are simply curt to their customers without realizing how they come across to the patron. No one wants to be treated as if they were an ignorant person even if they are. It is extremely important to explain what you are doing as you go along.

A student came in the library with a citation wanting to get a copy of an article. Forty five minutes later we requested a copy from interlibrary loan. The journal was a Canadian journal which we did not have, nor was it in any of our consortium libraries, nor was it available through our Electronic Journal Center. In the middle of the search the server went down so we were going from one computer to the next to try to get re-connected. Finally I went back to my office which is not a public terminal and got connected. I searched Ulrich's to find the ISSN number, then I searched WorldCat to find owning libraries. We then had to get the professor's social security number in order to request a copy of the article. We then filled out a request form. After all of this I had to back-track, and show the patron how I had gathered some of the information. She was grateful as she had learned much that she did not know and hopefully will remember for the next time.

Do It Once so Do It Right

The longer you take to deliberate, the less time you waste. Communications have a way of breaking down when people get in a hurry. They leave out intricate parts of the problem, so you may be working on only part of the problem and not see the full picture. Returning to the question several times often helps clarify the real information sought. When sitting there waiting for the system to respond, it helps to ponder the search strategy and the concepts one is trying to research. I have spent the good part of a half an hour just getting the request solidified. Without this clarification, you may be barking up the wrong tree and not even know it. Taking time to do a proper reference interview also shows that you are not only actively listening, but that you genuinely care about getting the right stuff for your patron. If it appears the question is going to take longer than either of you anticipated, explain this to the patron, get a time frame in which the question must be answered, and have the patron return a little later, which gives you room to wiggle.

Research usually takes twice as long as people think it will. I always tell people to ask for help at the beginning of their project not at the end as so many do. Often I will take a request, ponder on it a little bit and ask the patron if I may have some time to work on it. Here is an interesting paradox with business questions. Every time a patron says he has a quick question, it turns out to be just the opposite. On the other hand, if a person thinks the request is going to take a long time, it often takes just a few moments to satisfy the request. So much information is generated today that it is sometimes very difficult to retrieve that same information at a later date. One day a Ph.D. student came to me with a very skimpy citation she had retrieved off the Internet and she was trying to retrieve the article again. Of course she could not remember her search strategy nor the web site where she had found the article. We tried at least a dozen different search strategies to no avail. We never did get back to where she had been on the Internet. Here is a word of caution, always write down the full citation and URL. This was a typical example of a student being in a hurry and not having enough time to write down the full citation or backing up her data. She may have been in a hurry at the time, but I can guarantee she spent much more valuable time trying to re-find that article.

In other countries and other settings, research may take even longer than it does in the United States. The materials may be older or out of date, one may not be able to borrow materials in a timely fashion, one may not have Internet connectivity. Materials that one needs may not be available to the person wanting them. Many libraries have closed stacks so one cannot browse. This brings me back to my experience in high school. I was researching the poet Emily Dickinson. Since I lived in the Washington, D.C. area, I went to the Library of Congress to do my research. It took a long time to find the books I wanted in the card catalog, write down the citations, hand them to the clerk and wait for them to fetch the books. Since there was no borrowing, I had to stay in the library and do the research taking careful notes as I progressed. Just physically having to get to the library, retrieving the materials, and reading them took a very long time. Turn this into several trips and yes it took more than twice what I thought it was going to take.

Another Case Study

Every day holds surprises for a reference librarian. One afternoon I took a telephone call in which I acted as the typical librarian trying to pass the buck. The caller identified herself as a student from San Jose State University in California. She was looking for documentation on the Accounting Hall of Fame. I asked her why she was calling me. After all I was in Ohio and I was sure San Jose's library had some of the same databases that we had. She explained she had searched the Internet and found nothing. Then she explained that the Accounting Hall of Fame was housed at the Ohio State University's Fisher College of Business. This was for a paper she was working on, but could not find anything on the subject. I went into the Accounting and Tax database to which we subscribe, but San Jose State University did not, and found twenty four articles for her. I asked her if she had access to a fax machine. I then explained to her that I could make copies of the citations and fax them to her. She said, "You would take the time to do that?" I said yes I would be happy to do that. I then explained to her that she should take them to her librarian who could her help retrieve the articles. She said she would greatly appreciate that. I made copies of the citations and faxed them to her. I asked her to call me back if she needed more informa-tion. She called me back with a request for several articles from magazines which our library contained, but their library did not have. I made copies and faxed those articles to her. Needless to say she was a very happy student because now she really could write her paper.

Ask What They Have Done Up To This Point

The reference situation has changed so dramatically over the last five years. Now when people seek out the reference librarian's help it is because they have exhausted every other means they know. Don't reinvent the wheel. It is paramount to ask where they have looked, what it is exactly they are trying to find, and why they think the information even exits. In some of these situations I am lost because the patron certainly knows more about the subject than I do. However, I know where to look. I know what databases contain what kinds of information, what books address certain subjects, and what is or is not available in my collection. So much time can be wasted by not knowing what previous steps have been taken.

During a conversation with a fellow librarian the other day, she expressed total frustration and exasperation because the more she helped the patron the more help the patron wanted. Is this not a good thing? I listened to her very carefully as she was expressing my very feelings with some of my sophisticated patrons. They know what they want. For instance, they know we do not presently have the electronic version of the International Monetary Fund statistics service although we should. We are one of the top research institutions in the country. Even though we receive the paper version, it would cost an additional eight hundred dollars for the electronic version In order to provide this service hours, weeks, even months would be involved. The patron's grasp of the English language is substantial, their grasp of the databases is substantial, and they know the information exists in paper format as well as electronically, but we do not offer the electronic version which often is free if we get the paper version, but in this case it is not. These patrons are not in a hurray. They have been wrestling with the problem for a while. They want to be able to extract certain data and download it into an excel spreadsheet. This would make life so much easier. We are working on the challenge.

The other kind of patron is the one who feigns ignorance. They know what steps they have already taken, but they will not offer this information to you. They know the difficulty of their request, but they will not disclose this to you either. They have what I call half truths; they are covering up what they know for whatever reason, maybe just to test you. This can be very annoying to say the least. The reason I know this is because hours later they will feed you a crumb. This is the difficult patron who soon becomes your most dreaded patron and the screening process begins. We all have our good days and bad days. If you are having a bad day and do not feel you can handle this difficult patron have someone take a message and tell them you will get back to them. There is no rule that says you have to be perfect all the time. Just get somewhere by yourself until you get your composure back as well as your patience. This is a must if you are going to continue to offer a top notch service.

Show Respect By Genuine Caring

A little respect can go a very long way and it is often revealed by our body language. There is no substitute for this and it is impossible to feign. Each of us has many ways of communicating and our attitude is probably the most obvious. If you really have no regard for people who are black or Hispanic or french or Middle Eastern this will come across loud and clear. I can hear the reader saying to himself, "Well I guess I have to fake it." You cannot fake it. Americans are in terrible need of an attitude adjustment which can only come about from understanding other people and their cultures. We are the only ones I know who live by the clock. Most of us do, but there are others who do not. Next time you observe someone who is not wearing a watch make a note to yourself that time is no big deal to this person. Otherwise they would be married to their wrist watch like most of us. Often these are your artistic types or people who come from a collective society.

For all our failures with customer service/customer care, Americans really have developed the concept of customer care more seriously than any other country. The English, some 20 years ago, also became involved in "customer care" and between the two countries (and obviously similar cultures such as Canada, Australia, the U.K., et al.), there began to be standards which is, for many Americans, simply the expectation of *perfection* in customer service. Obviously such standards of service were never achieved, but at least in Western culture (especially in the U.S. and the U.K.) there is an interest in achieving something close, which is why it is important for Americans, the British, and other countries that aspire to customer care to understand how important it is to seek standards of service for all customers (but *especially* for those coming into the present culture from a different one).

The other day I went to the 12:30 Mass. This Mass is said in Spanish and is specifically intended for the Hispanic part of our community. Meri was looking at her watch every minute after the appointed time. Finally, the Mass began at 12:45, fifteen minutes late! However, the Church was not really full until 1PM. Father knew this, in fact, everyone knew this except me. I was sitting on pins and needles. I do not know why. There was nothing I really needed to do after Mass. It was just that Mass was supposed to start at 12:30 and end at 1:30. Fat chance. Now I have a decision to make. Either I go to an earlier Mass which I really do not want to do, or I learn to cope with another culture and learn something, maybe even how to slow down a little bit and stop to smell the roses for a while. It may take getting over some uncomfortable feelings, but in the long run it will be so much better for me and for my fellow community members.

Closure

Part of the genuine caring is following up on the patron's request to see if they are finding what they need or if they need further help either in finding the resources or reconfiguring their search strategy. Without this closure neither you nor the patron knows if the journey has been a success. A library is not usually a place one stops by on the way home. People come to it for very specific reasons. They are looking for a place to chill out, the library contains the materials they need to do a certain job or they need help. Service is what a library provides. The service is only as pro-active as the people providing the service. We should not be wall flowers when it comes to interacting with our clientele.

A prime example of this whole problem just occurred in the library. The librarian walks in from her short break to find five students behind the desk, all of them looking very confused, with the patron standing on the other side of the desk also looking very confused. The librarian drops her coat and book and asks what is the matter. According to the catalog the 1973 volume of the Journal of Marketing should be on the shelf but the patron could not find it. No one had volunteered to go up to the shelves to help him look again. The librarian, knowing the set up of the library, immediately goes to the shelves and finds the desired volume. Again, the patron does not know this library or how it is set up. Less than five minutes later in comes another patron with a call number stating that he is an Engineering student and not familiar with this library. The students are still standing around looking puzzled. The librarian, who is staff, immediately pulls out a map of the second floor and proceeds to tell the patron how to go up the stairs, shows him the beginning of the collection, where the collection ends, and approximately where he will find his book. **This is not customer service**! I call this point and show. He has already told you he has never been in this library, he doesn't appear to want a lesson on how to fully utilize the library. All he wants is to find a book that is supposed to be on a shelf in this library, one of eighteen libraries on campus. I take him up the stairs and help him find the book on the shelf. In another scenario the student whips out a map following the example of the staff librarian. I immediately turn to the student and tell him, "Don't be so lazy. Take the gentleman up stairs and help him find the book." The student hops right to it. And believe it or not the book was right on the shelf where it belonged, a rare happening. This is customer service. Think of the perception of these patrons about the library staff and their ability to help. If we are acting like the pesty retail sales lady, they will let us know immediately. This is the problem as I see it. So let us proceed to assess our goals and the methods with which we can attain them.

Chapter Two

Welcome

Why the Problem is Important and Why Place Matters

To illustrate the importance of the space a library occupies I would like to quote Lillian Gunter, who was a librarian at a Carnegie Library in Gainesville, Texas back in 1923 and I do not believe the environment has changed much today as yesterday.

> The monthly report must be handed in to the new commissioner's court and it is not yet finished. The assistant librarian is at home, ill with the flu. I have a reference to look up, "Find a copy of a mock marriage." A high school history teacher . . . is looking up books with my assistance, to put on reserve. Ten children want to use the same number of the "Reader's Guide." Ten more want to find a recitation or declamation. Six or seven are hovering around the loan desk to have their books charged or discharged. A branch librarian is selecting books to take back with her. Two teachers from the country want help with their work. The phone rings way back in the office. I take up the receiver. No answer, so return to loan desk. Ring number two. Leave everything and walk the 20 feet back to the office again. Take up receiver. In answer to my rather gruff "Hello," a sweet voice says "I just wanted to ask if you have St. Elmo in the library so I can get it when I come down-town tomorrow.
>
> (Van Slyck p. 521).

Creating a Comfort Zone

The very first thing you want to do is create a comfort zone for your clientele that is conductive to learning. "*Smile* at People. It takes 72 muscles to frown, only 14 to smile." (URL http://www.dallas.net/~barker/1.htm). "When truly genuine and freely given, the Smile elicits almost instant trust and friendship. No frown can ever do that: And it takes such very little effort and energy." (Crawford PR "Celebration of the smile." Journal de l'association Dentaire Canadienne 55(3):159, Mar. 1989). An introduction, a gesture to be seated, or some indication that you have all the time in the world will help those living in a "blurred" society to take a deep breath and get focused. As an example, I will sit down next to the international person at the computer and show him/her how the information is organized in the computer. I also show how easy it is to get a full text copy of an article from that computer. After the session he/she has more confidence in using the computer and in building search strategies. I often explain how our particular library is set up so he/she has an understanding about the "reference shelves", "index tables", the "periodical room" and the "stacks" and what is housed where.

Conveying a welcoming environment may not be all that easy when dealing with a complete stranger, especially if the stranger is a guest in your country. There are a thousand ways misunderstanding may occur. I was talking with a student the other day who I assumed was from France since we were hosting 67 students from France one particular quarter and his accent said to me France. After talking to him several days in a row he told me he was not from France. He was from Bulgaria! Was I embarrassed. I made the mistake of assuming which by the way makes an ass out of you and me (Ass u me). Always ask in order to clarify and clarify why you are asking. People from other countries often ask very personal questions of us Americans and we tend to be offended by it. When asked your age one could respond, "Oh, I am in my thirties" instead of "I am 39." Foreigners see us as a very rich country and are very curious about how much money we make. They think everyone is a millionaire. On the subject of money explain to them the wide range of salaries in America from the minimum wage to the President of a large Fortune 500 company. And that we also have poor people in this country.

Try to get out of your comfort zone and into theirs. Americans do not understand why other countries hate us so. Stop and think about it for a while. We are rich, we think only about ourselves and we are arrogant. We are also very richly blessed as we see it. In some other countries, the rich one is the one who owns nothing! First we must understand our own culture. This is not easy to do. I cannot understand the senseless shootings and violence in black communities. I can understand that in that kind of culture one cannot think about the future since one might be dead by tomorrow. I as a white female cannot understand how it feels to be discriminated against or made to feel inferior.

One of the most important aspects of reference work is teaching the clientele. It has been said: It is better to teach a man how to fish, rather than giving him a fish. This way he can fish for his entire lifetime. This is the way I feel about research. If you just give your client the answer he has learned nothing. If you show him how to find the answer, he will know how to do it the next time. Teaching is one very important aspect in dealing with an international clientele.

One day I was coming out of my office. There were four or five Asians standing there looking very perplexed. I asked if I could help them. They asked me where are the stairs? I showed them the stairs. Then they showed me a piece of paper with citations on it. I took them to the reference section and showed them a book listing our currently received periodicals with their call numbers. We then looked up the title of one of the journals. I explained that older journals are bound and arranged on the shelves by their call numbers, carefully explaining the call number. A light bulb when off in their mind. We then looked up a second journal title and wrote the call number next to the citation. They got very excited and thanked me several times for showing them how our system worked. Then I took them to the computer and showed them how to find the record for the journal title **American Economic Review**. I explained the call number, the location of the journal and the status of the journal. We then went to the shelves and I helped them understand how to read the call number on the shelf. Obviously, this was a real learning experience and one they would carry with from now on.

Another time I noticed a student at the computer and the screen looked a bit funny. I went up to her and asked her what she was attempting to do. She was looking for information on "household audio and video equipment", but she was in the wrong database. I showed her how to go to the ABI/Inform database to look for articles on that industry. However, once we got there then we had to decide on the terminology of the database. Each database has its own terminology. We first searched "Household Audio Equipment" and found zero results. We then searched for "Electronic Equipment" and the result was over 17,000 hits. So now we were on the right track.

Countries – Introductions and Gestures

The following excerpts have been taken from a series, entitled "*Passport to the World*" published by the World Trade Press. This publisher is one of the few I have found that produces practical information on international business.

Argentina

Argentines greeted each other with a handshake until recently. Now one is more likely to be greeted with a kiss on the cheek, but in the formal business environment a handshake is still used. To break the ice, ask them about Soccer. They are avid Soccer fans. Titles are used in Academic and Professional settings. Doctor or Doctora (for women) is used for lawyers, economists, researchers, the same as in this country, for those having a Ph.D. *Licenciada* or *Lic* for short is used for someone with a college degree. Business cards are not as likely to be given out as they are for other countries. However, if one is going to be doing a lot of business with someone from Argentina, it is best to get a business card if possible because it will have a direct telephone line to the person or that person's email. Communications across countries can become very frustrating and time consuming. Their typical greeting to close friends is a generous handshake, a hug, and a pat on the back which is accompanied by a kiss on the cheek. Women usually greet each other with a kiss on the cheek whether or not they know each other.

Brazil

Brazil is the largest country in South America and its official language is Portuguese. Approximately ninety percent of its population is Catholic either practicing or non practicing. There is a great disparity of income in Brazil. Either one is fairly wealthy or very poor. Those visiting the United States are as well educated as the reference librarian and understand English very well even if they do not speak it well. There are many English language program schools in Brazil. Although they use the first name almost exclusively, do not be surprised to be called Doutor or Doutora as anyone with a college degree is assigned this name. Brazilians stand closer than most when maintaining a conversation so try to refrain from backing away. Everyone shakes hands in Brazil even the children. If a hand is extended by all means shake the person's hand. They are a very passionate and friendly people. However, their sense of time is not the same as ours. They take a 90 minute lunch, which is the big meal of the day, and punctuality does not exist for them. If you make an appointment for 10 am they are likely to show up at 11 am because something else got in the way. They truly believe that God is Brazilian and they are a blessed country with a wealth of natural resources, rich rain forests, and beautiful weather. They are very proud of their country and can speak for hours on the subject.

Brazilians are as informal in their greeting as the Argentinians are formal. Practically everyone with a college degree is called *Doutot* or *Doutora*. They mostly use their first names so Cas Heuer would be called *Senhor* Cas not *Senhor* Heuer and an older woman, regardless of her martial status, would be called *Dona* Mary for instance. The president of a company is called *Presidente*; the vice president is called *Director superintendente*. Next down the hierarcy is *Director* for director and *Gerente* for the general manager.

China

In China age is of utmost importance. The Chinese extend a gentle handshake; the older the person the more gentle the handshake. They do not exactly bow as do the Japanese, but they will lower their eyes when meeting others. Sometimes the handshake is accompanied by a nod. To show an expression of warmth, they may cover the normal handshake with the left hand. Since China is a communist country, the word "comrade" is used only by the communists. Americans should never use it.

It is not always clear who is in charge. Top communists officials carry two business cards. To foreigners they present their business side, but to their fellow communists they are first party members. The person in charge usually has a "deputy" or "vice" in their title. The following are Chinese titles with their English translations:

Dongshizhang – Chairman of the Board
Zongjingli – President
Fu Zongjingli – Vice President
Bumen Jingli – Department Manager.

France

The French are a very formal people. The "vous" is always used; the "tu" is reserved for intimate friends or children. Keep in mind that when a person makes the transition from "vous" to "tu" he can never go back to the more formal address. It would be an insult. First impressions are very important because the French are a very instinctive people and can size up someone rather quickly. Madame is used for Mrs., Monsieur is used for Mr., Mademoiselle is used for Miss. The French love titles. The President-Directeur General is the Chairman of the Board; an Administrataeur is a senior officier. The Directeur-General is the head of a department. This in turn is divided into Directions headed by the Directeurs. Further down the corporate ladder are divisions, services, and sections headed by chef de division, chef de service, and chef de section.

The French shake hands both on entering and leaving a room. When meeting a total stranger they will shake hands, but never smile. The hand shake is usually accompanied with a personal greeting such as Bonjour, Monsieur Hill. As is true in almost all countries one might be visiting, when a business card is presented take a moment to read it before putting it away. It is a sign of respect. The French are sticklers for savior faire and etiquette. One of the first test one might run into is the "Bataille de la Porte." When exiting through a doorway the rank and gender are of utmost importance. Ladies first, then senior executives, and finally junior executives. Manners are very important to the French and if you show ignorance in this matter, you must be ignorant in other more important matters. Good friends can expect a double kiss on the cheek both when greeting and departing. It usually starts with the right cheek. Another common greeting which means hello and goodbye is the word "Chow." This is also true in many other European countries.

Germany

In 1994 a law was passed that abolished the use of double surnames. Therefore, now wives can use their maiden name which was not allowed before the law was passed. A child's given name must be chosen from a list approved by the municipal authorities which excluded non-German names. Herr is Mr., Frau is Mrs. Fräulein is a young girl and a young man is also Herr. It used to be that any unmarried woman was called Fräulein, but today if she is over 18 years of age, she is called Frau. The Germans are very formal and polite when meeting a stranger or in a business setting. In introducing an important person one must include all their titles. So if one is introducing a person who is a professor and has a Ph.D., he would be introduced as Mr. Doctor, Professor Hill going from the least important to the more important titles. One always takes the spotlight off that person and puts it on the other person. For instance, if a Mayor is giving a speech, he would say something like "I am pleased that you have given me the opportunity to be here." In other words one takes it from the "I" and puts it in the "you." On greeting someone, always a right, affirmative hand shake is offered. When a person is leaving and has done a favor for someone there is always a hand shake and a "Thank You."

Hong Kong

Greeting and names are very complex in the Chinese countries. When being introduced to someone from Hong Kong, they will usually give you their surname followed by their given name. However most of them have four names, one given at birth, another during puberty, a third at adulthood and one each person uses privately. China is such a large country and although there are approximately 440 family names, 100 common ones (the Ancient One Hundred Names) are used for ninety percent of the country. It would be like Smith in our country. Age is so very important that beside the name often an adjective is added. For instance lao means honorable old one, xiao means honorable young one, and da means honorable middle-aged one. They should be addressed by Miss, Madame, Mr. or their title Doctor Li. Today in the United States many Chinese have taken on an American name because they can sense how uncomfortable we are in pronouncing their names. They will change their way of life in order for us to save face, because this is such a big thing to them. To be on the safe side, always ask them how they prefer to be addressed. Also if you do not know someone's surname, it is fairly common to address them by their title, for example Teacher Meri or Doctor Meri. This also applies to managers, directors and high ranking officials. The traditional manner of shaking hands is by saluting another by making a fist with the left hand, covering it with the right palm and shaking the hands up and down. It is also a way of thanking someone and showing reverence. One of my students has used this hand shake to mean all three things – greeting, thank you, and showing reverence. However the Western hand shake has taken over. For the Chinese it is a very gentle hand shake and can last as long as ten seconds. Do not try to shorten this process because it is a way of showing respect for you and what you do and how wise they perceive you. The hand shake is followed by giving you their business card. It is also very important not to rush this process. The card is handed to you with both hands, holding each card corner between the thumb and forefinger. Study the card on both sides. One side may be in Chinese and the other in English. The Chinese are very socially conscience and those visiting our country probably rank pretty high up there. It is critical to give them the respect they so deserve.

Confucian morality lectures humility and collectivism so showing independence and arrogance will most decidedly offend them.

India

The *Namaste* is India's traditional greeting although *ji* (pronounced gee) is fast replacing it because it can be used regardless of age, by both sexes, and for almost any occasion. One presses the palms together with fingers up below the chin and says *Namaste* or in the South, *Namaskaram.* To show respect for one's elders or superiors a slight bow is added. Women are not touched in public by a man. Therefore a simple "Hello" is acceptable. However, when addressing a superior it is better to be more formal with a "Good Morning" followed by their title such as Professor. Muslims use the right hand for a *salaam* gesture of greeting and farewell. Indians do not use their hands with lots of gestures as it is considered impolite. The soles of one's shoes should never be seen and if one's foot should touch some else an apology should immediately follow. Western-style name order is becoming increasingly popular. Among young students the first name is followed by *ji.* For example Michael-ji would be appropriate. Indians always ask permission before taking leave from others.

Indonesia

When greeting someone from Indonesia it is of utmost importance to convey respect. It is also essential to know the proper titles, name order and protocol. Many a business deal has fallen through because the wrong person was being addressed. When dealing with a group it is better to inquire who is in charge than guess. Some Indonesians have one name, some two and others several. To be on the safe side always use Mr., Professor, Doctor, etc. Engineers have their own title wich would be "Engineer Muhammad." Chinese women keep their maiden name. For example Mr. Chew is married to Mrs. Chow. Her full name is Chow Le, surname first, given name second. Do not hurry introductions as it is considered extremely rude. Indonesians shake hands with a very light touch, slightly bow their heads, and smile. Even though the hand shake is light (what we Americans call a fish hand shake) it is for a very long duration, possibly up to 14 seconds. They may bring their hands back to their chest showing the greeting comes from the heart.

The traditional form for Mr. is *Bapak*, the shortened term *Pak* is often used. *Ibu* is used for Miss, Mrs. or Madam. As in other Chinese cultures, the business card is a very important expression of the person's status and rank in his society. The Indonesians like flashy cards that are embossed rather than printed. The card has as much information on it as possible especially academic titles and qualifications. It is presented with both hands, with the print facing the recipient, or with the right hand with the left hand supporting the right wrist. The latter way is even more cordial. Gold ink indicates prestige.

Israel

In Israel everyone calls everyone by their first name regardless of who you are. The egalitarianism of Israel's socialist founders encouraged equality among all. That is why Golda Meir was called Golda not Mrs. Prime Minister. Therefore the greetings are very informal. Shalom is the most common greeting meaning Peace. It is used as a greeting and parting phrase. It may be followed by *Ma Nishma?* (What's up), or *Ma Shlomcha?*, a more formal greeting for How are you? Hand shakes are common with additional touching hugging or kissing. Women might hug or do the double kiss on the cheek; men might hug and give a slap on the back or shoulder. Waiters, hotel clerks, bellhops and taxi drivers treat tourists just like everyone else. Here bus drivers make more money than doctors. They do not understand titles, corporate ladders, or societies with a hierarchy. Even school children call their teachers by their first name. This very religious people does not touch in public.

Italy

Always address an Italian by his or her title and surname. If someone has an aristocratic name use it. That is how they wished to be called. The most common title is *dottore* widely used by all levels of university graduates. *Professore* is used by middle school teachers and higher while *maestro* is used by elementary school teachers. Men shake hands when greeting and departing. Male friends may embrace and slap each other on the back. The handshake may include grasping the arm with the other hand. Men meeting women may shake their hand, but are more likely to kiss her hand. Chivalry is still alive and well. Women for the most part touch cheeks and "kiss the air." *Signore* is used for Mister or Sir, *Signora* is used for Mrs. or Madame, and *Signorina* for a young lady or an unmarried women. *Ciao* (pronounced chow) is the most common greeting or departing phrase. *Buongiorno* means Good Morning and *Buonasera* means Good Afternoon or Good Evening. In certain regions in the South nodding the head up and down means "no". Italians are known as the people who could not hold a conversation if their hands are tied behind their backs. In fact there are so many different gestures that there is a dictionary on the subject. They often communicate with their hands rather than words. Removing one's shoes in the presence of others is considered impolite. One covers one's mouth when sneezing or yawning. This is a very passionate and vibrant people with a true love for life.

Japan

Japan is a very formal culture. Greetings and partings are both very important and elaborate. A bow is the traditional greeting between the Japanese. While some appreciate it when Westerners bow, others do not, especially when the two people are not acquainted. Bowing is a sign of respect not subservience. However a nod of the head may be just fine for a Westerner. If you are going to bow, the question is how much and who goes first. The short answer is you (the guest), and not too deeply. A proper bow is executed from the waist. For men, hands should be at one's side; for women hands rest on one's thighs. For foreigners a hand shake is more appropriate. Given names often reveal the gender of the person. For example a female's name would end in "ko" or "e" and male names would end in "o" or "ro" much the way certain names in English indicate the gender. The suffix "san" represents Mr., Mrs., and Miss. So Mrs. Dada would be Dada-san. The word for teacher is *sensei* so Meredith would be Meredith-sensei. If one really wants to be very respectful one can use the honorific phrase *samma*, but use it very sparingly. *Meishi* (the business card) is a very serious tool for establishing business contacts. Failure to present one at the first meeting can mean that will be your last meeting. Protocol dictates that the person of lower rank present his card first. It doesn't hurt to take the first initiative. Here again are some guidelines for the exchange of business cards for most Asians. Be formal and present the card with both hands, thumbs on top and fingers underneath, with the print facing the receiver. Always show respect for the most senior or highest rank and present the card to them first. Take your time. This is the beginning of a relationship which hopefully will last a long time. Do not deface the card in any way by writing on it, bending it, dropping it or leaving it behind. That would be the rudest thing you could do. Read it carefully, look up at the presenter again and then carefully put it in your pocket. Then gently shake the presenters hand.

Korea

How one is greeted is very important and depends on one's age and social standing relative to the greeter. A bow is the traditional greeting and is usually accompanied by a handshake between men. As a sign of respect, the left hand may support or rest under the right forearm during the handshake. Women shake hands less often than men because one does not touch a women in public places. Names are considered very personal and are rarely used in communication. A Korean's family name is spoken first, followed by a generational name, followed by a given name. So the name of a friend of mine is Lee Changhun and he would be called Mr. Lee. A female does not loose her maiden name when she gets married. She would be referred to as "the wife of Mr. Le." Professional meeting for the first time exchange business, presenting and accepting the cards with both hands after a handshake. A common greeting is *Annyong haseyo* which means are you at peace? Names of position and titles are very important. The title comes after the name so President Bush would be Bush *Taet'ongnyong*. The phrase *Son Saeng Nim* is a overall honorific name meaning "teacher" or "honored one." It is not uncommon to see a Korean man walking with a male friend with his hand on his shoulder. One passes and receives with both hands. When yawning or using a toothpick, one will cover the mouth. Beckoning with the index finger is considered rude. Facial expressions are often more important than body language in communicating unspoken messages. When embarrassed, a person may respond by laughing or smiling in order to save face. Eye contact is important in conversation among peers, but not with elders. Because personal space is so limited in Korea, pushing and crowding is common and generally not considered impolite.

Mexico

Mexicans usually greet with a handshake or a nod of the head. Close friends usually give a full embrace. Women often greet with a kiss on the cheek and men may greet close female friends in the same way. Common verbal greetings are *Buenos dias* for Good Morning, *Buenas tardes* for Good Afternoon or Good Evening and *Como esta?* for How are you? The casual greeting is *Hola* for Hello. Mexicans always have two given names and often two surnames. The first surname comes from the father and the second from the mother. Coworkers address a person by their title and first name. Without a specific title a women is called *Senora*, a man is called *Senor,* and a young lady is called *Senorita.* Older, respected people are call *Don* or *Dona.* If you do not know how to pronounce someone's name simply ask. Do not make the mistake of calling someone by their second surname which is their mother's maiden name. Legal documents should contain the full name. The conventional practice is to address all female office personnel, except executives, shop workers, waitresses as *Senorita* regardless of age or marital status. Other titles include: *Gerente* – manager, *subgenerte* – assistant manager, *director de mercadotecnia* – marketing director, and *Agente de ventas* – sales-person. Mexicans shake hands a lot.

> If a Mexican business associate greets you and says goodbye with an *abrazo* (hug) – by grabbing your arm or putting his arm around your shoulder and punctuating it with a couple of claps on the back – it's a signal that you've begun to gain his trust. Don't insult him by shying away from such contact.

Mexicans may take a long time to say goodbye. In this society, your host may walk you out to your car, bend your ear a little longer and before you know it a half an hour has passed. Farewells may be repeated several times. These pleasantries tell you that your host is in no hurry to see you go and that he likes you. *Hasta luego* means See you later and *Buenas noches* which is a greeting and a farewell means Have a good evening.

Philippines

Filipinos follow the Western style of a given name, middle name, and family or last name. A Filipino male often has two first names such as Jose Maria. Sometimes he will incorporate his mother's maiden name into his own such as Jose Maria Guerrero y Rivera – Guerrero being his father's name and Rivera his mother's name. Initial greetings are friendly and informal. Handshakes are typical but only verbal greetings are also accept-able. To show respect one places the free hand on top of the handshake or uses it to pat the other person's shoulder. Hi and Good morning are as common a greeting as other greetings in their native tongue. One will always be on safe ground by using a title and the last name, for example, Chairman Guerrero. However, special effort should be taken to properly pronounce the names of those with whom you will be working. If the title is not known Sir and Ma'am can be used rather than Mr. or Mrs. The handshake is just a formality. What is looked for in the visitor is warmth, graciousness, an understanding of the local culture, and the ability to fit in with a group. Filipinos do use various gestures to communicate. Raising the eyebrows can mean "yes" or "hello." A quick nod of the head can mean "I don't know" and a widely opened mouth means "I don't under-stand." Men offer bus seats to women. Women commonly walk hand in hand or arm in arm while men may put their arms around each others shoulders. Displays of affection between a man and a women in public is considered inappropriate.

Poland

Believe it or not the Polish are more courtly and formal than the British. The regular forms of address are *Pan, Pani, Panna* before the last name and are more closely translated into Sir, Lady, and Mademoiselle than

Mr., Mrs. And Ms. There is even a professional title for the wife of a Doctor. Pan Doktor's wife is called Pani Doktorze. The use of the first name is unacceptable when there is a relationship between a younger and older person such as a student and a professor or if there is much difference in rank. The use of the French "Madame" is prevalent while the other two forms of Monsieur and Mademoiselle are not. For example, Madame Suhocka is as acceptable as Pani Minister Suhocka. Friends greet each other with *Czes c* a way of saying "Hi." Some common Polish greetings include *D-jen dobry* – Good Day, *Dobry wieczor* – Good Evening, *Do widzenia* – Good-bye and *Dziekuje* – Thank you. When the Poles sign their name, they sign their family name first and then their given name.

Russia

Addressing a Russian solely by his or her first name is considered an insult. The Russians are a very formal people. Be sure to use the *vy* rather than the *ty* form because it is more formal. Russians use the courtesy titles of *Gospodin* (Mr.) and *Gospozha* (Mrs.) if there is no title to be used. Otherwise always use the title with the person's last name such as Director-General Koslov. They in turn will call you as Company (Nike) Director Smith or Company (Nike) Treasurer Jones. Russian women will add the letter "a" to the last name of their husband. So it is Mikhail Sergievich Gorbachev, and his wife is Raisa Maximovna Gorbacheva. Their names are listed in the same order as in the West, first name, middle name, and last name. The quirk is that the Russian middle name is a patronymic – a name derived from the first name of one's farther. So in the name Mikhail Sergievich Gorbachev, the middle name means literally "son of Sergie." Your Russian counterpart will eventually invite you to address him or her by their patronymic. To not do so after having been invited to is an insult. Like many who find their names difficult for Americans, they may substitute a nickname and you may be asked to call them by that name. Once they have established the use of the name, use it always even in written format. Friendship is extremely important in Russia. Russians are warm and open with trusted friends. They rely on their network of friends in hard times and will go to great lengths to help friends whenever possible. When meeting, Russians shake hands firmly and say *Zdravstvuyte* (Hello), *Dobry dien* (Good day), *Dobroye utro* (Good morning), *Dobry vecher* (Good evening) or simply *Privet* (Hello) which may be easier for Americans to pronounce. Pointing with the index finger is improper but commonly practiced. It is impolite to talk (especially to an older person) with one's hands in the pockets or arms folded across the chest. To count, a Russian bends (closes) the fingers rather than opens them.

Singapore

Greeting customs vary according to age, ethnicity and situation. Chinese people shake hands, sometimes adding a light bow for older people. Along with the individual's name, the introductory greeting will usually include some sort of biographical guide such as this is Miss Song a colleague of mine or this is Vice President Lee, he is an Ohio State University graduate. Titles and the family name are used in the formal or business setting. Chinese names begin with the family name, followed by a generational name, followed by a given name. So, a single woman named Lee Hwi Chern is properly addressed by her full name or as Miss Lee. Chinese (especially Christians) adopt Western names, which come first. So Catherine Tan Leng Yan is addressed as Miss Tan, but Catherine to her friends. Introductions are made from the top down: the higher ranking to the lower ranking: Minister Chan this is my assistant Greg Smith, the elder to the younger: Mr. Curtis meet my son Jason Lee, or the woman to the man: Mrs. Hassan, please meet my assistant James Beard. Introductions among equals do not require a specific order. Muslims, particulary Malay men, may after a hand shake, touch their hands to their chests, symbolizing a heartfelt greeting. The traditional hand shake is a gentle squeeze that lasts from ten to twelve seconds instead of our normal eight seconds. In both Malay and Indian cultures, religion dictates a more reserved greeting, just a nod. While it is mostly a rare case, the best response is to simply offer a smile with a nod of the head. It is acceptable for women to shake hands with both sexes, but they are responsible for initiating the gesture. More often than not they will simply nod. Touching another person's head is not only impolite but banned in some countries. There is a superstition that such a gesture would bring harm to that person's soul. It is impolite to point the bottom of a foot at someone or to use the foot to move objects. Also pointing the finger or making the OK symbol are considered rude in this country.

South Africa

Everybody, but everybody shakes hands. The English, the Afrikaners and the black Africans have distinct forms of greeting each reflecting their collective personalities. The English speaking white South Africans follow the British styles of greeting not overly sincere but polite with an exchange of pleasantries. The Afrikaners say *Mora, meneer* which literally means Morning, Mister. The black South Africans are less structured and the introduction may be quite lengthy as they will want to know about your trip, your family, your health, etc. The tradition of long greetings stems from a time when Africans walked miles to visit neighboring villages on a social call. Most Africans understand Hello and Good Morning. Expect to be called by your last name with a title such as Mr., Mrs., or Miss by people in the service industry.

"I could tell there was something bothering Margaret, my housemaid, for weeks, but I couldn't put my finger on it," recalls an American lawyer who was residing in South Africa. "She seemed eager to avoid me and rarely spoke. I just couldn't figure it." After cornering Margaret in the kitchen one afternoon, the lawyer discovered the source of her maid's unhappiness. Weeks before, the lawyer had instructed Margaret to call her by her first name, Catherine. "It seems Margaret couldn't handle it. She was so uncomfortable with it, she just avoided talking to me." The solution: Margaret reverted to addressing her employer by her last name and title."

(Passport South Africa P69)

It is imperative to understand the culture in which one is living. People do things differently in other countries and visitors need to understand and adjust to that culture. Africans and mixed-race people frequently use hand gestures in conversation, but it is impolite to point with the index finger, stand too close during a conversation, or stand with hands in both pockets. These gestures are so American that a concerted effort must be made not to do them when talking to people from other countries. Receiving an object with cupped hands is polite.

Spain

Spaniards usually go by their first name, their father's last name and their mother's last name. So if a Spaniard calls himself Francisco Badilla Sanchez, his first name is Francisco, his father's name is Badilla, and his mother's name is Sanchez. In business they are very formal. Men usually greet each other with a handshake. Good friends will add a pat on the back and even a hug. Women shake hands when greeting. However close friends usually give each other a kiss on each cheek. Professional and business people use the formal salutation *Senor* (Mr.), *Senora* (Mrs.) and *Senorita* (Miss) with the surname. Typical greetings are *Buenos dias* (Good day), *Buenas tardes* (Good afternoon) and *Buenas noches* (Good Evening). *Hola* is a very casual Hi. Friends or young people may ask *Como estas?* (How are you?) rather than the more formal *Como esta?* reserved for older people to show respect. When parting they say *Adios* which literally means "Go with God" and *Hasta la vista* means "So long, see you soon." Eye contact is also important and is often maintained longer than in other cultures. To refrain from shaking hands send the message that you lack trust. Spaniards speak loudly, laugh and smile a lot. Pointing at others is impolite and showing emotion in public is acceptable for women but not for men. It is common for men to open the door for women.

Taiwan

It is very common for Taiwanese males to introduce themselves in English using the initials of their given name followed by a simplified version of their family name. So Chiang Teng-kuo would become T.K. Chang in the English version. Women are not required to adopt their husband's surname, but many do while traveling abroad. When being introduced, Taiwanese, like many other Chinese, will nod their head, smile and offer a quick, gentle handshake. It is considered rude to address someone by their given name until asked to do so. Mr., Mrs, Miss, and Madame are perfectly acceptable forms of address. Calling someone "Ms" is very confusing and in these circumstances should not be used. Titles such as Doctor or Professor are also acceptable. After initial greetings, polite questions may follow. Adults often ask the young about their school work and the elderly like to be asked about their health. Often the Taiwanese will adopt an American name while in the United States. Whatever name or initials one chooses to give you, respect their wishes and call them by that name. Do not make the mistake of asking someone what is their "real name". This would be an insult. It is best to ask for someone by their full name and to include their job title. Business cards are a must and lots of them. Lack of a business card is rude and indicates that a person is unprepared. The card is presented with both hands and the lettering facing the recipient. The card should be carefully studied and then neatly put in one's pocket. It is a good idea to have one side of the card in English and the other side in the language of the country you are visiting. If you have the business card of the person you are meeting, it would make the receptionist's job easier if you presented it to her as many people have the same surname.

Thailand

The most traditional and common greeting in Thailand is called the *wai*. How the gesture is performed depends entirely on the relationship between the people and there are many variations. Generally, a person places the palms of the hands together, with fingers extended at the chest, and bows slightly. Women curtsy. The younger person greets first, the more senior person responds with a *wai* in a lower position. When bows and curtsies are more pronounced it shows greater respect. The *wai* is given to a peer or superior, but never to an inferior. If you return your hotel maid's *wai*, she will think you are very ignorant. The correct response to a *wai* from someone of lower status is a smile and a nod. In general, Westerners should not use the *wai* but a handshake will do just fine. You may initiate the handshake. If there is a large age discrepancy the senior does not return the *wai*. Buddhist monks never return the *wai*. The formal honorific title in Thailand is *Khun* It is an all-purpose, gender-free title. The Tais use nicknames often given at birth. If your name is too difficult to pronounce, you may be given a nickname also. Body posture and physical gestures are extremely important in polite company and will speak volumes about one's character and regard for others. A person's head is considered sacred and one should never touch one's head or pass anything over it. The bottoms of the feet are the least sacred part of the body and should never be pointed at another person. Tai avoid stamping their feet, touching people with them, and using them to move or point at objects. Placing one's arm on the back of a chair in which another person is sitting is offensive. Women must never touch images of Buddha or a Buddhist monk or offer to shake hands. One passes and receives items, especially gifts, with the right hand only, never the left. For heavy items, one uses both hands.

United Kingdom

There are several classes of people within England. There is, of course, the Royalty, the lesser nobility, Lords of the Manor, Knights and Dames, and the commoners. When being introduced to Royalty wait to be introduced. Never speak first. Giving a little bow or curtsy will put you in good standing. Every one runs in their own circle. As Ferggie put it "It is very dangerous to go outside your circle" speaking about Princess Di. The lesser nobility are addressed as Lord or Lady followed by their surname such as Lady Spencer. Many of these titles have been handed down in the family since William the Conqueror who in the year 1086 commissioned these lordships. They are entitled to sit in the House of Lords and vote on major political issues of the day. Lordships should not be confused with "Lord of the Manor." This is an honorary and fairly meaningless title. It can be bought at auction for thousands of dollars and often by Americans who want a distinctive title. Knights and Dames are quite another matter. These titles carry with them a distinct honor and are awarded in recognition of extremely successful careers in business, politics, government or the arts. Nicknames are not acceptable to the British so refrain from calling someone Chuck when the real name is Charles. In fact do not even call them by their first name until asked to do so which may take some time or may never happen. Aside from the queen Mother and other royalties, stick with Mr. or Mrs., or Director or Managing Director (equivalent to CEO in the US). The British are reluctant to handing out business cards, so one may have to ask for it. They are a very reserve people that do not like showing loud and demonstrative behavior. They keep their distance during a conversation and manners are very important. Touching is generally avoided.

United States

Both men and women smile and shake hands when greeting. The American handshake is very firm. Good friends and relatives often embrace when they meet, especially if they have not seen one another in a long time. Friends also may wave to one another or give the "high five" gesture. Except in formal settings, people who are acquainted address one another by their given (first) name. In formal settings titles such as Mr., Mrs., Miss, Doctor are used with the family name. So Professor Meredith would always be used. This shows respect for the person being addressed. The handshake is usually accompanied with the phrase "Hello" or "Good Morning". When meeting someone for the first time, Americans usually say "It is nice to meet you" or "How are you?" There are also regional greetings such as *Aloha* in Hawaii and *Howdy* in the West. People whom one does not know can be address by Sir or M'am or Miss. Military and Police should always be addressed by their title or rank. An example would be Colonel Hill or Officer Bridge. Direct eye contact is a must for Americans. A person may be regarded as untrustworthy if there is not direct eye contact. In a business setting minimal physical contract is the rule of thumb. Americans point a lot with the index finger. They will also give the "thumbs up", the "OK" signal, or the victory signal during a conversation. They usually do not think about who else may be in the room or may be offended by these gestures. Also, they may prop their feet on chairs, place the ankle of one leg on the knee of the other leg, cross legs at the knee or sit with legs spread apart. They also speak with both hands in their pockets. Many of these gestures are considered rude in the international arena.

Vietnam

Vietnamese shake hands when greeting formally, but otherwise greet verbally, standing about 3 feet apart with a slight bow of the head. Names in Vietnam are structured with the family name first, followed by the middle name, and finally the given name. Over half the population carries the surname *Nguyen*, so people are commonly addressed by their given names that are prefaced by Mr., Mrs., Miss, or Madame. For example Nguyen Minh Tuan would be called *Bac Si Tuan*. In other words first comes the title followed by the person's given name. I would be called Mrs. Meri. The wife no longer takes her husband's surname. It is also acceptable to use a professional title in conjunction with the Mr. or Mrs. I would be addressed as Mrs. Doctor Meri. When introducing yourself, stick to the format of your home country. For very formal occasions and with very special guests they give a two-handed shake, with their left hand lightly holding their right wrist. The showing of both hands is a gesture that symbolizes respect and a lack of hidden agendas. The initial greeting will often be accompanied by a invitation to a home or restaurant either for a meal or a cup of rich Vietnamese coffee. Seniority plays a major role in Vietnamese organizations and it supersedes knowledge or skills. The formal greeting between strangers is *Xin chao*. Among friends *Chao* is popular. *Chao* is very popular around the world and stands for Hello and Good-bye. The Vietnamese are almost as fanatical about business cards as the Japanese. Hand shakes precede the distribution of business cards. Like many other countries, the proper way of handing the card is with both hands with the print facing the recipient. In a meeting, occasionally, a woman may not extend her hand. If this happens, respond with a slight nod of the head and a smile. Use discretion when handing out your own business cards. Keep in mind that anyone receiving one will consider the gesture significant; they may even use your card as a reference. And that reference may come back to haunt you. Vietnam is a country where networking and name dropping rule the day. A casual but unscrupulous acquaintance may use your card as a introduction to another business deal. One does not touch another person's head, the body's most spiritual point. It is rude to summon a person with the index finger. Instead one waves all four fingers with the palm down. It is impolite to cross one's index and middle fingers as we do in this country for good luck. As in many other countries, it is common for members of the same sex to hold hands while walking. Public display of affection is frowned upon.

Chapter Three

Respect

Respect for Oneself and for Others

The second thing we must keep in mind is the continuous educational environment in which we all work so being *polite* is paramount. The learning process lasts a lifetime. With constant change there is constant learning which can be fun or very laborious. Try to brainstorm with your clients. This creates a proactive environment in which students can act as teachers and teachers can act as students learning from each other. When a client feels you are taking him/her seriously, they will feel *respected*. As Maya Angelou said in her Bill Clinton inaugural poem *On the Pulse of Morning,* "Here on the pulse of this new day You may have the grace to look up and out And into your sister's eyes And into your brother's face, Your country, And say simply Very simply With hope –Good Morning." (Angelou p. 10). When you treat a person with respect it builds their confidence. For some reason our clientele have difficulty reading certain call numbers. So after six years of dealing with this problem, I walk them to the stacks and help them find the item. It is not easy explaining why HF5415.127 comes before HF5415.3 on the shelf. Once they see the difference they have a better understanding of the structure of the library.

All About Respect

There is a web site about respect. The URL is http://www.allaboutrespect. net. One of the articles at the web site is about making judgment and greetings. It is about a program aimed at fifth graders to increase tolerance of other people's differences and how not to make mistakes in judging others. The first assignment is to interview their parents and grandparents in order to understand the richness and diversity of their own heritage. The second assignment is to write an essay about a time when they made a judgment about a person they really did not know, and to discuss if this judgment turned out to be true or false. One student told about her experience as a Puerto Rican moving from a culturally diverse neighborhood of Port Richmond to a mostly-white neighborhood of Rossville. She recalled some of the things her class mates said about her that really hurt her feelings.

Another exercise was about greetings. The fifth graders had to greet each other in different cultures and they discussed how they felt greeting someone differently than with a handshake. Then a rag doll was brought forth named "Maria." The younger students pretended to be intolerant toward her. Every time they called her a name, the teacher would put a rip in the doll. The students were asked how they could patch things up and they apologized to "Maria." Every time they apologized, the teacher put a piece of Scotch tape over the rip. But underneath the scars remained. This left a lasting impression on the students who had been taught "Sticks and stones can break your bones, but words will never hurt you." They had just learned that words really can and do hurt.

The class was divided into two groups. One group of students was given pink cards to display. The students who wore the pink cards had privileges taken away and they could not drink from the water fountain or play with their friends. They began to understand what it feels like to be discriminated against. A discussion followed on how they could promote acceptance and respect.

In order to create a climate of respect one needs to build a rapport with another. Rapport is the ability to see the other person's point of view. In other words seeing the world through the other person's eyes, hearing the way the other person is hearing. This does not mean one must agree with the other's point of view. This does mean one has to have the skills to observe different points of view. Robert Frost once said "Education is the ability to listen to almost anything without losing your temper or your self-confidence."

Respect by others is earned through integrity. A person tells the truth or keeps a promise or does not lie. This we say is a person of integrity. Respect is earned through humility. The bible tells us to be humble and treat others with dignity. A humble person is rooted in God standing tall with a sense of security in a greater good. Respect is earned through dependability. If others can depend on you to keep your word, show up when you should, perform your work with the best quality you can, then respect will follow. Respect is earned through generosity. When you sincerely give of yourself, others can see that and will respect that extra mile you go. This is especially true of international students. The are appreciative of any time you spend with them. If your goal is to teach them well with kindness, they can see that and you will help them build their confidence.

Kaba Abdoulaye in a paper reviews the state of library and information science in Malaysia. There are three universities in Malaysia that offer a master's degree in library science. They are the University of Malaya (UM), the International Islamic University of Malaysia (IIUM), and the University of Technology MARA (UiTM). Only the UiTM offer a library science degree at the undergraduate level. All three use the IFLA *"Guidelines for Professional Library/Information Education Programs – 2000."* These guidelines or standards are quite stringent. Interest, aptitude, intellectual and educational backgrounds and diversity should be addressed in the criteria. All schools require a bachelor's degree and some require three years of work experience. He/she states that although the standards for admission should be applied consistently, differences exist among the schools.

The ideal curriculum should have both practical and theoretical courses and that an awareness of professional concerns should permeate the program. The courses are grouped into six categories: the information environment, information sources and services, access to the record, access to information content, management, and underlying competencies such as information technology, library automation, and research methods. A majority of the academic staff, ranging from 14 percent to sixty three percent, hold a Ph.D. Most of the Ph.D. faculty obtained their doctoral degrees in the USA or UK. He/she leaves us with a thought to ponder. It is not clear whether the one-year master program is sufficient in preparing today's informational professional for the current challenges. (Abdoulaye P 11).

According to Oded Shenkar who was working as a faculty member at a university in Israel, his experience with the librarian was great until that librarian left and another one took his place. The new librarian just would not support his research for whatever reason. He found this situation to be very frustrating but there was not much he could do as the librarian was married to the mayor of the city. Some librarians are not customer driven, but more budget driven. Often this problem arises when the head librarian sees him/her self as head of the library institution rather than a support facility for the department or university.

On the first encounter with a student the reference librarian should listen carefully to the student's question. It is good to remain open-minded and objective and consider the question carefully. Avoid interrupting a student. Wait until he or she is finished and then give deliberate feedback on what you interpret the question to be. Respect the student's personal space as this may be distracting to him. Use friendly gestures such as an open upturned palm. If you are not reading the question correctly the student will let you know immediately. You might use their given name, but in my environment where I encounter so many students a day, sometimes as many as 90 per day, I seldom get to a name calling level. The physical level is very important in the encounter. If the student is standing I stand up. If the student is sitting I grab a chair and sit also. In dealing with children I try to get to their eye level. It just makes everyone more comfortable. The student has to think you are taking his question seriously.

With Respect to Our Asian Friends

Fifty percent of the students I work with are of Asian decent. I cannot stress enough the importance of helping them save face. The following is an example of what I mean and you will see how subtle this can be. The student came up to the circulation desk and stated there was something wrong with the copy machine. There was a little flashing light on the machine. Now I know it is Summer, the machines are not being used very often so they go into a energy saver mode. When this happens it takes a minute or two for them to warm up. She had walked up to the machine, inserted her copy card, put the document she wanted to copy in the machine and hit the copy button without any response. It tells you it is warming up. You must wait until it say "Ready" before you can make the copy. Being in a hurry, as all student are, she could not figure out how to get the thing to work! When I reinserted the card and hit the copy key the machine made the copy right away. I could see the embarrassment in her face. So I immediately began teaching her the intricacies of the copy machine. First the flashing light did not mean anything was unusual. Then I explained about the energy mode and what one had to do to get it out of that mode. Her face lit up because now she was not an idiot, and she had gained some very good information on how to make a copy when the machine was in an energy saving mode. She thanked me very much and was on her way.

The most serious mistake an American can make when interacting with an Asian is to be insensitive to our differences because they seem so "Westernized" in our current affluent and technologically advanced state. Asians are not likely to confuse the outward appearances with the inner reality. If you notice a difference, realize the difference in itself may not be so important. What is important is what you don't notice. In almost everything in Asian countries there is some unseen or unstated meaning which is usually not pointed out but which everyone is supposed to know. When being introduced to a group, it would be acceptable to ask who is in charge and then you will understand the pecking order. The "We" always comes before the "I" as everything is decided by group consensus. It is really hard for Americans to think this way. Sometimes when we are listening to an Asian he is offended by our direct and fully focused pose. They see this as being arrogant and overbearing.

There are many ways in which Asians publicly acknowledge their social hierarchy. There is a right way to exchange condolences, a right way to greet a superior, a right way to greet the new year, a right way to offer a drink, a right way to accept a gift or decline a compliment. When giving a compliment you are making them stand out like a sore thumb and their philosophy is harmony, being one with the group. There is a Chinese saying that the nail that stands out will be hammered down. These cultures are thousands of years old and many, many traditions have evolved over time.

Here is a fact to ponder. If four fifths of the world's population consists of people of color, why are they called minorities? As the world's population changes those who were once in the majority are now in the minority and visa versa. This means those who were intolerant must reverse their roles and become tolerant of cultural differences. In order to do this, one must understand these cultural differences and develop an appreciation of them. Tolerance is the ability to recognize and respect the beliefs and practices of others. It is exciting to work with people who comprise this rich variety of America's changing culture. Patience and time are a large part of making this process successful. It may take the reference librarian only ten minutes to answer a question posed by an American student and it may take as much as three times longer when posed by an Asian student because one may have to explain things in much more depth. The goal is to fully educate each student. We will all need to rethink our attitudes and see others as worth appreciating instead of taking away our jobs, getting our "A" in class, or our place in the classroom. Becoming tolerant results in learning more about our fellow man, fearing differences less, and becoming more self confident and comfortable in all kinds of situations.

In Columbus, Indiana, USA about twenty years ago a group started an event called "Ethnic Expo." It started out representing about 10 countries. Today this annual event probably represents about forty counties and it just keeps growing. The booths have food, crafts, clothing and art from around the world. The event has grown from a one-day event to a three-day event. What better way to education our children about Flamingo dancing, the Polka, and the Irish jig? The people are happy, but more importantly they are fascinated with what they are learning.

When looking at our diverse citizenship consider these differences: single parents, heterosexual marriages, homosexual marriages, lesbians, gays, Koreans, Japanese, Germans, Asian Indians, West Indians, Italians, French, British, Saudis, Malaysians, Chinese, poorly educated, highly educated, rich, poor, those born with disabilities, those suffering from illnesses such as depression, diabetes, obeseness and the list goes on. Now think about how these people may be struggling with self respect. Just a simple smile may increase their self respect or the smallest kindness. It takes so little to do such good. There are three things that keep us from showing respect to each other. The first is Racism, the belief that people of other races are inferior. It began in this country with the American white man thinking he was superior to the black slave and the Indian savage. Of course he was not, but he did have the money and owned the land. The West was expanded on the backs of the blacks and the Chinese. The second stumbling block is Prejudice, a feeling against or for something or someone without any good reason. Prejudice leads to a lot of violence because it has no reason behind it. The third is having a Bias which is a preference that keeps one from making a fair judgment. People are not always aware of a bias. They just think that is the way it is.

According to the National Public Radio's "Prejudice Puzzle" teacher's guide:

> By age three, children already exhibit prejudicial tendencies toward people based on physical characteristics. If these ideas are reinforced by people around them, they will develop into full-blown prejudices.
>
> From ages four to five, children stereotype gender behavior, express racial reasons for not playing with others, and show discomfort around disabled people.
>
> Between ages seven and nine, children develop what psychologists call "true racial attitudes", likely to be long-lasting.
>
> By 12, children develop a complete set of stereotypes about all ethnic, racial, and religious groups.

Diversity has always been very apparent at the university level, but this was not the case at the elementary and high school levels until recently. There has been a resurgence in immigration over the last decade which has changed the face of America. White Caucasians now comprise only twenty four percent of the population. The rest are people of color with various levels of education. Where I went to school there were no African American students. There were students from all around the world, but not one African American in 1960. Of course all of that has changed, but look how long it took to do it. In just eight years, from 1990 through 1998 some 1.139 million people have immigrated to the United States.

Conflict Resolution

There was a cultural misunderstanding when a Cambodian and a black student bumped into each other. The black student tried to speak to the Cambodian student, who refused to look at him. The more the black student tried to talk to the Cambodian student, the more he turned away. The incident ended with a chase and a fight. During mediation, the black student explained that he felt the Cambodian was being disrespectful by not making eye contact. The Cambodian explained that he had been confused, and that he was trying to prevent a fight by not looking at the black student. In the Asian culture it is considered rude to look someone directly in the eyes. The following guidelines may help to resolve such a conflict in the future.

1. State your feelings clearly, without accusing the other person. Begin with "I feel . . ."

2. Never interrupt or finish another person's sentences.

3. Concentrate on what is being said, not on what you are going to say when the other person is finished talking.

4. Maintain eye contact with the other person.

5. Ask questions to make sure you understand what the other person means.

6. To let the other person know that you are listening and you understand his or her side of the story, repeat what you think the other person is saying.

7. Never put down the other person. (Meek p. 46)

Learning about Diversity

One way we can lean about diversity is to follow the example of a group of fifteen students from Birmingham, Alabama. They get together one afternoon each month to discuss their different racial, ethnic, religious backgrounds. They come from different schools and neighborhoods. They share their frustrations, fears, hopes and ideas. They discuss how they feel when they encounter sexist or racist jokes, jokes about obese students or elderly teachers. They are learning that America has a very rich diverse culture and that this melting pot offers great opportunities to all its citizens. They are exploring their feelings, brainstorming solutions to problems, role playing with other members of the group. The result is they are gaining a greater confidence to confront real conflict and to speak up for themselves and their classmates. (Duvall p. 24). Today, even in an average size city, residents have access to movies in foreign languages, Mexican craft demonstrations, Haitians art exhibits, Chinese and Laotian dance troupes, as well as restaurants with Mexican, Chinese, Tai, Korean, Creole, Malaysian, Cajun, and South American foods. Where else can an immigrant from India buy a food cart and make a fortune selling food on a street corner? Where else can a person with a fifth grade education become a millionaire?

Another way to start respecting differences is by asking questions. Ask which country they call home. If you know anything about their country share your knowledge with them. They will be very surprised and delighted that you have some understanding of their country even if it is just small. One student told me she was from South Korea. I asked her if she was from Soul? She asked, "Do you know Soul?" I said no but that is where the last Olympics were held and I had watched them on television. This immediately put her at ease and we continued with her request for help in finding some information. It is sometimes quite difficult to get the foreign students to ask questions. They are ashamed of their broken English. Elders in their country are highly respected and so they must not waste my time or bother me. After all I have valuable things to do such as writing this book. I actually have to explain in great detail that my job title is "Reference Librarian" and my job is to help them with their research needs. This is a new concept for many students not just students from other countries. Not long ago I visited a Public Library and was talking to a reference librarian. Her comment was that she never dreamt her major role would be to police the computers and make sure people did not stay on them more than 30 minutes! With the proliferation of information on the web, people are seeking help when they cannot find something on the web. We librarians should not be insulted by people searching the web, we should be educating ourselves to more efficient ways of searching the web. Lets get some of these little surfers to educate us. We need to respect from whence they come and their search for knowledge.

Developing Respect

In order to develop respect one must first develop self awareness. Learning to appreciate who we are, our ancestory, our values and beliefs. When we have this self awareness, we can begin to appreciate others and where they are coming from. A friend of mine and I were discussing our backgrounds, education, and beliefs. It turns out we have very similar backgrounds. Her parents are Republicans, my parents were Republicans; she was educated in a Catholic environment, so was I; she loves horses, so do I.

When Not Feeling in a Respectful Mood

It is not always possible to be cheerful, perky and have a positive attitude one hundred percent of the time. When I start feel frustrated or overwhelmed, I get the hell out! This is important because first impressions make a huge difference on how the service is perceived. If one has been working eight straight hours at breath-taking speed, and it is all one can do to answer another reference question, just excuse yourself and make a disappearing act. In a large university setting the demands can be quite high. By simply stating that you have been very busy and need a short break is acceptable to most patrons. However, there have been times when I prayed for patience and forged ahead. I remember one Asian student in particular. She had approached me several times over a several week period. She was working on a research paper. I had showed her the indexes that would yield the best articles on her subject. In fact I had even found some with full text which was rare back then. After a while it became quite apparent this student did not want to read or could not comprehend English well enough. She wanted me to do the reading for her, make an analysis and in essence write her paper for her! I finally ended up telling her that she was a student in one of America's top ten universities, a top research university and that it was her job to learn not only English, but to understand the university library system and to learn to do research on her own. Like most of these students, once you explain what is expected of them and that it is very difficult, they put their noses to the ground and really start working.

Since my undergraduate major was in French, and I spent nine months in Paris, I know how difficult it is to learn to speak, write and read a foreign language as well as live in a foreign culture. I made friends with many Frenchmen and came away with a very positive experience. Of course falling in love with a Frenchman did not hurt the great progress I was making. The French are a very intelligent and complex breed and I felt the good Lord sent me the best mentors who were well versed in the finer things in life especially the conditional verb and seven course dinners. I worked as an "au pair" for Madame DeSoucy who had two children, one five and one two years of age. Talk about children who can be rude and disrespectful. However, Madame stepped right up to the plate and firmly put her foot down. It was a great learning experience for all involved. When visiting another country, it is especially important to learn the culture and the dos and don'ts of that culture and to be flexible enough to live according to their laws and regulations . . .

Being respectful when not feeling like it:

1. Say a little prayer "Lord give me patience and I need it right now."

2. Count to ten and then restart the conversation.

3. Ask yourself if you are understanding where the person is coming from and if you don't, start asking questions.

4. Apologize and restart with something like "I'm sorry, where were we?"

5. Never imply a person is lazy. Their agenda may be different, but never mistake slowness to action as being lazy. It is probably more a contemplative mode, trying to completely understand the environment in order to save face.

Patience and Tolerance

Recently I was standing at my reference desk when an older professor approached me with a very time consuming research question and believe me she knew it was time consuming. In hind sight she should have called and made an appointment with me. I told her I was in the middle of teaching a workshop. She explained she was from the Marion Campus, a two hour drive from me, and when she called no one explained to her that I might be busy. I learned she is a native New Yorker. So when she walked into the library she expected to get my full attention on this very difficult primary research project. Anyway, while the workshop students were working on their questions, I began the reference interview with her pointing out several primary sources she could use now and that I might get interrupted until the workshop was over at 6:30 PM. We started hashing out how she could locate the information she needed which involved locating information on certain businesses in New York city from over a thirty year period. Of course we were interrupted several times by the students, but I managed to juggle the two tasks simultaneously. At one point I said to a student to come with me and shouted orders to the professor to stay put! I was amazed when she totally complied with my barked orders. When the workshop was over, I turned my complete devoted attention to the professor. We must have talked and brainstormed for an hour. When she left she seemed pleased that the trip had been well worth it. I had given her at least ten leads or directions to think about, practical ways of getting at this information that was going to be so difficult, if not impossible, to find. I am sure she will be calling me several times over the next six months when the project is due.

It has recently occurred to me that we need to rethink our attitudes and see other people as worth appreciating. We have all been asked to be vigilant since the attacks on the World Trade Center. I do not know if it is vigilance or just being more aware of our surroundings, but this morning I was on my way to a food market to get some milk for my upset stomach. As I was cutting through the parking garage I noticed an elderly gentleman trying to leave the garage by inserting what looked like a credit card. Since only people with a keycard can park in that garage during the day, I knew something was wrong. I stopped to lend a hand. He said his son had parked the car in the garage, had left him the card but he was not able to make it work. It is a visitors garage at certain times of the day and evening. However, at the time he was trying to exit, it was a keycard only garage. I told the man to stay there and I would go get help. I went over to the Traffic and Parking Station not far from the garage to get help. Low and behold the Station was closed and was soon to be permanently closed. There was a phone number posted to call for help. I then took out my cell phone which I use only for emergencies and called the number. When the person on the other end answered and I told her about the situation, she just laughed and said she had never heard of such a thing. She did inform me that she could not help me, but would connect me to someone who could. As I walked back to where the man was standing by his car, I was connected to a very nice person who knew what he was doing. He told me to tell the gentleman that he needed to put $4 in the machine. The elderly Asian man pulled out some money from his pocket, found a $5 bill and tried inserting it into the machine. Of course the machine would not take the old, crumpled bill. We tried three or four times and still no luck. Finally, the person on the other end of the phone pushed a button and the gate went up. The man got into his car after thanking me profusely and drove out of the garage.

The above situation would not have occurred even during the last quarter because there was always an attendant at the gate from six in the morning until ten in the evening and then the gates are opened. Since the university has had large budget cuts, one less person is working in the garage and it looks like the near-by Traffic and Parking Station is about to go away also. Was I treating the person with respect? I certainly was, but the situation called for going that extra mile to help someone who was all alone and totally confused in an abandoned garage. I do not know if anyone else who might have come along would have done what I did, but I certainly hope so. A reader's response to the above situation might be that they would not have had time to do it, but if that reader was in the same situation, wouldn't he hope there would be a me instead of strangers rushing about with no concern for another's situation? It is time to rethink our attitudes.

I find meeting people from other countries fascinating. They bring with them their rich heritage and knowledge of a different world than ours. One can learn from Asians about the various healing effects of teas on the human body. My Korean friend told me that if I eat water-melon during the summer, I will stay healthy during the Winter. Is this an old wives tale or is there some truth to it? I know I see a lot of very old people eating watermelon in the MCL Cafeteria.

There are several reasons for developing a more tolerant attitude toward those who are different from us. The more we learn about others, the less we have to fear about others. Tolerance makes life more inter-esting. We get to see life through others' eyes and this can be just down right fun. People who can be tolerant of others have more self confi-dence and are more flexible in different situations. In this day and age it is difficult to know who owns the store or that gas station. It may be an Arab or an elderly black gentleman.

The bible talks about respecting others. It tells us to "Do unto others as you would have them do unto you." It also tells us to "Love your neighbor as yourself." In order to receive respect one must show respect. Manners are a very important way of showing respect. I was raised according to Emily Post. My mother was a Washington, D. C. socialite; my father a colonel in the Army. Being polite and minding my manners was not a choice. I was taught how to dress appropriately, speak to my elders with respect, and that there were certain behaviors that were absolutely unacceptable. One never talks with food in the mouth, one always leaves the silver ware in it proper place, one always has the napkin on the lap and so on and so on. Consideration and high regard for the other person generates respect. Our thoughts are the soil from which all behaviors grow. If we think in a negative way, we will be negative and depressed. If we think in a positive way, we will respect others and bring out their positive side also.

Often Americans do not realize they are being disrespectful. It was brought to my attention that one of our student workers had been rude and disrespectful to one of our patrons at the circulation desk. The patron was an older Asian who had just received an overdue notice on a book he had borrowed and there was a fine on his record. Apparently, the student had laughed or smiled at the patron who interpreted the students gestures as being gleeful that the patron had a fine on his record. Our students are for some reason a very happy up-beat group of people who are always joking around. The student may have laughed or smiled out of embarrassment of the situation not realizing how upsetting it was to the patron. Several things come into play here. Asians often smile or laugh to conceal embarrassment. This could well have been what the student did. However, in the eyes of the Asian, the student was being a typical American, rude, arrogant and shallow. There was a double whammy because the student is young and in Asian countries elders are treated with great respect. So the age of the student added insult to injury. If the student had been more aware of the seriousness of the situation or even had an understanding of the patron's culture, the scene may have been very different. The fine on the book meant the patron had done something very wrong and had lost face. It was a much more important situation for the patron than for the student. To rectify the situation, the student should have apologized which he did not. The patron was so upset that he approached management. At a staff meeting later that week a long conversation ensued on how to teach our students to act respectfully toward all our patrons. Needless to say, that student acted more seriously with future encounters with the Asians.

One of the most difficult ways for Americans to show respect is to learn to be patient while waiting one's turn. The other day I was walking into the MCL Cafeteria when one of our patrons just flew past me in the walkway. I noted to myself just how rude he seemed. After all there was a line and he had to finally stand and wait like the rest of us. This was another elderly person so the behavior seemed even more rude. One can understand if it were a young person because they are always in a hurry. I see this behavior on the highways and streets with cars speeding past each other. It amuses me when someone in a huge hurry passes me and I catch up with him at the stop light. One way I try to show respect in my automobile is to leave several car lengths between me and the vehicle in front of me. It is not just good driving practice, but it allows driver's waiting to pull out to do so.

In all parts of the world there are some gestures that instantly show respect to another person. Primarily, the smile is one of those gestures as is the nod of a head and more people are using just a wave of the hand. All mean "Hello." I can show respect by learning from others and their ethnic groups. I can show respect by carefully listening to others' ideas without judgment or putting down those ideas. I can show respect by setting a good example and by taking responsibility for my duties. My whole appearance shows the amount of respect I have for myself. If I am well groomed and have clean hair, clean hands and clean shoes, it tells the world I respect myself. And if I respect myself, then I am capable of respecting others too. A clean car, a clean office, a clean apartment or house, or a clean working environment all convey a respect for things given us by our creator.

Some people make a point of disrespecting others' property and belongings. Skateboarders ruin property. People who spit out their gum on sidewalks or carpet show disrespect not only to those who own the property but to others walking in the same path. The way some people dress these days makes me wonder about their living conditions. What kind of parents let their children out of the house with their pants half falling off?

I go out of my way to make people feel welcome in the library. I hold the door for someone else entering or leaving the facility. I make a point to say "Good Morning" or "Good Evening." If a student has a confused look on his face I ask if I can be of some help. I often go to the stacks to help someone find their book. After all it is easy for me, I work there. Even though I am a librarian, I am frequently lost in other libraries, especially public ones. There is a public library in Upper Arlington, Ohio in which I simply cannot operate without help. They have a children's collection, a young adult collection, an oversized collection as well as young adult fiction and adult fiction. Then there is a non-fiction section, reference and ready reference. I cannot even operate the computers without help.

Strangers in a Strangers Land

Americans, especially librarians, are being forced to operate as if they are strangers in a strange land. We do not have to travel the world, the world is coming to us in the form of patrons from Europe, Asia, the Middle East, Africa – the seven continents! We would do well to refrain from judgment until we have familiarized ourselves with the basic differences that exist be it philosophical, political, psychological, social or economic. There are several basic codes of behavior. The one in America is almost identical with that of Great Britain and the countries developed by Britain and it is similar to that observed in Scandinavian countries, norther Germany, and Holland. The code in France, Belgium, southern Germany, Austria, Poland, the Check Republic, Italy, Hungary, and the Balkans stems from the Latin conception of a group consensus rather than an individualistic code. These differences make the Latins consider Americans as somewhat cold and abrupt; the Americans sometimes interpret the Latin's warmth as insincere and excessive.

When I was working at Cummins Engine Company, the company decided to build a plant in Mexico to cut costs and save money. After they had built the plant and hired local employees, the company ran into some major "opportunities". The first of course was the language barrier. The American managers had to learn Spanish, but not just Spanish, but idiomatic Spanish used in every day life in Mexico. To add to the confusion was the language of the shop floor employee which was different from management and executive styles of communication. To make matters even worse was the use of the metric system used by the rest of the world but not the good ole US of A. The icing on the cake was the daily "siesta" two hour lunch which was their way of living. There was literally no nine to five work regime. This was very frustrating to the American managers who had to justify things back at corporate headquarters.

To further differentiate between the codes of behavior is the simple introduction of one person to another. In the United States and Great Britain introducing is done as little as possible and in large gatherings one can talk to any other guest without an introduction or it is quite possible to introduce oneself. The Latin concept becomes the "Continental code" in the system of introductions. On the Continent introducing oneself is considered bad form. The system demands that one must ask to be presented to older or ranking guests, either by the host or hostess or by anyone who had been properly presented to them. *All* men must arrange to be introduced to *all* women in *all* but large gatherings. Two men may introduce themselves to each other, if no one is on hand to make the introductions, but a man and a women or two women must never do so.

People like people who are like themselves. One way to quickly show respect is to observe the other person's behavior. If that person speaks softly, you speak softly. If the person speaks in a fast tempo try to maintain that tempo. This is a difficult one but try to match the person's mood. Some people are all fired up at eight in the morning. I am not even awake at eight in the morning. That is why I have a flexible schedule and work from ten in the morning until seven in the evening. I am a lot sharper by Noon than I am at ten. That makes me an night person. I try to observe the person's language system. There are three basic linguistic systems – visual, auditory, and kinesic. If a person says "I see what you mean." that is a visual person. Auditory people prefer to hear an explanation rather than seeing something. They will say something like "I hear what you are saying." The kinesic person feels something or senses something. This kind of person might say "I feel confused about this question. Can you help me?"

One of perhaps the easiest things to change about our behavior is to stop pointing with our fingers. In many cultures this is considered quite rude, but Americans do it all the time. Instead try teaching yourself to use the full hand open with an upturned palm. It is a tiny thing, but it will make people from other regions of the world more comfortable. In some instances this is impossible of course. If I have to point to something on a screen I use the mouse or a pen. That makes it less personal. We have many students coming and going into the library. One of the little courtesies we give each other is holding the door open for someone else who is entering or leaving at the same time. This little courtesy developed out of necessity. The doors to the library are extremely heavy so since one person had expended so much energy to open the door, one might hold the door open for the next person to catch. An added benefit was it make the person coming in behind you feel welcome. Such little things go a long way. On the other hand, failing at some of the little things can create an environment that is not welcoming or just down right intimidating. Being polite is always appreciated. However, being polite means putting others before oneself which is rare in this day and age. Some people do not believe in being polite. There is a saying in the United States, "Always look out for number one." The number one mentality is part of America's culture and individualism. Otherwise people run over you or take you for all you are worth. Respect prohibits violence, humiliation, manipulation, and exploitation all of which run rampant in today's society. We must turn this around if we are to survive.

Chapter Four

Speak Slowly and Distinctly

When communicating with an international visitor it is best to remember to speak slowly and softly. You may have as much difficulty understanding them as they do you. I thought my friend said "high school" when in fact he was saying "hi score." Some Asians not only have difficulty pronouncing our "r", but they construct sentences according to the syntax of their language. This means they may place the verb at the end of a sentence. It is especially important not to use slang. "Where is the Restroom?" is much better than "Where is the bathroom?" because "Restroom" is what they are probably more familiar with since it is the word used in public places. Saying "I do not know." is preferable to "I don't know" because they hear something they cannot understand. Most international visitors who have studied English, have studied just that – English. So when they get to America and are confronted with the American language, they are greatly confused. It is not the language they were expecting. Gestures (See Chapter 2) can be a big help in enhancing the communication process. However, there is one gesture that we Americans should refrain from using when dealing with an international visitor and that is pointing the finger. This is an obscene gesture in many countries.

The Quick Question

It is perfectly acceptable to ask an international visitor to repeat a question or even write it down if you are really experiencing difficulty in understanding the question. Why is it that whenever you think there is a lull in the reference arena, your most difficult questions come roaring at you. Just yesterday a Ph.D. Asian student came to me wanting some data on a foreign exchange rate. One would think off the cuff that it was a fairly simple request. Not so simple, since he wanted the Sterling pound to the dollar on a weekly basis from 1970 to the present in electronic format. I, of course, had not a clue as to how to find this data, but I did know Datastream could probably answer this question with its 30,000 time series. Those people at Datastream are wonderful and they have an 800 number with a real live expert at the other end, answering the phone. So I tried to translate the question as best I could to the Datastream expert. This did not work, so I handed the phone to the student who talked with the expert for several minutes. He was very uncomfortable speaking on the phone, so he handed it back to me as quickly as he could. After several attempts, we found the correct code and time series and voila – we had exactly what the student wanted. However, he did not have a disc with him so I loaned him one of mine. Actually, it belongs to the library. This session was by no means over. I had to take the disc back to my office to make sure we had really downloaded the data into excel. After checking, I told him that yes we had been successful and he was welcome to take the disc to his office. I told him he could keep the disc, but he would have no part of this. I have to make the assumption that discs are very expensive in his country, and he could not accept it as a gift. He insisted in only borrowing it until he could transfer the data and then he would return it to me. When I finally agreed to this, he left a very happy camper. This is not the end of the story.

The next day he said he needed two sets of data. One was the spot foreign exchange rate and the other was the current foreign exchange rate. So here we are back on the phone talking to Mark, a Datastream expert, trying to get the right code and time series for both sets of data. Low and behold without too much anxiety, we managed to find both and download them into excel. This may sound like a fairly easy feat, but it actually took months for the IT people to load excel on this computer and make sure it worked with the Datastream database. So much for the quick reference question.

Many Asians students are very self conscious about their ability to speak English. They always say to me, "My English is so bad." I tell them their English is better than my Chinese which is nil. This makes them laugh and builds their self esteem. Suddenly, they are not afraid to ask a question. When speaking with someone not familiar with English, it is very important to speak distinctly. Americans so often slur their words or run them all together. This makes comprehension very difficult. I always try to do active listening and restate the question to make sure I am hearing what is actually being asked. Sometimes, I am actually hearing the exact opposite of what is being asked. So this feedback has been essential to a successfully answered reference question.

Often the students will come to me with just a call number written on a piece of paper. They have no title, no author, or status of the book. I then need to go to the computer and put in the call number to find the location and status of the item. More likely than not it is a book in the stacks and can be checked out. However, sometimes it is in a different library or is already checked out. I can show them on the screen wherein lies the problem. If it is on the shelf, I ask them to come with me to find the book. We find the book together. This way they learn the size of the library and just how large our collection really is which is very large. This can be daunting even for our American students. One can imagine what it is like for an international visitor. Trying to put yourself in their shoes, can be an enormous help both to you and them.

Some Things Take Time

I found out that one of my South Korean friends is a Catholic. I decided to invite him to attend a mass with me. He had been attending the university for four years and had never gone to mass at the Newman Center. He asked me how long the mass lasted. After mass was over, he said he had no idea how many people were Catholic especially South Koreans. It had taken three attempts before we finally made it to mass. The first week he did not show up because he was feeling ill. The second week he simply forgot. The third week we finally managed to meet and go to mass. The following week he emailed me that he could not go because he had to study for final exams. The point I am trying to make here is that it takes time to get things accomplished when dealing with an international clientele. There are many things that can go wrong when communications break down. The important thing to remember is to never accuse or get angry. When an apology comes, accept it with grace and reassure the other person that everything is fine. This way they save face and you keep the relationship in good standing.

Uncovering the Real Question

There are times when a student or patron is just standing around the reference desk, but not too close. To me this is a clear signal to approach that person and ask them if they need some help. Note, they will not approach me. I have to make the first move. Usually I approach them with a smile and say some cheerful word of greeting. This breaks the ice for what follows. When the opposite happens and the patron approaches me with the phrase, "I have a quick and simple question," the question is usually neither quick nor simple. Hours later you are still working on that quick and simple question. Information is packaged in a myriad of different ways. It may or may not be packaged the way the client thinks it is. One day I received a phone call asking for information on a UK company. The question was very broad in nature. She just needed any information on this company that I could find. After looking in all the normal places and finding nothing I called her back with my findings.

She then informed me where she had looked, Dialog and various other databases to which she had access. As the conversation ensued it became quite apparent that the person on the other end of the line was not just your average library user, but was an information professional like myself. She then asked me if I had access to the Dun & Bradstreet database. I told her that although I had searched our D&B Million Dollar database, I still had found nothing. The conversation ended with her telling me the company only had twenty employees. That meant the company located somewhere in the UK with twenty employees was probably private and there was no information to be found. This was an information request for which there was no answer and she ultimately knew it, but she wanted confirmation from the expert!

Another client, who shall remain nameless, and who has called frequently over the years left a message on my answering machine at 8PM one night. She needed some negative information on a certain software company by early the next morning because she had a meeting and needed some proof to back up her statement. This was Thursday night. So sucker that I am, I logged into the libraries' databases from home and found some negative information on the company. This information I conveyed to her later that night. The next day, Friday was my research day which means I do not go into work. Later that day I called to see how her meeting went with her client. She told me they had cancelled the meeting, but my boss had told her the stock price had gone from $35 to $10 in the last several months. The information I had found was that the company's earnings had not met expectations for the last two quarters. Apparently my findings were not good enough. Being able to access what a person's real informational needs are versus what they say they need can be a very tricky business. This is why I encourage people to start their research with a reference question instead of ending their research with a reference question. There may not be an answer to the question.

So how do they handle this is other countries. It is my understanding that the head of the library in India will certainly have an advanced library science degree, but the assistant librarians probably have an undergraduate library science degree which is true in several countries. The assistant librarians are the ones who work with the users. Most of the library staff are polite and helpful. Once a new user gets to know the procedures, he/she will not require additional help from the staff unless a book/journal is not traceable. The only environment in which new visitors descend upon the library staff for help would be in an university library setting with a new batch of students for the initial few days of classes. The librarians help a lot in locating some things. Also in India the cataloging system is different but just as affective. Bar codes are not yet being used, but it is my guess that they are not too far away from becoming implemented as they are already implementing automation in their technical services departments. (Dr. Rajanala)

According to one of my students, Hussain Kahn, who is from Saudi Arabia, the staff work with patrons of importance, not student workers. One does not interrupt someone until they are finished speaking. Smiling is being friendly according to the Islamic religion. And the first thing the librarian would say, "Is there anything I can get you?" as in a glass of water. In greeting one shakes the right hand and then puts the hand to the heart. The older person is to be seated in the front of a car. A kiss on the right shoulder is reserved for royalty or extremely wealthy people.

How They See Us

When international visitors come to this country what they are expecting is what they have seen in American movies and television. They think everyone is rich beyond their dreams, that we are an immoral people who thrive on sex and violence. Nothing could be further from the truth especially in our library systems. Therefore, it is up to us to set the record straight. I think Laura Bush is putting forth our true image. She is a librarian who is publically promoting the development of reading skills in our children. Often our visitors are at the same level of reading as our children and we must keep this in mind when interacting with them. Right now I am working with a visitor from South Korea. Since it is Lent, he and I are reading some bible passages together. He is reading them out loud and I am correcting his pronunciation as he goes along. His comprehension is fairly good, but he needs help with certain sounds. Talking more softly, moving at a slower pace and showing consideration may help to dispel the image they have of us as fast moving, loud and violent people. Speaking slowly and enunciating each syllable will enhance the reference experience for them. They already feel embarrassed to even come to you. Often just a word of encouragement will make them feel more confident.

The Art of Translating

The art of translating is a must in this business. A student will come to me with an assignment in hand. This particular instance the student had to find liquidity and activity ratios for a company. Not everyone knows that a liquidity ratio is also called a quick or current ratio. However, if one consults a ratio book, it will tell you this and how to calculate this ratio. I am still working on what the professor means by an activity ratio, but I think something like inventory turnover tracks the activity of a company. This can make for a very long process if the student is a visitor and does not have a firm grip on business terminology. One professor made an assignment that entailed finding six main economic indicators for three countries over a five year period. Some of the indicators were the GNP (Gross National Product), the GDP (Gross Domestic Product), and the GNP at the PPP (Purchasing Power Parity). This translates into 90 data elements. I could not find a single source that had all three in it. This is when the reference librarian has her work cut out for her. Even my boss could not believe that all six indicators from three countries over a five year period could not be found in a single source. Usually if a source has the GDP, it will not have the GNP and visa versa. The only source I have found to date for the PPP is the *World Development Report*. Anyway, we ended up gathering the data from seven or eight resources, each with different arrangements and different ways of saying the same thing. If this is difficult for me, imagine how daunting it is for our visitors.

We are Professionals

There are two very different perceptions our visitors may have of us and it is important to communicate the truth to them. Many see us as very busy people and therefore they should not bother us. In some instances this is true, but not always. So how do we let them know that one of our jobs is to help them in their research? A key strategy I use is by being pro-active. I stop long enough to access the situation or I just ask if they need some help. Sometimes I wish that I had not done that, but failing to do so would be failing to do my job.

The second perception is that I have nothing to do and should be at the beck and call twenty four seven for them alone. This of course is not true either. These kind of people, be they visitors or not, tend to be lazy and want you to do their work for them. These are the ones who want everything simple, packaged just the way they want with no brain work necessary. There is a fine line between helping certain students get a jump start and doing their assignment for them. Some may see this as spoon feeding, but if it helps them to get up and running what is the harm?

I will never forget an Asian student who kept coming to me with her assignments. I would show her how to get to the database, help her formulate a search strategy and she would find some very relevant articles. This was not enough. She expected me to read the articles and tell her how to do a SWOT (Strengths, Weaknesses, Opportunities, and Threats) analysis. I ended up telling her that it was her job as a student in a large American University to learn English and understand it. She had to learn to think for herself and to learn to think critically, and learn to read between the lines. Many years later I learned that her culture did not teach students to think critically or analytically. Besides, in her country librarians are perceived as servants who do everything for the students including making copies of articles for them! The United States is a self serve nation, many others are not. Also in her country students learn by rote, memorizing and repeating what they are taught. It is impolite to be critical. It shows disrespect for your teachers and elders.

There is no doubt that our guests perceive us as arrogant and a wealthy people with very wasteful ways. One of the major difficult issues for them is the buying of textbooks that can cost as much as $600 per quarter. They see this as an unnecessary expenditure for each student to have his own book for each class. They think it makes more sense to share textbooks. Frequently, I am asked if a certain textbook is on closed reserve. They do not understand the premise that sales of textbooks puts money into the professor's pockets. Many professors in our country feel they are overworked and underpaid. The sale of these books means a certain commission for the authors. The more one sells the higher the amount of commission is attained. Also at the core of this practice lies a fierce independence. If each student has his own textbook for the class, he can study when he wants to study. He can also mark the book in a way which helps him learn the material. He does not have to share. This is such an alien concept to so many of our visitors.

When the international student approaches the reference librarian, there are a couple of things foremost on his mind. The first is to communicate the question correctly with as good English as he can muster up. The second is he needs you to show him so he can do it on his own the next time. We have all had questions that were the exact opposite of what was really needed. The real trick is to come to that conclusion with the student saving face. One thing I try to do is break the question into steps. If the student is looking for six main economic indicators on three countries for a five year period, go after the easiest first. This is not one question, but rather six questions with a total of ninety data elements. Breaking them into time series helps make the project more manageable. It can still be very time consuming, but these students are coming from a very different time frame than us. They are not in a hurry like our students. To them time is not money. Time is not of the essence. Time is what it takes to do a thorough job. They understand the process of coming to a consensus and that this process is a long and slow one.

Students come to me from all different walks of life. Some come with a chip on their shoulders; others are totally embarrassed to be there. It is imperative to access the situation quickly and put the student at ease. I have watched other staff members go into a long explanation as to why a question cannot be answered. This is not what the student wants to hear. The student is looking for a solution. Give him one regardless of the difficulty or simplicity of the question. Help him to find that book, even if it is not in your library, but in another library. At least point him in the right direction. Show him how to request the book. Show him how to check his circulation record. Of course, you cannot do this unless you know how to do it yourself.

Listening Comprehension

International students read English often much better than they speak or hear it. This is because they have had years of studying it, but not listening to it. One of the first steps in their research process is to learn how to use the *Reader's Guide to Periodical Literature* in its paper format. Here the student can see the way the information is organized as well as the way it is not organized. If, for example, one were looking for information on "human resource management" there are two full pages of See Also references. One must look under the terms "Personnel" or "Employees", etc. Then various topics on the subject are further sub-categorized. This quickly shows the student the various possibilities under which the information can be found. The "See Also" leads to synonyms for further exploration. This opens up a whole wide world of research processes and possibilities. Conveying this concept is much more difficult to accomplish in the listening mode. In the listening mode one has to hear, translate, and comprehend. Much can get lost between the hearing and the comprehension. It has been said that an international student actually only hears every third word a person speaks in English. One can imagine the difficulty in this conversational process. I know from personal experience since I experienced the same problems when I arrived on the shores of France. For three whole days I had to speak French since not one soul spoke English. I must have said "Pardon" a million times. To my amazement everyone was very polite and patient with me. I wish Americans could be as "gentile". Of course, the "conditional" phrases are the most difficult to learn and very few do unless they become completely fluent in the language. The point here is that it takes time to hear, see and finally comprehend that which is being said. When one can show or demonstrate, the learning process becomes much faster. An added benefit is less opportunity for misunderstandings or confusion. What you see is what you get.

Explaining English Phrases

A phrase such as "capital allocation of a company" might be very difficult for an ordinary person let alone a person whose primary language is not English to understand. First one needs to define the separate words in the phrase. When one talks about capital, one usually means "money" or capital asset which is long term money or property that is not bought or sold in the normal course of business. The term also includes "fixed assets" which are buildings, land, equipment, furniture, etc. Allocation is simply another word for distribution. So capital allocation is the way in which a company's value is distributed. How much of the value is in long-term debt, how much of the value is tied to real estate, how much is in plants and equipment, how much is in operations, etc.

A request to find the "portfolio management of a company" is not likely to ever be answered. One reason is that this information is private and proprietary information and only a few top executives know the structure of the portfolio. However, this may be incorrect wording, when what was really being sought was the structure of the company. In business communication, a portfolio consists of money allocations into three investment sectors: stocks, bonds, and cash. The management of that portfolio is the percentage of money in each sector. For example, if the portfolio contains fifty percent of the entire value in stocks, it is considered a more aggressive portfolio than one which has thirty three percent in stocks, thirty three percent in bonds, and thirty three percent in cash. This is a very conservative portfolio. One can certainly find the names of the investment managers or the analysts for a certain company, including which investment company the company is affiliated with and a telephone number and even the recommendations of a manager, but that will not tell anyone exactly how a company's portfolio is managed. So much clarification is needed in order to understand the exact request.

What does "membership dues" mean? This was a question from a Korean friend of mine. He understood "due" to mean a time line, deadline as in "The paper is due on August 24th." He could not understand the combination of the words "membership dues". In one instance the word "due" is a verb and in another it is a noun. The English language has so many words that are like that with two meanings depending on how they are used. Some of the international students are just so hungry to find someone who will speak English with them or explain how to go about finding information. It seems they go days without speaking to a real person except other students from their own country. They often express their sincere gratitude for me just taking the time to teach them what they need to learn.

I have learned more from talking to you in this last 30 minutes than in my four years here

One day a student came in with a piece of paper with four call numbers written on it. He declared he could not find the books. He was in a big hurry so he left me with the piece of paper and said he would return. When he returned about a week later, I took him to the computer and searched each call number and pointed out the status of the book. Two of them were in the depository because they were so old, one was in another library, and one was in our library. I explained to him they were too old and asked him what he was trying to find. He wanted information on "Food Brokers". However, this was not really what he wanted. What he really needed was information on the food service brokers industry, specifically food service distribution brokers in the dairy and frozen food industries as in "Schwan". I went to several of the databases and showed him records on the Schwan Food Company and other companies operating in the same industries. In the process we determined that Schwan was indeed a private company, not a public company, as he had assumed. I showed him how to find information on the competitors, on the dairy industry, on the frozen food industry and on the distribution operations in these industries. I also showed him how to search the Wall Street Journal electronically. Then I took him to our paper resources which have different kinds of information. I also showed him the Associations Unlimited database in which he could target those associations within those industries. This whole time of course I was explaining where he needed to go to get the different kinds of information. I finally ended up telling him that he could have access to some of this information even after he graduated if he became a member of the alumni association. Now that was some valuable time spent helping a patron learn the merits of research.

Explaining the Information Seeking Process

During the reference process it is so important to take one's time assessing the situation. An elderly gentleman called me on the telephone the other day. He said he was looking for the price of a certain stock on May 5, 1976 in order to determine the cost basis. I took down his name and telephone number and said I would call him back with the information. As usual, it got very busy in the library that afternoon so the next morning I started looking for the answer to the stock question. I thought this was going to be a very easy task since 1976 was not that long ago. I could not find the stock in the *Wall Street Journal*, I could not find it in the *Stock Guide*, and our IPO (Initial Public Offering) did not go back that far. I did find something in the *Capital Changes Reporter* so I called him with the information I had found. He then explained that he had talked with numerous other librarians and had been working on this problem for two weeks! It seems his wife had bought the stock as an IPO as a favor for a friend. The wife had died twenty years ago. He had the stock in hand but no way of knowing what she had paid for it. I told him I would look in several other places and call him back. I searched the *Bloomberg* and found the stock. From the price, together with the information from the *Capital Changes Reporter*, we could ascertain the approximate IPO price and the fact the stock had a two for one split. I made a copy of the page from the *Capital Changes Reporter* and sent it to him. He called me and thanked me for having done such a great job. He then asked me for my name and the name and address of the director of libraries. He was so impressed by my skills, thoroughness, and my social skills he wanted to write a letter on my behalf. He did just that.

Chapter Five

Communication

Everyone is Special

Communication may be defined as the means through which people exchange feelings and ideas with one another. Unlike things, feelings and ideas are difficult to exchange. What do writing in a diary, watching television, talking with friends, speaking on the telephone, and reading a menu have in common? They are all forms of communication. It has been estimated that people spend more time communicating than they spend in any other complex activity in life. Even so, communication is a word that most people have difficulty defining and talking about (Encyclopedia Britannica Online 2003).

Communication encompasses a great deal more than the above definition. There is verbal and non verbal communication. There are posture, facial expressions, gestures, body language and movement, and attitudes. The way we groom ourselves, the clothes we choose to wear, even our hair style and the shoes we wear tell others about who we are, how we have been raised, from what economic background we may have come, even how well we have been educated. There is a popular saying in the United States, "You can take the boy out of the country, but you cannot take the country out of the boy." It basically means one can move from a rural area to an urban area, but it will still be apparent that he was raised a country boy. Another saying is "The fruit does not fall far from the tree." This means you are who your ancestors are and your actions will reveal what this means.

In this chapter I will discuss ways to better understand those people and their cultures who have come to us as our visitors, guests, and students, either on a temporary or a permanent basis. When I teach my workshops, I encourage my students to come in out of the hot or cold weather into my library. It is clean, warm, dry, and a peaceful place to be. They may use the facility for quiet study, group study, research, to socialize or even grab a quick nap between classes. Now wouldn't you want to come to such a place?

First impressions are the most important. In trying to create a welcoming environment, we hire students from countries all over the world and have them work at the circulation desk. This way, if a shy Asian student sees someone from her own country, she will feel more comfortable approaching another Asian student. Our students come from Hong Kong, the People's Republic of China, Singapore, Malaysia, Saudi Arabia, Yemen, Mexico, Brazil, Turkey, France, Germany, etc. You get the picture. We also have African American, Indian American, Chinese American, Native American, European American, and Latin American students. It is very difficult to tell who comes from where. It is a totally international environment. Language is often a barrier. The other day I asked a student if he had managed to get in touch with a student who had left his student identification at the front desk. His response was, "No, he is engaged." I did not have a clue about what he was saying, so I said back to him, in kind of a question, "engaged?" Another student quickly told me that the phone line was busy. The student from Singapore speaks the King's English and that is how they say the phone is busy in Singapore!

My reference desk is the first thing one sees upon entering the library. I always try to greet the visitor with a "Good Morning" or "Good Afternoon." My desk is on their right. The circulation desk is on their left. There is always someone at one of these two desks which means there is always a warm person to approach with a question. I also communicate in other ways too. I always dress professionally, have a ready smile on my face, and do a slight bow to the Asian students. They seem to really appreciate this as it tells them I know a little something about their culture. I try to be inviting, open, and gracious sending the signal that they are important to me as is their assignment. This first encounter is not always easy and certainly not fast. It can take quite a long time to ascertain what the real question might be and which resource would be the best introduction for them. Many times they will tell me they have class and will have to return at a later time. This is fine. We have at least begun the relationship.

Active Listening

Active listening is a tool I use to get a better understanding of the situation and the person with whom I am dealing. First, I let them ask the question fully without interruption. I then repeat back to them what it is that I think I heard. This is followed by a discourse or further explanation. Just this morning a student came to my office. She sat down and told me that I had helped some of her friends in the past and could I help her even though she was in the College of Human Ecology not the Fisher College of Business. She is looking for articles and journals that would give her the top 10 or top 100 companies in the Apparel Industry. She is from South Korea, so her English and pronunciation were not that great. I wanted to take her to the reference section and show her some of the major resources, but she had a exam in half an hour so we set up an appointment in several days. We had quite a discourse in only about five minutes, but everything I had said above about not interrupting was totally forgotten. Whenever I did not understand a word, I asked her to repeat so the conversation proceeded fairly quickly. This was due in large part to the fact she spoke and pronounced English better than some others from her country. Each encounter is different and must be approached accordingly. Because of her skills, she was probably sent as the envoy for her group.

Since this conversation had been so successful, I tried to analyze it further:

Show Respect – "Please have a seat."

Smile – "I am from South Korea and my friends have told me that you have helped them."

Listen intently – "I am from the Human Ecology Department." (Meaning I know helping me is not part of your job, since you are the Business Librarian.)

Ask open ended question – "How may I help you?"

Totally listen to the full reference question and decide if it is indeed something you can actually help them with in their research. Be sensitive to their level of confidence – She has a fairly good grasp of English, did not feel shy about asking for my help, and alluded to the fact she had confidence in me.

Communicate Empathy – I told her that we have several resources that could help her, but that it will take some time to do the research.

Later that week she returned with her friend who was much more knowledgeable about what she wanted to prove with her research. I asked them to be seated and we sat and talked for several minutes about the project and how easy or difficult it would be to obtain the list she wanted to put together. Actually it was a list of the top 100 mail order companies that sold women's clothing. If one looked at just mail order companies, such companies as Home Depot popped up and if one looked at just stores that sold women's clothing many did not have a mail order department. Basically she would need to pull up over 500 companies in order to obtain the names of those that not only sold women's clothing, but lots of other things too. I showed them several SIC codes they needed to work with and several databases in which one could search by the SIC code to get a listing of names. I also explained how they could do this research from home or a computer lab. They were very excited about this bit of news. Then I took them out to the Ready Reference section and showed them a paper resource that listed mail order companies on a national basis. They now had a thorough understanding of the task ahead of them. They thanked me profusely and left to tackle the job in the comfort of their home. I made sure to tell them to return with their final results so I could be sure their findings were correct. They assured me they would do that.

There are many who come to this country who have learned English, though it be British English, and speak and write English very well. They come from countries who are now independent, but who were under British rule at one time. Thus their social language is English. In an interview with Dr. Rajanala, he says that most of the Indian scholars in the US will not have a large problem with the English language, except probably the accent. Indians have learned English from the U.K. point of view. However, there are exceptions from the pronunciation aspect. Their understanding and vocabulary is far better than most of the Asians being referred in my manuscript which discusses many encounters with students from China, South Korea, and Taiwan. This is due to the fact for most of the schools in India, "English" is the first language. The local mother tongue, such as Telugu, is the second language. The National language is "Hindi." Most people with "Hindi" as the mother tongue also learn "sanskrit" as their third language. However, the problems that Indians face in the US are new phrases as mentioned in page one, short cut spellings, and very localized expressions which can't be found in British English. So the expression "I don't know" is alright, but "I dunno" is difficult to understand. Other words/phrases are "sucker", "licked", "chip on the shoulder", and "beck and call". Asian is too broad a term. It is better to identify the country of the student than the broad term Asian (Dr.Rajanala).

Verbal Communication

What you say and how you say it makes all the difference in the world. If you are soft spoken, your message will get across much better. Many of our visitors come from soft spoken countries. I am sure the level of noise in this country is very uncomfortable for them. To be soft spoken is not the same as whispering. I grew up in the days when the good nuns would hold up their finger to the mouth and say shush. I vowed the reference area would never be a quiet area. Here people need to talk out loud. By its very nature, it is not a quiet study area of the library. I often have to inform the client that they do not need to whisper, I need to be able to hear the question. Once that matter is cleared up, I can visibly see them relax and begin to concentrate on their informational need. When they see that I am genuinely listening to their question, repeating back to them what that question may entail, and explain which resources we have in the library that will help, I see a sigh of relief.

I know many cultures do not like to hear the word "No", but there is one situation in which they are greatly relieved to hear it. That situation is when they come to my office and ask "Are you busy?" Ninety-nine percent of the time the answer is "No." I may not be telling the truth, I may be very busy trying to write this book, but my job is to help anyone and everyone who needs help in the Business Library. This is my top priority. One of the things I love to tell people is that their question is not as complicated as it may first appear. Then I show them where the answer can be found.

It is difficult to know the emotional state of the patron. One day a student came to me with what I thought was just a typical reference question. She needed to do an analysis of a company and an industry. From my perspective it was just a basic reference question which I had answered thousands of times before. I took her out to the public terminals and showed her how to get to two key databases, both of which contained company and industry analysis. This is a fairly standard operating procedure for me, but as I showed her the different elements of the databases she kept trying to hold back her tears. I have no idea how long she had been trying to find the information, but it was obvious she had been struggling with this for some time. I tell the students in all my workshops, "Please ask first, seek later. You will save a lot of time."

Verbal communication needs to be kept as simple as possible when dealing with those who are struggling with the English language. The use of jargon, abbreviations, libraryese, and slang sayings should be avoided at all costs. Although we librarians do have our own jargon, we should try to be other oriented, and stop to listen how something might sound to the receiver on the other end. I have been asked many times what ABI/Inform stands for as if there was a big secret about the letters. Visitors need to have everything spelled out for them. If they give you a blank look or an expression of confusion, rephrase in a more simplistic manner. Even regular American visitors sometimes have to tell me that it is the first time they have been in my library. At that moment I know they are about as clueless as any other stranger so I ask them what exactly are they trying to find. I often have to explain the basic rules to them such as a book may be borrowed for three weeks, but in order to check out a book one must be a *current* faculty, student or staff. Since we have such a magnificent collection, this rule does not make outsiders very happy. However, they can join the "Friends of the Libraries" for an annual fee and receive borrowing privileges. Now they can even join the Alumni Association for an annual fee and not only check out books, but they also have access to five large online databases from anywhere in the world. These are the Ebscot databases.

Avoid Jokes

Avoid jokes! They will backfire every time. To show you how sensitive this topic is I will demonstrate an attempt at humor which for some reason left me feeling hurt. I was getting out of my car and two guys were tossing a football back and forth. I said "Good Morning" and one of them replied with a smile, "Good Afternoon." Well yes it really was afternoon instead of morning, but the fact that a much younger person was correcting me hurt a little. I am not usually a sensitive person and that comment would normally have rolled off my back. Maybe, just maybe it was the tone of his voice. When I use a humorous line when talking to my friend from South Korea it takes me about ten lines of explaining before he fully understands what I am trying to say. Just today he came to me asking for an explanation of a certain sentence. The sentence read, "Since the Association has seen a decline in its members, the revenues have also declined because of the dues decrease." He did not understand the word "dues" as in "membership dues." I explained to him that dues means a membership fee in the Association. Then it was clear to him.

Speaking Out Loud

I find that reading out loud can help the student better understand what he is reading. It really helps their pronunciation of the English language. It is the same gimmick we use with our children. We point to something and say what it is, then you get them to say the word. This may be uncomfortable for the student in the beginning, but it makes their learning so much faster. One student asked if he could read the Bible out loud to me. We did this several times and it was a very slow process because he had to stop every few words to ask for clarification of a certain word or sentence. It did help him have more confidence in speaking English. Years ago when I was teaching English for Berlitz to Spanish speaking people, we would look at a word and ask the student to put it into a sentence. A light bulb would go on for the student because he could associate the word with a concept. However, the sentence needs to have meaning for the student. Such everyday happenings need to be part of the conversation. When one says, "I ran to the bus stop," who has never had to run to the bus stop to catch the bus. We all have had to do this sometime in our life.

Saving Face

Please understand the concept of "saving face." It not only means to maintain one's pride, but it means avoiding any kind of embarrassment what so ever. When communicating with Asians it is very important to do it in a gracious and methodical way. They can easily take offense if you are not careful. Use the I instead of the you. For example if you are having trouble understanding the student, ask him to repeat the question. Never say, "Your English is difficult to understand", say instead, "I am sorry, but I am having trouble understanding you. Would you please repeat the question?" If this does not work, have them write it on a piece of paper. This almost always works. For those of us who use the word "no" all the time, it is a real struggle to refrain from using it with people from other countries. We also have a tendency to take what others say literally. When someone from another country says, "I agree.", this does not mean the same thing as "yes." or if they say, "I understand" it does not always mean they understand. In fact it may mean just the opposite, but they do not feel they can say that. The following is a real example of communicating both verbally and non verbally at the same time. "The Filipinos rarely say 'no' as we do. They resist confrontation and may say 'yes' verbally while putting down their heads to indicate 'no.'" (Pacther p. 306)

My friend from South Korea was preparing to make a presentation to his class. He was representing his group. He was very nervous because he could not make a mistake and embarrass himself, but more importantly the group. He worked many hours on both the written and spoken presentation. It was of utmost importance that nothing go wrong. He asked me to help him with his pronunciation. The English language has been very difficult for him to grasp both in written format and spoken format. I finally understood the importance of "saving face." According to his culture, harmony within the group is necessary in order to achieve the group's goal. It is a very collective philosophy in which all must come to a consensus so that the group speaks as one. He explained that in his country no one likes the person who is the over achiever, who is the smartest, who is the one better than the others and so to maintain harmony, the one that sticks out is hammered down to fit into the group. This is just the opposite as in my county in which the over achiever climbs the corporate ladder. This also explains why the Chinese may fight among themselves – in order to achieve harmony. In his writings he kept talking about the "intent." I could not really understand what he meant until one day he wrote, "The intent and purpose of this meeting . . ." Then it clicked with me. He is meaning "goal" when he is using "intent" because in his country everything is done to reach the "intent" or as we would say "the ultimate goal" or heaven.

Communicate Patience

Communicate that you have all the time in the world for the person in front of you, on the telephone, or by e-mail. Your job is to provide service to that person, the best service in the world. One day two MBA students came to my office with a request for help. I asked them to be seated and they continued to explain their dilemma. They had been given an assignment to do some market research in the analytical chemistry industry. I have a business background as do they so I asked them to define "analytical chemistry." They did not know what it meant either. We first went to the catalog and found a book on the subject, an elementary book. I explained to them that they spoke "business" and that I spoke "business" and the chemists spoke "chemistry" or "science." Therefore, we did not speak the same language. The next step was to meet with the chemists to further clarify the area that needed to be investigated. I also gave them the telephone number and e-mail address of our chemistry librarian. I told them I would make an initial call to the chemistry librarian to get some guidance. I called the librarian and he was sufficiently rude and told me he would not even continue to talk to me unless I could further refine my request. What he meant was that the discipline of analytical chemistry was so enormous we had to determine which subset we wanted to investigate. At that point he had not heard from the two students. A couple of days went by and I received an e-mail from the chemistry librarian. I wrote him back asking him to call me so we could discuss our plan of action. Then I encountered an incident that really shocked me. My colleague was trying to reach me by telephone to set up a meeting with him and the two MBA students to discuss the resources the students might use to work on the project. An American student was answering the main switchboard telephone and tried to transfer the phone call to my office. I was sitting right at my desk waiting for the phone call. For some reason it did not transfer so she explained to him that she would have to try it again. Showing a total lack of patience, he said never mind. He would try later. When he tried to get me later, he was told that I was at lunch. Before the second student could even ask if he could take a message, this colleague hung up the phone. The second student, an international student, was very offended that someone would just hang up on him. When I finally did manage to get through to this colleague, I told him there was no excuse for him to be rude to my students. After a long pause, we proceeded to discuss the resources he needed to use to help the students with their project. He had wanted to set up a meeting on Friday but I was not going to be in on Friday and he was going to be gone Wednesday and Thursday which would have pushed things into the next week. So I asked him to give me an example of a subset and I walked him through one of my business databases on how to search in this database. I told him I still thought his chemical databases would yield better market research on that subject because "spectroscopy" would be indexed in his databases not mine.

Non Verbal Communication

We probably communicate more non verbally than we do verbally. We tell others about ourselves in the way we dress, wear our hair, wear our shoes, in our general appearance and attitude, as well as our posture, touch, facial expression, eye contact, and distance with which we stand. We can even guess how well educated and how financially well to do a person is by their attire. Are they carrying a Coach handbag, are they wearing a Burberry raincoat, are their clothes filthy dirty?

When sitting at the reference desk one should be aware that several things shout out at a patron and they are not complimentary. I used to chew gum at the reference desk until I encountered a fellow librarian at a reference desk chewing gum and I realized how non professional she looked. While doing my research, I discovered that chewing gum in most Asian countries is just not done and in China one can be put in jail for it. It is against their law of importing gum or chewing gum in public. You do not see many Asians chewing gum because in their country it is prohibited. Another non verbal insult to the potential customer is remaining behind the desk thus forming a barrier between you and the person needing help. It makes me so mad when librarians do this for several reasons. It communicates that they are superior, they are the professional behind the desk and you are not. I also think to myself, "Those lazy bums. Why can't they get off their derriere and help me?" Also there is a tendency to point someone in the right direction such as all our books on cats can be found at this call number. I do not want all the books on cats. My question was "What does it mean when my cat is kneading her claws?"After going to two different libraries in search of a particular book entitled "Why Do Cats Do That?", I finally went home and did a search on Google and found my answer. They do that if they have been taken away from their mother before the 12 week period; they do that before making themselves comfortable; and they do that to show their affection for their owner. Thank you, now was that so difficult?

Facial Expressions

Facial expressions can be the most powerful nonverbal communicator for many people. I think we all tend to arrive at a conclusion about another person just by observing that persons facial expression. I know there are faces that I automatically warm to and others that scare the daylights out of me. I can look at a person and observe that he is chipper today, or not well (a pale face), or recovering from a hang over from too much partying the night before (glazed eyes), or is worried, or is curious, or is bored out of his gourd, or is just oblivious to his surroundings. I believe they call this "people watching." Faces can be very ambiguous or very honest. Faces can be very stern (as was my father's) or aristocratic (as was my mother's). It is really difficult to hide one's attitude in a facial expression. If someone is in a lot of pain or very angry it is very difficult to hide this in the face. A person's smile may indicate one's lack of seriousness which might be interpreted as an insult to a person from another country especially if the smile does not fit the situation. The smile, for instance, can be very genuine or it can look as phoney as a three dollar bill. A smile can be welcoming or connote the message that the person would rather not be communicating. Years ago I worked with someone who really hated working with the public and when she was required to she would put on this really phoney smile, if she smiled at all. Anyone could tell she was uncomfortable in that setting. She was just an unhappy, nosey, jealous type of person and it showed through every time. A smile usually means a greeting in almost every part of the world. However, sometimes a smile covers up an embarrassment or an angry emotion. One day I was observing a couple having lunch together. The young man was the typical young American male trying to show off to his lunch partner who was a young, beautiful Asian looking young lady. As the conversation continued, his voice got louder and he was making an attempt to be funny. I could not really hear the conversation, but I did notice the young lady smile while covering her mouth. Right then I knew she was attempting to cover up an embarrassing moment. I never saw them again together. A smile accompanied with laughter might be fine among friends, but would be very insulting to someone in the reference area seeking help no matter how funny the question may appear. This happens a lot at the circulation desk among the American students who fail to comprehend the seriousness of the patrons on the other side of the desk. The students are not very professional whereas the patrons, especially in a business setting, are very serious and keen on getting serious help.

Some people use facial expressions to intimidate or to show anger in order to get their way. This is used more by Americans than anyone else although I have seen people from other countries use this tactic too. It can easily backfire and the person gets the exact opposite of what they were wanting. A frown can have various connotations. It can mean a person is in deep thought or expressing disapproval or disagreement. It can mean a person is really concentrating on what is being said or that someone is unhappy or sad. It can simply mean a person is not feeling well or is just tired.

In my line of work, I smile briefly and then put on my serious face of listening carefully to what is being said. The person in front of me would not have come to me unless he needed my help. I need to convey to him that I take his informational needs seriously, but it might take some time to figure out what he really needs and how to satisfy that informational need. I try to keep it as simple as possible, but, of course, this is not always possible. I definitely try not to have anything between me and the patron, like a desk, that would distract us or make one feel superior to the other.

Eye Communication

Eye communication varies greatly from one culture to another. Below is an eye contact guide taken from Barbara Pachter's *Complete Business Etiquette Handbook*:

Eye Contact Guide

How	Where
Very Direct eye contact (Shows sincerity)	Middle East, Latin America, France, Italy
Direct eye contact (Shows interest and that You are listening)	USA, Northern Europe, Canada
Avoid direct eye contact (Shows respect)	Asia, India, parts of Africa

Knowing and using the various types of eye communication when dealing with people from other countries is really important for successful interactions with our new neighbors or visitors. If we continue to communicate the American way, we will not only insult, but intimidate those who come from other countries. There was an incident between an Asian student and a black student who was trying to apologize to him. The Asian would not look the black student in the eye and this made the black student furious. He kept shouting at the Asian student who would just not look him in the eye. The black student started hitting the Asian student. Finally someone stepped in. When the situation had calmed down, the black student said, "Why won't you look at me?" The Asian replied, "In my country, I was showing you respect." This is how serious eye communication can become. I have to consciously tell myself, "You are dealing with an Asian or a black person or anyone else who may be feeling not quite "OK" in this situation so remember the Eye Communication Guide. In our country direct eye contact means interest, attention to what the other is saying and lack of direct eye contact means a person is shady, or dishonest, or just showing a lack of respect. It means quite the opposite in other countries. I read somewhere that in Asia there is a superstition that a person can steal part of another person's soul with direct eye contact!

It is certainly considered rude to stare at another person for any length of time. I was having lunch today and the waiter just kept staring at me. There were only two other people in my area of the restaurant, and the waiter looked funny anyway. He did not look too bright and he looked weird and scarey to me. The longer he stared at me, the more uncomfortable I became. He finally turned his attention to the television. I was beginning to have thoughts of him taking me out back and chopping me up into little parts. Now I really know I watch too much television. Since I had only frequented the restaurant a few times, he was probably trying to place where he had seen me. I know he had been there at least a year and I had been in only three times.

Many people are not aware of nonverbal communication styles even among the subcultures of their own culture. I am totally clueless of the African-American's nonverbal communication style and sometimes it is even difficult for me to understand their verbal communication style. They have their own idioms, their own sentence structure and even their pronunciations leave me clueless as to what had just been said. When I project my own nonverbal communication style onto them, they can misinterpret what I am saying and visa versa. Americans have a way of looking directly into the other person's eyes continuously as they are speaking. I know of no other culture that does this. Both Latinos and Asians may look very briefly into your eyes and then look away as you are speaking. An Asian told me once that she cannot look at the person speaking because it distracts her and she finds herself not really listening to what is being said. She is concentrating on the other person's facial features instead. Latinos look very directly but only for a moment. Then they look away. The American can misinterpret this as not being interested in what is being said or not listening to what is being said. In the Latino culture, prolonged eye contact means the other person is challenging you or angry at you.

Space

The use of space varies from culture to culture. The general rule of thumb is that people from Asian countries leave more space between each other than do Americans and people from Latin American countries have less space between each other. In Europe the further North you are, the more distance there is between people when communicating. The further South you go, the closer they stand to each other as is typical in Italy, France, Russia, and Spain. Arabs stand as close as two to three inches to each other and if you back away they are insulted. I have noticed this in my reference work and I have to make a conscious effort to stay and hold my ground and let them decided how far or how close they want to be. Asians, on the other hand, have a tendency to stand back. Depending on what they have had for lunch it still might not be far enough. By this I mean Garlic breath.

William Sonnenschein in his book entitled *The Practical Executive and Workforce Diversity* tells an interesting story about a visitor from Africa.

"An African worker tells the story of his first days in the United States. He boarded a bus late one evening and noticed only one person on the bus. In his culture he would have been considered rude and unsociable to sit anywhere but right next to the other passenger. The person he sat next to, a small white woman, complained to the bus driver that the large black man was harassing her." (Sonnenschein p. 55) She obviously did not know he was a visitor or what his motives might have been, but surely it frightened her late at night.

It is interesting to see how visiting students take on American ways after being here just a short time. When my friend from South Korea first met me, he would bow and give me the three gesture greeting. As time went on he would greet me with the V greeting. The other day he came up and gave me a hug. I was taken quite by surprise and felt a little uncomfortable to say the least. This is what we call taking on "native behavior." In academia this is definitely frowned upon because teacher and student must keep their distance with one another. I must find a way to let him understand that this is improper behavior, and at the same time, not embarrass him. Standing too close to someone is this country can be interpreted as flirting with someone which may be far from the truth.

Touch

Touching in this country is definitely a very intimate nonverbal means of communicating. It is not done in public. You may have to explain this to the younger crowd, but for the most part I just do not see many people showing that kind of affection openly. I do see young Asian female students walking arm in arm which is perfectly acceptable in their country. The French are also known for doing this. When one of my colleagues or students and I have become good friends, he or she will give my a hug when parting or, if they are from Europe, we will kiss on both cheeks in departing. I am such a touchy, feely person that I have to watch it in both business and social settings.

How we touch another person says multiple things to that other person. Just the handshake alone will reveal much about a person's personality. Have you ever had a hand shake that left you thinking I have a few broken bones? An Asian's handshake is usually very soft and gentle which is fine if you understand where they come from as opposed to someone who is American and extends the same soft and gentle hand shake. You immediately think, "What a wuss." As a teenager, I once had the opportunity of shaking hands with Lyndon B. Johnson. He was the Vice President at the time. I was with my classmates. We were in his office and as we left he shook each of our hands. I am a little person and he was very tall with an unbelievably strong hand shake. As I left I felt like he sent me flying through the door. Soft and gentle it was not!

In some countries, public touching is forbidden. In Indonesia, for religious reasons, men and women do not touch in public, not even a hand shake, and one never touches anyone on the head, especially not that of a child. In most business settings the only touching is the hand shake. There are occasions when a hug is appropriate. The other day a former student returned to say hello. We had formed such a bond, that when she was about to leave she gave me a big hug. She is from Latin America, but I would never expect a male counter part to do the same. Italians and Latin Americans are more likely to touch more than a hand shake in order to be warm and friendly. When I was going to Italy, everyone warned me to expect my behind to be pinched and it was. As long as we were in groups that was fine. American, Asians, British, Germans, and Japanese are not prone to touching. However, Hispanics and some Middle Eastern cultures touching can be appropriate. As Barbara Pachter explains, "Arabs will bump you on the street and touch you during conversation. Latin Europeans and Latin Americans may tap you on the chest or touch your arm as they talk with no sexual implications or any attempt to physically dominate you. You need to understand these gestures as what they often are: an attempt to treat you equally, even to show that you are accepted." (Pachter p. 311).

I found a wonderful web site on communications in the different countries. Below are some of the countries and their rules for communications.

Argentina

- Italian and German are second and third languages
- Good conversation topics: soccer, history, culture, home and children, opera
- Bad conversation topics: the Peron years, religion, Falkland Islands conflict

  (http://www.cyborlink.com/besite/).

Brazil

- Music and long, animated conversation are favorite Brazilian habits. When conversing, interruptions are viewed as enthusiasm. Brazilians enjoy joking, informality, and friendships
- Good conversation topics: soccer, family, children
- Bad conversation topics: Argentina, politics, poverty, religion, and the Rain Forest

  (http://www.cyborlink.com/besite/).

Canada

- English is spoken in most of Canada. French is spoken in Quebec, and some areas of Nova Scotia and New Brunswick.

- Be open and friendly in your conversation. If you are naturally reserved in your behavior, you will appear confident and credible.

- Don't be boastful and don't overstate you product or service capabilities. You could implicate your company in a legal situation.

- If you are from the U.S., don't say, "we Americans", inferring you are including your Canadian hosts or guests in your reference. Canada is a distinct country with its own wonderful history and culture.

  (http://www.cyborlink.com/besite/).

China

- Being on time is vital in China

- Appointments are a must for business

- Present and receive cards with both hands. Never write on a business card or put it in your wallet or pocket. Carry a small card case.

- Chinese value rank and status. Let them know your credentials.

- Develop a working knowledge of Chinese culture

- Many Chinese will want to consult with the stars or wait for a lucky day before they make a decision

  (http://www.cyborlink.com/besite/).

France

- If you do not speak French, it is very important that you apologize for your lack of knowledge

- The French have a great appreciation for the art of conversation

- The French often complain that North Americans lecture rather than converse

- Be sensitive to the volume of your voice. Americans are known to offend everyone in a restaurant, meeting, or on the street with their loud voices and braying laughter

- Eye contact is frequent and intense, and can often be intimidating to North Americans

  (http://www.cyborlink.com/besite/).

Germany

- Germans love to talk on the telephone. While important business decisions are not made over the phone, expect many follow up calls and faxes.

- Germans guard their private life, so do not call a German at home without permission

- Titles are very important to Germans. Do your best to address people by their full, correct title, no matter how extraordinarily long that title may seem to foreigners. This is also true when addressing a letter.

  (http://www.cyborlink.com/besite/).

Hong Kong

- A round of applause may greet you during your visit. The Chinese like to applaud. You are expected to return the applause out of respect

- Appointments are recommended. Punctuality is expected

- Use only black and white materials for presentations, as colors are very significant

- Patience is important. The Chinese do not make decisions quickly

  (http://www.cyborlink.com/besite/).

India

- The word "no" has harsh implications in India. Evasive refusals are more common, and are considered more polite. Never directly refuse an invitation, a vague "I'll try" is an acceptable refusal

- Do not thank your hosts at the end of a meal. "Thank you" is considered a form of payment and therefore insulting

- Titles are very important. Always use professional titles.

  (http://www.cyborlink.com/besite/).

Indonesia

- For religious reasons (Muslim and Hindu) men and women do not touch in public in this culture period

- One important honorific title is for Muslims who have made a pilgrimage to Mecca. *Haji* is the title for a man, *Hajjah* is for a woman

- "Yes, but" means *no* when someone is speaking to you

- Do not use red ink when writing, or having printing done (Chinese) (http://www.cyborlink.com/besite/).

Israel

- "Tsk." Instead of saying "no, " Israelis make a loud "tsk" sound with their tongues
- "Ech? Ech?" means "What?" or "I don't understand."
- "Nu?" with different inflections is a Yiddish word that can mean almost anything, but often means "How are you?"
- To indicate "Oh no!" or "Now what?": Put hands on your head, then lift your shoulders in a shrug.
- To indicate "Great!" or "Yesss!": Make your right hand into a fist, with the thumb pointing upward. (Rosenthal p. 76)

Italy

- Avoid talking about religion, politics, and World War II
- At social gatherings, it is considered insulting to ask someone you have just met about their profession
- Good conversational topics include Italian culture, art, food, wine, family, and films

  (http://www.cyborlink.com/besite/).

Japan

- If you are greeted with a bow, return with a bow as low as the one you received
- Take special care in handling cards that are given to you. They are given and received with both hands. Read it carefully. Business cannot begin until this process is completed
- The Japanese prefer to use last names. Do not request that they call you by your first name

  (http://www.cyborlink.com/besite/).

Korea

- The Korean language encompasses a refined spoken etiquette. The three basic levels of the language include polite form (superiors and elders); intimate form (friends and equals); and a "rough" form (directed at people on a lower social class)

- Avoid physical contact. They do not like to be touched
- Keep your distance. Westerners are generally taller, hence the closer, the taller
- Remember your status. No hands in the pockets, no shoes on the desk or chair, no crossing the legs, especially showing the sole of the shoe
- Posture matters. Sit and stand ramrod straight to enhance your dignity
- Never point to anyone or anything (Keating p. 65)

Mexico

- Do not use red ink anytime you are writing someone's name
- The traditional toast in Mexico is *Salud* (Sal-UUD)
- Mexicans refer to people from the United States as North Americans
- Good conversational topics are Mexican culture, history, art, museums, and fine cuisine
- Never discuss the Mexican-American war, poverty, illegal aliens, or earthquakes

    (http://www.cyborlink.com/besite/).

Philippines

- Avoid pointing a finger at anyone while speaking
- Filipinos are quite skilled at saying "No" without actually saying it
- Know that being touched on the arm or shoulder indicates that the person speaking to you feels quite comfortable with you
- Listen and listen carefully
- The formal Tagalog greeting is *Kumusta or Kumustra po*

    (http://www.cyborlink.com/besite/).

Poland

- If someone tells you you look very well, you may wish to go on a diet. For Poles, looking well means well fed
- When a man wishes to go drinking with his "buddies,", he flicks the side of his neck with thumb and index finger
- Poles usually spend a few minutes talking about "cabbages and kings" before they broach the real subject for discussion

- Good conversation topics include sports, literature, Poland's culture and economic progress
- Exchange business cards and handshakes with everyone in the entire group (Kissel p. 66)

Russia

- Speaking or laughing loudly in public is considered rude
- Many Russians speak English, as it is often taught beginning in the third grade
- Russians are highly literate, and have almost a 100% literacy rate
- Good topics of conversation include peace, the current changes taking place in Russia, and their current economic situation

  (http://www.cyborlink.com/besite/).

South Africa

- Use titles and surnames to address people
- Appointment should be made starting at 9 a.m.
- Do not rush deals. South Africans are very casual in their business dealings
- Business cards have no formal exchange protocol
- South Africans prefer a "win-win" situation

  (http://www.cyborlink.com/besite/).

Spain

- Spain has four official languages: Spanish, Catalan, Gallego, and Euskera
- Lunches and dinners are an important part of business life in Spain. Most communication will take place during them
- During business negotiations, rules and systems are only used as a last resort to solving a problem
- During business meetings, doors are usually kept shut
- Business colleagues often dine together, but different ranks within a company do not mix

  (http://www.cyborlink.com/besite/).

Taiwan

- A nod of the head is an appropriate greeting

- Women rarely shake hands but this is changing

- "Have you eaten?" is a standard greeting. It is more of a rhetorical question

- Always wait for introductions

- Punctuality is of great importance in Taiwan

  (http://www.cyborlink.com/besite/).

Thailand

- When greeting someone put your hands together as in prayer and lift them to your face

- Thailand is called "The Land of Smiles." the smile can mean many things. Often, it indicates genuine friendliness, as Thais are warm and hospitable

- As in most Asia, a nervous giggle indicates embarrassment

- A sudden brief laugh for no apparent reason is a frequent reaction to *farang* rudeness (Wise p. 67)

United Kingdom

- In England, English is the official language, but it should be noted that the Queen's English and American English are very different

- Ordinary vocabulary can differ extensively between the two countries. When the English say, "I'll knock you up in the morning," contrary to what you might think, it is merely an announcement that you will be given a wake-up call in the morning

- One gesture to avoid is the V for Victory sign, done with the palm facing yourself. This is a very offensive gesture

- If a man has been knighted, he is addressed as "Sir and his first name" as in Sir John

  (http://www.cyborlink.com/besite/).

United States of America

- Offer a firm handshake, lasting 3–5 seconds

- Good eye contact during business and social conversations shows interest, sincerity, and confidence

- Introductions include one's title if appropriate, or Mr., Ms, Mrs and the full name

- A smile is a sign of friendliness

- Always ask permission to smoke before lighting a cigarette or cigar. Many places have banned smoking in public places

  (http://www.cyborlink.com/besite/).

Vietnam

- Don't Point. If you need to indicate something, do so with your whole hand, with the palm opened upward

- Keep your distance during conversations. The further away you are, the less physically threatening you are

- Speak softly and keep your hands down. They probably will not understand your gesture

- Posture matters. Balance is a highly valued principle in all aspects of Vietnamese life (Curry p. 76).

As you can see, most of the world does not believe in equality or equal rights for all citizens. Titles and punctuality are very important in most countries as well as formality and civility. It is also very clear that most people in the world do not run on the motto "Time is money." as we do here in the United States. When dealing with people from other countries, I think it is very important to slow down your whole process and approach each encounter very carefully so as not to offend the person with whom you are interacting. One last word, when someone from another country is late for an appointment, be understanding and gracious. They are probably very embarrassed at being even a little late. Let them know it is fine and continue with your business.

Chapter Six

Etiquette

Basic Etiquette

Etiquette is defined as the forms prescribed by custom or authority to be observed in social, official, or professional life. Many people scoff at the concept of etiquette, but these people are neither well-bred nor well-educated. It behooves everyone, especially those working with visitors from other countries, to develop skills of etiquette so as not to embarrass the visitor or oneself. Basic etiquette is taught to children from the time they are very young. Children are taught to listen and learn. They are taught to speak only when spoken to. They are taught acceptable table manners. They are taught not to interrupt. They are taught to sit still and be quiet, and not to speak in church. They are taught to be polite to their elders, addressing them as Mr. Or Mrs. Or Yes Sir or No Mame. I was raised in the South where proper etiquette was the norm. When I was about 10 years old, I would go to the local gas station to get a candy bar. I would say to the gas attendant, "Yes Sir", or "Thank you, Sir" or "No Sir." This drove the kid crazy, he was probably about 16, and perceived this formality to be for only older people. Well to me he was older, old enough to be a grown up.

When Inside, Remove thy Hat

My heritage is English and I was raised in an Upper Middle Class family. I attended a private college preparatory school with the daughters of ambassadors from all over the world, senators, representatives, and Prime Ministers. Believe me the good nuns taught us proper etiquette. We wore hats and white gloves to church. We curtsied before we spoke to any nun or anyone with real authority. One day I was talking on the telephone to one of the good nuns and I curtsied as I hung up the telephone. The other girls around me laughed and told me I did not need to do it over the telephone. This is how ingrained these customs had become for me. Much etiquette has flown the coop in today's society, but much still remains and most of it is just common sense and a sensitivity to others. A gentleman should always rise when a lady enters the room or open the car door for a lady. Hats should be removed in the presence of a lady or at least lifted for a moment. Hats should never be worn by a man when inside any structure, be it a house, office building, unless coming or going, a church, a library or a restaurant! Today I see so many uneducated youth wearing hats in the library or restaurant and I just want to say to them, "in polite company, the gentleman always removes his hat."

The Roving Librarian

Throughout the book I have tried to stress some of the basic etiquette skills as they apply to the different countries and cultures. Politeness in itself is etiquette. I recently attended a workshop titled "The Reference Process: How to be a roving librarian." There are three basic steps to the process. One is becoming approachable, two is the reference interview, and the third is the closure. I was some what amused that all of this was new to these librarians, when I had been doing it all my life. The first step involves customer service. There are two librarians on the reference floor at all times. One answers the telephone and mans the desk. The other walks around making sure people are finding what they need and assisting whenever or however it is needed. This particular public library, like many others, has five or more separate collections housed in different parts of the building. There is the children's collection, the young adult collection, the fiction collection, the non-fiction collection, the media collection, a Spanish area, the reference collection, the ready reference collection, etc. all in different areas and some on different floors. It is the job of the roving librarian to walk the patron to the area where the particular items that is wanted resides. That means if the patron is in the reference collection and the item sought is in the media collection, the librarian walks with the patron to the media area and stays with the patron until they both find the item. In this way you guarantee the patron has been satisfied. We were told to stop reading at the reference desk, go to the terminal with the patron to help them search, and to allow absolutely no barriers between you and the patron, i.e. arms folded, hands in pockets, hands on hips, etc. Sometimes these postures come as second nature to us. I like to put forth my hand and introduce myself and give the visitor a greeting such as "Good Morning" or "Good Afternoon" so the patron knows who I am and why I am there to help. Most people will reciprocate with a handshake.

The Importance of Posture

The greeting or salutation in most countries is much more important than it is in the United States. This means in person and on the telephone. Our international students get very upset when someone just hangs up the telephone without a good-bye. They say "You Americans are so rude." It is true. It takes but a minute of politeness to make all the difference in the world. We are living in a much too much hurry-up country. No place lives the motto, "Time is Money" like we Americans. Another etiquette skill that many of us lack is sitting tall, standing tall, no slouching. To slouch, believe it or not, is considered very rude in many countries. It shows a lack of respect for others. That is why our parents were always correcting our posture. I had to learn to walk with a book on my head. I also learned to ride a bicycle with no hands. That is what is called balanced and for many cultures balance is an intricate part of the cultural harmony. The Chinese, Confucius, could not tolerate the suggestion that virtue is in itself enough without politeness, for he viewed them as inseparable and saw courtesies as coming from the heart, maintaining that when they are practiced with all the heart, a moral elevation ensues. Etiquette is simply a system of rules of conduct based on respect of self coupled with respect of others. According to Emily Post, "Best Society is not a fellowship of the wealthy, nor does it seek to exclude those who are not of exalted birth; but it is an association of gentlefolk, of which good form in speech, charm of manner, knowledge of the social amenities, and instinctive consideration for the feelings of others, are the credentials by which society the world over recognizes its chosen members." (Post p. 3)

Asian Etiquette

Manners are something that can be learned very easily just by observing someone else's manners. One of the key gripes that Asians have in this country is the fact that Americans refuse to remove their shoes when they enter the house or apartment of their Asian friend. This is a case of sheer arrogance on the part of Americans. To the Asian, home is a very special and clean place and they do not wish to track the filth of the world into their homes. It makes so much sense that we all should follow their example. But from the American point of view, when in Rome do as the Romans do. They fail to recognize that this custom is completely ingrained in the Asian mind. The Asian American Services Committee of the Chicago Public Library has a web page on Asian Etiquette. It is mainly taken from Roger Axtell's *Do's and Taboos Around the World* and Elizabeth Devine's *The Traveler's Guide to Asian Customs and Manners.* Here are some of the highlights:

Do's

When visiting an Asian's home, remove your shoes at the entrance and leave them at the doorway. (India, Indonesia, Japan, Korea, Thailand) In some homes the visitor will be given disposable slippers.

To show respect for people, use both hands when handing an object or receiving it. (Japan, Korea) This is very important for librarians to remember when exchanging business cards.

When you are greeting individuals in a group, always greet older people or those in authority first. One may politely ask who is the leader or the person in charge of the team.

They also say to show special honor when greeting older persons, especially relatives, use the terms ?lolo' and ?lola. For greater honor, place their hand on your forehead. (Philippines) I am not at all sure I would feel comfortable with this and in some countries it would be down right wrong to touch another person's head.

Don'ts

Don't write a person's name in red ink. Only the names of the deceased are written in red ink. (Japan, Korea) So librarians, when in public refrain from using red ink at all.

Don't kiss when saying "hello" or "good-bye", even with close relatives. Asians rarely make physical displays of affection. (China, India, Japan) Even a handshake might not be appropriate. Just a slight bow is all one needs to do.

Don't pick up your chopsticks to begin to eat until those older than you at the table have done so. (Japan, Korea) This is just worldwide etiquette. I was taught as a child to always wait for the elders to begin, but you would be surprised how many people do not know this.

Don't praise an object in the home of your host because they will feel obligated to give it to you. (Pakistan) This is true in many situations, but a slight mention of praise of art or anything pertinent to their culture will probably be appreciated.

Never joke about "Uncle Ho" or "Mr. Ho" (Ho Chi Minh). He is regarded as the father of his country and is a venerated figure. (Vietnam) This can easily be overlooked by Americans because we are so familiar with the Santa Clause's Ho, Ho, Ho. Jokes are often misunderstood and do nothing but embarrass the person from a different culture.

Many people use the word ethical when asking questions about etiquette, but these two words mean different things. Ethics pertains to morality and values. It is unethical to lie on your resume. It is unethical to steal or cheat someone. It is not unethical to drink from your soup bow; there is no dilemma in this. It is, however, a breach of etiquette to drink from your soup bowl at a formal dinner. Etiquette rules are guidelines for proper and accepted social behavior in the company of others, where as ethics deals with morality and values. It is a breach of etiquette to drink directly from a milk carton shared by others, but it is not unethical.

Reach Out

I started writing this book because I wanted to address some of what I consider to be the large issues in libraries. The first and foremost is the lack of acknowledgment of a patron entering the library. I see it in public libraries. I see it in academic libraries. Librarians do not approach you; you have to approach them and often I get the impression they are too busy to bother with me. This must be corrected if libraries are to remain viable. Everything is customer driven these days and librarians had better learn how to be customer driven. It irks me no end when I enter the reference room, obviously seeking help, and no one even acknowledges my presence. Not even a greeting is spoken. The librarian should assume that the patron is stepping into this area for the very first time and has not one clue about using the facility. So please move away from that desk, move away from that computer, and let no barrier come between you and the person in front of you. Be bold and put out that hand. Put on that smile and become the gracious host or hostess your job required you to be. You are representing your country, your community, and your library. Be neatly appointed with clean hair and nails and shoes. Wear conservative clothing. In failing to do so, you may unconsciously offend the person coming to you for help. Remember it is the little things that count.

Etiquette requires a sensitivity of the situation at hand. Think before you speak, think very carefully before you speak and do not make any assumptions about the patron. It is really easy to stereotype people. When I think about stereotyping people I recall the time a farmer came into the library seeking some information. Of course, he was dressed in overalls, mud all over him, dirt under his nails. He was certainly scraggly. I asked him how I could help him. He needed some agricultural statistics. We went to the *Statistical Abstract of the United States* and found what he was seeking. After he left, my boss asked me what Mr. Owens wanted and I told him. He said to me, "I bet you did not know he is the wealthiest man in our community." I did not know that, but it made no difference to me whether is was the wealthiest or the poorest. He was simply another human being in need of some help. We can never judge a book by its cover, nor should we ever try. Manners are the little things like letting a person go before you in a line or giving an automobile the space to pull into line.

Table Manners

A word about table manners. Americans eat with their fork in their right hand and the knife in the left hand. We eat a lot of things with our hands which was not done years ago. I was raised to eat everything with the proper utensils, not to slurp my soup, not to blow my nose at the dinner table, elbows did not rest on the table and my hands should rest in my lap. In other societies just the opposite is true. Hands should never be below the table and elbows should be rested on the table. In Japanese society it is considered polite to slurp your soup or noodles to show one's appreciation of one of the country's cheapest meals. However, young people are scoffing at this 400 year old tradition and prefer to eat more quietly. Most Europeans eat in the continental manner with the knife in the right hand and the fork in the left. When I went to France this took some practice and I still have never been able to conquer the chopsticks. Your Asian friends may say it is OK, but you can tell on their face it really is not. It is so easy for them.

When visiting an Asian home remember that bones are never placed back on the plate. A separate plate is provided or one may place them on the table next to the plate. In Italy it is considered a compliment if one burps at the table indicating an excellent meal. In America this is considered rude. I have several friends whose table manners I consider quiet crude. I think one should always follow the example of the host or hostess. If your host places the knife and fork in a perpendicular manner after finishing the meal follow suite. Many people do not follow this rule of courtesy which just indicates their lack of observation skills. It is considered rude by some people to mix their food like combining lima beans with mashed potatoes. One does not eat asparagus with the fingers. This is considered rude although I love doing it. Never cut up your lettuce, fold it over until it is a manageable size. This is a real stickler in France where they have the best table manners known to man.

French Cuisine

During my visit to France, a dear friend of mine, Monsieur Bonhomme invited me to an excellent restaurant to enjoy a seven course dinner. I was overwhelmed as I had no idea how to use half of the silver in front of me. The table was impeccably set with white linen and a white linen napkin. Sitting at my place I observed a large plate in front of me with a linen napkin on it. There were several forks on the left and several knives and spoons to the right. There was also a spoon and fork at the top of the plate. A small butter plate was placed to the northwest of the plate and there were several different shaped wine glasses as well as a water goblet. As we proceeded through the meal I learned much about good table manners and haute cuisine. One always starts from the outside of the silverware and progresses inward. The first utensil to be used is the appetizer knife to the far right to be used for the appetizer of Pate de Foie Gras Natural. The appetizer plate is placed on the place plate. It is replaced, on the place plate, with the soup course – only served in a flat dish. This is to be eaten with the soup spoon, the next utensil on the right. At the end of the soup course the place plate and soup dish are removed and only from the left. Place settings on the right are removed on the right. As the place and soup plate are removed together, the warm plate for the fish course is immediately substituted. The fish course is accompanied by white wine. After the fish course has been removed the "roti" appears, always hot, though not necessarily roasted, arranged on a beautifully garnished platter with vegetables. Red wine is served with this course. The next course is the Salade du Jardin followed by a cheese course. Sometimes they will be served simultaneously. The next course is the fruit course. A standard dish would be a half a cantaloupe with port wine in the center. Nothing is offered a second time except for water and wine replenishment. The last course is dessert consisting of Petits Fours, cakes, chocolates, etc. After dinner, if this were in a home, the ladies would retire to the polar for coffee and the gentlemen would retire to the library for Cognac and cigars. The entire meal takes at least two full hours. Fine dinning is always an exhilarating experience.

Civility

The following paragraph from Emily Post's *Etiquette*, Chapter 29 titled "The Fundamentals of Good Behavior", 1922, is the essence of the meaning of civility. She writes, "All thoroughbred women, and men, are considerate of others less fortunately placed, especially of those in their employ. One of the tests by which to distinguish between the woman of breeding and the woman merely of wealth, is to notice the way she speaks to dependents. Queen Victoria's duchesses, those great ladies of grand manner, were the very ones who, on entering the house of a close friend said, "How do you do, Hawkins?" to a butler; and to a sister duchess's maid, "Good Morning, Jenkins." A Maryland lady, still living on the estate granted to her family three generations before the Revolution, is quite polite to her friend's servants as to her friends themselves. When you see a woman in silks and sables and diamonds speak to a little errand girl or footman or a scullery maid as though they were the dirt under your feet, you may be sure of one thing; she hasn't come a very long way from the ground herself."

This paragraph speaks volumes on how one should treat others. Do unto others as you would have them do unto you. We are all human beings traveling our journey from one side to the other. We never know what little kindness or gentle word of support affects others and how they take that bit of kindness and pass it on to someone else. It is important to be as generous with your time as possible because the opportunity staring you in the face may never resurface. One of the key etiquette skills in reference work is the open question. Any question that can be answered with a yes or no is not an open question and does not allow for further negotiation. An example of an open question would be "How may I help you?" or "What are you looking for?" This way a conversation or the negotiation process can begin and further clarification made.

Etiquette is simply being smart enough and sensitive enough to the other person as to not cause embarrassment or an uncomfortable situation. There is a world of difference between "May I help you?" and "What do you want?" "What do you want?" in itself implies several things. First, that you are peeved that person is front of you taking up your precious time. Secondly, that the person is needy. No one likes to feel needy, even if they are. It is not just the words, but it is also the tone used in asking the question. Ask something with the wrong tone and the patrons will go running for the hills. Many students approach me with an apology and I immediately let them know that my job is to help them with whatever it is they are struggling to find.

The Children's Library

Probably the most valuable experiences I learned about librarianship were the ones I gained from my practicum as a children's librarian at the Monroe County Public Library under the tutelage of Jennie Richie. I believe she is the best librarian I have ever had the pleasure of knowing or working with. She taught me lots and lots of things. First and foremost, in order to be a good children's librarian I had to know my collection inside and out. I had to know the titles in a series; I had to know all the characters in a book by name; I had to know the color and size of the books and series; I had to know the sequels in the series. In other words, when a child came up to me and asked for the next book about Madeline, I knew not only what she was asking for, but where to find it in the collection. Children have no patience, are extremely sensitive, and want it right now. Actually they are not too different from all of my patrons. Also, collection development played a very large role in what we chose to buy and what we felt was better left out of our collection. This library was in a university town. The patrons of the children's department were for the most part children of professors and people connected with the university. Thus the parents' expectations of the children's collection were very high. They wanted their children reading books with excellent qualities with good wholesome morals and values. No 'trash' for these kids. We had multiple copies of the Newbury Medal winners. This is really where I learned much of what I know about etiquette. I learned how to put a smile on a face where there had been a frown or a tear. I learned how to negotiate with the most unnegotiable child. I quickly learned how to present choices so they walked away somewhat satisfied. If you ever what to know how it feels to feel totally incompetent, volunteer in the children's department of your local library.

The Epitome of Etiquette

Aside from the "Please" and "Thank you", etiquette is picking up after yourself, busing your table in a fast food restaurant, putting clothes back on the rack in the same place where you retrieved it, and not pulling into the lane when you are passing someone until you see them in your rear view mirror. Etiquette is not one-upmanship. It really peeves me when a person introduces himself as Professor Collins or Mr. Collins. I am a professor also, but my name is Meri Meredith. I have a first name and a last name. This form of introduction is pure snobbery. I guess some people feel so inferior they have to come across as superior. They are not. As my mother always said, George W. Bush puts his pants on the same as any other man, one leg at a time.

Chapter Seven

Diplomacy

The word "diplomacy" has many different meanings from foreign policies to international relations to simply tact. I am using it in the context of tact and international relations in reference work. Diplomacy is nothing more than common sense rules for politeness or just plain courtesy and thoughtfulness expressed in an outward manner that everyone understands. It is a sort of sign language which tells a distinguished person that he is recognized for what he is or what he represents. It is an expression of culture that cannot be taken lightly or only partially practiced. Americans should not miss a single opportunity to sell themselves, their ideals, and their goals to a single foreign visitor, especially a foreign dignitary, who travels in the United States. Americans already speak the international and universal language of common sense, courtesy, gentleness, and good manners; but it does no good to slap a foreign visitor on the back in a gesture of praise and friendship if such a gesture is offensive to him. A person from Sweden would be very offended. It does not benefit the national intelligence or plain common sense to make believe that it is right to give no time to proper recognition of international guests in America. (Lott p. 1).

Diplomacy also encompasses the rules and regulations of a country. By not following certain protocols, one might find himself in the local jail. For instance, in China all gum and chewing of gum is against the law and even having it in one's possession is breaking the law. Chewing it in public will certainly land you in jail. However, Singapore has recently lifted this ban on chewing gum. I am using the term "diplomacy" more in a sense of negotiations in the reference interview when one needs to understand what kind of information is needed and that it exist in the way the patron thinks it does. This process may be very brief or it can take quite some time to figure what is being sought and the amount of assistance needed.

Francois de Callieres, in his book *On the Manner of Negotiating With Princes* (1716) listed what he considered to be the best qualities of a good negotiator. Among them were "an observant mind . . . a spirit of application which refuses to be distracted by pleasures . . . penetration which enables him to discover the thoughts of man . . . a mind so fertile in expedients as easily to smooth away the difficulties . . . presence of mind to find a quick and pregnant reply . . . and equable humor, a tranquil and patient nature . . . an address always open, genial, civil, agreeable . . . with easy and ingratiating manners. (Diplomacy p. 143) Sir Harold Nicolson in his book *Diplomacy*, first published in 1939, believed that the qualities of an ideal diplomatist were "truth, accuracy, calm, patience, good temper, modesty, and loyalty." Taken for granted were, "intelligence, knowledge, discernment, prudence, hospitality, charm, industry, courage, and even tact." (Diplomacy p. 143) So librarians, as you can see, you have your work cut out for you. It is not easy to remain calm when the patron in front of you is agitated and in a hurry. Many of you are finding yourself in a situation where you have to justify your positions and libraries. Going that extra mile to make sure the patrons see you as valuable is extremely important today. The patrons are your justification for your position and your library.

Power of Observation

Let us take a look at some of these qualities. An observant mind means the power to observe the patron and the situation. We often see but do not observe. When asked what someone was wearing could you fully describe the attire? When asked to describe a situation such as an automobile accident, how accurately could you describe it? The power of observation is a skill that must be developed. It does not come to us automatically. Observing lets one go beyond seeing to creating an open and responsive atmosphere. It also allows one to get out of oneself and frees one to be objective and reflective of a situation. Observing allows one to create a respectful and appreciative environment, but the most important thing it allows is freedom from judgement. It is not achieved overnight. It involves thoughtful planning, asking oneself questions, making decisions, evaluating and re-evaluating situations. How could I have made that a better encounter? What am I really seeing in this person's behavior? Sometimes it is exactly the opposite of what is the truth. One of the students I work with seemed to me to be rude and sarcastic. After I observed her behavior for several weeks, I came to the conclusion that she was very shy and not at all sure of herself. When I started making positive and respectful comments to her, she seemed to do a complete turn around. The power to observe allows one to see the whole picture. The following is a true story.

In an article in *Perspectives in Behavioral Performance Improvement* in September 2002 a worker relates a true story of the Power of Observation.

The HAWKS Process is a process for improving work safety. The observer asked if he could observe these two workers who were placing chemical product into a dryer. The product is delivered to the dryer in drums that weigh 150 lbs each. Four or five drums at a time are put into a cage which is raised 30 feet in the air with a hoist and positioned on top of the dryer catwalk. From there the drums are removed and their contents are dumped into the dryer. While the operator above was controlling the hoist, I moved a short distance away and began readying more drums to put in the cage. During the feedback after the observation, the observer called my attention to an at-risk behavior he observed. He asked me, If the hoist failed or the cable broke, where would the cage fall? Wouldn't it land where I was standing? After the feedback I moved to a new staging area. Six weeks later the cage did fall. If it can happen, it will. Thanks to my change of behavior, the three drums and the cage weighing 450lbs did not fall on me. The observer had saved my life. (PBPI P 19).

Spirit of Application

The Spirit of Application means applying oneself one hundred percent to the task at hand. This does not mean immediately turning to your computer and going on the internet to see what you can find on what you "think" is the question. Then point to the section in your collection that might be relevant. It does mean going to the right reference section or resource or going to the relevant database which may answer the question. It may also involve referring the patron to someone else who has more expertise than you do in the subject discipline. It also means getting to the job at hand **now,** not five or ten minutes later. It does not mean leaving a patron waiting while you go on break or to lunch. Often I have gone to lunch one half hour or even later because the demand was so strong at that time. Applying oneself means pulling on all your past experiences and using them in the present situation if needed. It means taking the task at hand seriously and on being focused. One should never address the question as trivial or unimportant. It is very important to the patron. Otherwise the patron would never have asked for help.

One reference librarian told me that he insists that as soon as he is finished with a reference or ready reference book, he demands that it be put back immediately by himself or any of his staff. Why you ask. Because of his spirit of application. If the book is not on the shelf in its proper place, it cannot be used by the next person needing it. This assures that the collection is ready and waiting all the time. This is what we call customer driven service. I have seen it happen all too often in my own situation. I go to the shelf to fetch the book and it is not there. I have to leave the patron hanging while I seek to find the **vital** resource which is often sitting on the copy machine or on a shelf behind the circulation desk waiting to be reshelved or just sitting on a table where the last patron who used it had left it. We still work much of the time with printed resources and I do not believe this will change any time soon because of the sheer expense of electronic sources.

Discover the Thoughts of Man

"The negotiator must further possess that penetration which enables him to discover the thoughts of men and to know by the least movement of their countenances what passions are stirring within, for such movements are often betrayed even by the most practised negotiator." (De Callieres p. 19). A student approached me one day about finding book reviews on a particular book. It was for an English class, but the student was a business major. English is not my area of expertise, business is. The book was a classic written in the 1930s. This was not going to be an easy feat since I did not have anything going back that far and neither did anyone else as far as I knew. We tried several databases to no avail. The student was from another country so his ability to express himself and what he was thinking was very difficult for him. However, he knew me and had faith that I could help him with this very difficult assignment. I might have had better luck in the Main Library, but of course it was late on Thursday, a long weekend was coming up, and most of the reference librarians in the Main library had already gone home. So we just kept looking. When I finally found a few book reviews I was ecstatic. No, no that was not what he wanted. By now I am sweating bullets. We finally came to the conclusion that what he really needed were articles by people about the reviews, not the actual reviews themselves. That was a whole different search. Once I understood the real question, we found a couple of articles pertinent to his request and he was a very happy camper. I could not read this person's mind. I could only work with him long enough for him to be able to finally communicate the real information need. This is diplomacy.

Sometimes we think we can read another person's mind, but more often than not, we are wrong. I am amazed at how people think especially when it comes to information and libraries. Some people actually think libraries are free. Well they are to the users much of the time, because many people do not know that property taxes fund the facility, the budgets, the materials, the staff, and the board which makes decisions on the operations of the whole place. Many believe electronics will replace the materials in the library. When I walk into a modern public library I am amazed at the amount of movies, DVDs, talking books, videos and CDs that have been added to the collection and the number of books with the same title that a library contains. The face of these collections are going to change to become more relevant to community members from different cultures and to help all citizens understand our increasingly diverse society. The libraries' new mission is to promote literacy, provide equal access to information, and encourage the preservation of individual cultures. We as Americans, need to learn about other cultures, understand those cultures, how they think and what is important to them in every day life. The following is a story that Barbara J. Ford told in her Inaugural Remarks on July 1, 1997 as President of the American Library Association. It shows just how libraries make a difference in the lives of real people. This is what our future holds.

Kathleen Vereeren, of Pitman, New Jersey wrote: "In our small, comfortable town, it seemed that we would be untouched by the war in Bosnia. But that was not the case." Kathleen and her family had hosted a teenage girl named Aida from the former Yugoslavia as an exchange student. The family and girl initially stayed in touch, but Aida's letters became fewer and fewer. Then telephone calls stopped going through and mail service no longer reached her town. The family received a message from Aida via the Red Cross begging them to help her escape from her town that had been besieged for four months. After numerous phone calls and letters, Aida was again accepted as a foreign student. Back safely in Pitman, Aida was starved for reading but her English was weak. Bookstores were not able to help. Finally, the local library was able to obtain books in her language from another library. Not only that, it located a lifeline in the form of a librarian fluent is Serbo Croatian. Kathleen concluded her letter by saying, "As small as my town and library are, they were able to give Aida an important connection to her world across the ocean." (McCook p. 5) Barbara closed her remarks with, "I would like to close by reminding all of us that as important and exciting as new technology is, it is the local touch that sets our libraries apart and will ensure their future as treasured institutions in the next century and beyond." (Ibid p. 5).

Smooth Away Difficulties

In the library sometimes it is not so easy to smooth away difficulties. I have encountered many an angry patron. Library fines are our largest complaints and rightly so because our fines are outrageous. If someone has put a hold on a book, the person who has the book is given ten days notice to return it, after which fines are $10 per day. Often a patron will say he never received notification to return the book which may or may not be true as they receive notification through the email system which does not always work. A friend of mine tried to take out a book from his public library and he was told that he still had a fine on his record after 30 years! A supervisor should have stepped in and erased that fine.

Other patrons feel they are not getting help in finding what they need. Again, we need to be pro-active, step away from the desk, and walk with the patron to help them find the material sought. Discrimination is often an issue. People feel they are being ignored because of who they are. When they feel this way, they will not seek help. Much of the time it is a simple misunderstanding, which with a little education, can be resolved. However, sometimes it is really a control issue of who has the power, the patron or the librarian. It is amazing how ruffled feathers can be smoothed by using an ingratiating manner or by simply making an apology. Saying, "I'm sorry. What seems to be the problem?" usually gets the patron explaining in very intricate detail about the problem. Much of the time the patron is correct.

Presence of Mind

Presence of mind means being open to new situations, seeing things from more than one perspective, not reacting or making an instant judgement. It means being focused on the moment. It allows us to think and analyze. It incorporates intelligence, knowledge, discernment, and especially tact. One is in the here and now, not thinking about anything else. When negotiating one must possess adaptability which is the ability to put oneself in another's place so as to understand their position and the seriousness of the need. It means using self control in a crisis and demonstrating the ability to say or do the right thing in an emergency. An example of not having presence of mind is ignoring the fire alarm when it goes off, thinking it is just another routine drill.

Another example, which people do all the time, is "awfullizing." In other words, letting your thinking go awry. We assess, interpret, evaluate, and make judgments based on our beliefs. We tend to feel it is unnecessary and a waste of time to stop, inquire, and reflect on what is really going on. If you are confronted with strange behavior from someone you know well, it is best to step back and ask yourself why this is happening. One day I walked into the office at 8, as usual. It was a beautiful day and I was feeling great. That was short lived. A colleague called me on the phone to tell me that one of my best clients was sending out requests for bids to do the same kind of work that I was doing for him. Absolute panic set in. Why, I thought we had a very good relationship and things were going just fine. If I loose this client there goes my entire business. I will loose the house, I will be unemployed, and the list goes on. By 8:30 I was a basket case. Then I did what I should have done in the first place. I decided to analyze the situation, take a deep breath, act calmly, go see my client. During the visit, I learned that he needed some expertise in an area in which I had none. He was just expanding his business. Presence of mind is so important.

A Tranquil and Patient Nature

Some people have a much more tranquil and patient nature than others, but it is extremely important to develop this skill when working with people from other countries because they are uncomfortable and uneasy in the first place. Any one who is new to a situation can easily become frustrated. In order to print in the library one needs to have a certain card with money on it. Since we initiated pay-to-print I have kept a certain amount of money on my card for emergencies. It does not happen very often, but occasionally someone will need to print and they are usually in a hurry and do not have an understanding of how the system works. Ten cents here or twenty cents there off my print card has been a tremendous help for those finding themselves in a printing crisis. It immediately alleviates the tension and anxiety about how to get the job accomplished. One student needed to have a paper printed in color. There is no color printer in the library, but there is one downstairs in the lab. However, only business students have access to it. I found a business student, explained to him what we needed. I had the disc in hand. He said he was a proctor for the lab, but it cost twenty cents a page to use the color printer. I gave him two dollars. He went to the lab and printed the research paper on color paper. The student told me I had saved her day. We had managed to turn what had seemed an impossible situation into a very successful one, all within ten minutes. She gave me two dollars the next day. Sometimes it takes quick thinking and cooperation to achieve a tranquil situation.

Many people from other countries have a much more patient nature than Americans. They often complain about the impatience of Americans. To be patient is part of their philosophy of life. So when dealing with people from other countries, they usually do not mind waiting until you can give them your full attention. They want to build a relationship with you. They want to share with you who they are and their culture. Patience yields knowledge and understanding. One day I was on my break, sitting outside, when a student came out of the building. We started a conversation about how well his studies were going as well as his summer. We talked for about ten minutes when suddenly he said I have a 5:30 class. He had been politely conversing with me. When I find myself in a time crunch with students, I ask them to come back when they have more time. Research takes time. It also takes a lot of energy and patience. When we practice patience we allow time for observation which in turn helps us to evaluate the patron and his needs. If those needs are met successfully, that patron will return when another need arises. This is good for business which is also good for your job. When libraries fill the needs of their communities, they become viable institutions.

Always Be Open

Being open is very difficult for many people in this country. One of the reasons is our isolation from the rest of the world. Many people travel, at least the well-to-do travel to other regions of the world, but there are many who have never even left their town or city. Their only education is what they have learned in school, seen on television or in the movies. According to the *Statistical Abstract of the United States: 2003* of the 182 million persons 25 years old and over only 17.7 percent have a college degree. That means 82.3 percent do not and 15.9 are not high school graduates. (Statistical Abstract, p.154). That equates to many uneducated or minimally educated people. They live in their own world and find it difficult and uncomfortable to interact with others from other cultures. This is a major issue for our country which operates as a representative republic whose strength lies in its educated population.

Robert Frost once said, "Education is the ability to listen to almost anything without losing your temper or your self-confidence." This is a prime example of being open. We may not always agree with someone, but we should be able to listen and be open to other's opinions. Being open is fun. You meet new interesting people with new ideas. You learn things you did not know and your horizons are stretched. Asking open questions educates you. Attending local ethnic food festivals are great fun. The food is different, the costumes and the music are very colorful and uplifting. It does more than one might imagine to help bridge the cultural gaps in a community. When they come into your library, they see a familiar face. One that is not judgmental but welcoming. Just by your presence at one of these festivals, you demonstrate an openness to new environments.

In 1970, Asian/Pacific Islanders accounted for only 0.7 percent of the U. S. population. In 2000, there were 11.9 million Asian/Pacific Islanders, comprising 4.2 percent of the total population. (U.S. Bureau of the Census, 2002). Although there are significant differences among Asian groups, many of them share relatively common values, beliefs, and parenting styles that originated from the philosophical principles of Confucianism. In a study on acculturation, communication patterns, and self-esteem among Asian and Caucasian American adolescents living in the same neighborhood by Rhee et al. Asian adolescents expressed more difficulty discussing problems with their parents when compared to their Caucasian counterparts. Further, self-esteem was found to be significantly lower among Asians than Caucasians. Acculturation tends to be stressful for immigrants due to difficulties in attaining language proficiency, separation from familiar social networks, and potential cultural incompatibilities. Depression, anxiety, and psychosomatic disorders are the most frequently identified mental health consequences among acculturating individuals. The most serious difficulties Asian American children experience include:

unrealistic parental expectations in terms of academic and career achievements; parental over involvement in their children's lives; parents' overall tendency to exclude their children in the decision-making process; and negative attitudes toward their children's behaviors and lifestyles (Rhee p. 2).

Thus we can see the importance of being open to these students and encouraging them in any way we can to learn and adapt to our country. Having been a visitor to another country, I cannot tell you how beneficial it was for me to meet open and caring French men and women. They invited me to their homes for lunch or dinner. They really took me under their wing and I learned so much about the French and France. They showed so much courage and trust in dealing with a complete stranger. I just want to say "thank you" for being so gracious and hospitable. Since I spent a whole chapter on etiquette, the subject of **ingratiating manners** does not need to be addressed here.

Chapter Eight

Learning versus Teaching

Today undergraduate education is seeing a shift from a teaching mode to a learning mode. Barr and Tagg explain it like this: "A paradigm shift is taking hold in American higher education. A college is an institution that exists to provide instruction. Subtly but profoundly we are shifting to a new paradigm: A college is an institution that exists to produce learning ... We now see that our mission is not instruction but rather that of producing learning with every student by whatever means works best." (Barr p. 1) This is also happening in the library world. No longer is it a library's mission to provide books and service. It is our new mission to provide learning using whatever works best. Library collections now contains videos, DVDs, CDs, talking books, language tapes, art, Internet connections, databases, access to other library collections. Today it is common to see an information booth with a knowledgeable person to steer you in the right direction as you enter the library.

The Demo is Instant Learning

Students learn at different paces. Some are more successful learners when they see rather than hear. Many times a student will come in for help not realizing they have access to our many databases from home or a computer lab. I simply go to the computer, log into the library's home page, and go to the databases which will best help their information need. I make sure I am finding what they are asking to find. One student recently came in looking for help in analyzing a company on which very little information exists. Their assignment is to find financial information on BMG Entertainment which is a subsidiary of Bertlesmann, a German company. The company has been very closed mouth about its finances. I took the student to the Datamonitor database and searched for "Bertlesmann" and found nothing. I knew this was not right, because I had been successful at finding it the previous week. So I search "BMG" and found "Bertlesmann". Had I not done the search myself, and found a problem, the student would not have learned how to find the information. We found a SWOT (strengths, weaknesses, opportunities, and threats) analysis. She was very happy and said she would go to the lab and do the search because she has free printing in the lab.

I only had to show that student once, but some students need to see it or do it several times before it registers with them. One student came to me with a call number and asked where he might find this book. I asked him to show me the record in the computer. When we pulled up the record, I could see that our copy was checked out and that the Mansfield campus had a copy that was available. I pointed this out to him. He had looked at the record, but he did not understand what he was seeing. Thus he learned how to properly read a record. The students are given an assignment to analyze an industry. For years we only had one source for this, aside from articles on an industry. When we taught our workshops on how to use the library, their assignment was to find an article on a company and an article on the industry in which the company operated. The students had a terrible time with this assignment. The company assignment was easy, but they had difficulty comprehending which articles were about an industry. They had to do this three times. By the third try most of them had learned to differentiate between an article on an industry and one simply on a company within that industry.

Walk Them Through the Process

I often receive phone calls from students who are home and having trouble finding the information they are seeking. I also have people come to my office saying they have exhausted the Internet, but cannot find the one piece of information they need. What works best is for me to get to my computer and walk them through the process of finding a book, or searching a database. In other words, I am doing the same thing at my end of the line as they are at their end of the line. This allows me to see what they are finding or if they are finding what I am finding. This is very helpful to the patron because often they have missed a step or they are not scrolling down far enough to see what I am seeing or they have been using the incorrect path to get to the information. One of the major stumbling blocks for many patrons is always thinking "Internet". One patron was trying to go directly to Jstore and when he tried to pull up an article, he was prompted for a user name and password. I showed him how to do it on my computer and I was successful. They do not realize that they must get to the databases through the library's URL which verifies them as a valid user.

I do this with the print sources too. We have a directory which has 20 volumes. I show them how to look up a company in the master index, how to read the entries, and how to find the actual entry on the company. I know that if I do not know how to use a source, I cannot not teach the patron how to use the source. Some of the paper sources in tax and law are very complicated to use and it even takes me a while to figure it out especially when they are not searched very often. Some of the databases have several levels with lots of links. One such database is *Hoovers Online*. If you click on the competitors section, a subsection pops up as "competitive landscape." The only problem is that it does not exist on all companies just like a "SWOT analysis" does not exist on all companies and students can waste hours looking for something that does not exist.

Repeat Business is Always Good

I find that in dealing with students from other countries, they need to have things repeated and repeated. That is the only way they learn some things. Often I try to say something one way and then say it other ways so that if they do not understand the first time, maybe using different words will help them understand. What English they have learned is formal English which does not correspond to some Americanisms. I know a Korean student who told me he must read a chapter six times before he feels he really understands it. And often he will come to me for help in clearing up some language that he simply cannot comprehend. For instance the phrase "to raise the bar" is beyond his comprehension. To him a "bar" is a place where you go to get a drink.

Here are a few sayings from the Editorial Board of the Thought for the Day that would baffle anyone who has learned English as a second language:

"The bandage was wound around the wound."

"The farm was used to produce produce."

"The dump was so full that it had to refuse more refuse."

"We must polish the Polish furniture."

"He could lead if he would get the lead out."

"The soldier decided to desert his dessert in the desert."

"Since there is no time like the present, he thought it was time to present the present."

"A bass was painted on the head of the bass drum."

"When shot at, the dove dove into the bushes."

"I did not object to the object."

"The insurance was invalid for the invalid."

"There was a row among the oarsmen about how to row."

"They were too close to the door to close it."

"The buck does funny things when the does are present."

"A seamstress and a sewer fell down into a sewer line."

"To help with planting, the farmer taught his sow to sow."

"The wind was too strong to wind the sail."

"After a number of injections my jaw got number."

"Upon seeing the tear in the painting I shed a tear."

"I had to subject the subject to a series of tests."

"How can I intimate this to my most intimate friend?"

"Hi, Jack" could sound like "hijack" to the foreign ear. Can you imagine the look on visitor's face if I told him, "I got it straight from the horses mouth." That is why it is good to explain the words you are using if the person has a confused look on his face. Sometimes they are hearing words that have a very different meaning from what you think you are saying. When Clairol introduced its electric curling iron "Mist Stick" into Germany, it didn't know that "mist" was local slang for "manure." When Colgate launched a toothpaste in France called Cue, nobody mentioned the "Cue" is also the name of a notorious French pornographic magazine. "Got milk?" the centerpiece of U. S. dairy industry ads–became "Are you Lactating?" in the literal Spanish translation. Frank Perdue's jolly slogan, "It takes a tough man to make a tender chicken, " fell on Spanish ears as, "It takes an aroused man to make a chicken afectionate." And the phonetic rendering of Coca-Cola in Chinese came out as "bite the wax tadpole." (Micossi p. 1).

Be Pro-active

I approach people on a daily basis to ask if they need some help, especially people who are visiting from other countries. They are always grateful that someone has bothered to take the time to help them find what they need. From the day we stopped using the card catalog and started putting everything into a computer, library users need help in just getting started. The other day a visitor came up to me and asked where he might find the *Business Source Premier*. I took him to the computer, showed him how to get to the database, and asked him what he was trying to find. When he told me he wanted to browse the McKinsey Quarterly, I showed him which button to click on, I then typed in the title of the journal, and all the years came up on the screen. Then I left so he could browse the publication. As I was leaving, the thought occurred to me that he might not be a current faculty, student, or staff which means he does not have access to the databases from his home or his office. So I returned and asked him if he was a current faculty, student, or staff. No was the reply. So I showed him how he could email articles to himself. I did this by showing him how to do it. I added a few articles to the folder, then I clicked on the folder, then I clicked on email. Once the email box popped up, I explained that he had to put something in the subject box and if any of the articles were a pdf file he had to check that box also. This all took about 5 minutes. The point is that I did not leave him alone until I knew he knew how to manipulate the database. He had made a special trip to the library; he was paying for parking; and he knew that we had what he wanted. I saved him a lot of time by teaching him a few quick steps.

One day a visitor came to my office with a request for some financial data on the amount of money the Veterans Administration and the Department of Defense were spending on pharmaceutical costs. I approached it the old fashioned way. I pulled out the *Statistical Abstract of the United States*. I know this resource fairly well and I know how difficult it can be to find things in this resource because it has its own weird terminology. I looked under quite a few index terms and all I could find was prescription drug expenditures, but that is a bit more narrow in scope than pharmaceutical expenditures. This is not my area of expertise so I sent him to the person who is an expert at finding this kind of data. I sent him to our government documents librarian. But first I called to make sure she was available. I got her voice mail. Next I called the reference desk in the Main Library. Penny was on the desk. Now, this is where the pro-active comes into play. First Penny identified herself. I asked her if Sherry was working today. This may be her research day which means she would not be in to provide service. Penny said she did not know and she then gave me an option. She could transfer me to Sherry's phone or she could walk to the back and see if Sherry might be around. I explained that I had already tried to get Sherry on the phone and had gotten her voice mail. So Penny left the reference desk for a minute to go in the back to inquire about Sherry's whereabouts. She came back and told me that Sherry was at lunch. I explained this to the patron and he proceeded over to the main library. The point is I looked for the information myself. I did not pull a book off the shelf and say, "Here, you should find something in this book." When you work in a large campus environment like I do, you do not want to send people on a wild goose chase. Time is precious and parking is expensive.

A Picture is Worth a Thousand Words

When working with people who's second language is English, sometimes demonstrating is far quicker than talking to them. Another technique is to point out what they are seeing. I use this technique often by reading out loud what I am seeing. One student was looking for market share of a particular company. She was looking at only one chart. I began pointing out the various markets within that particular SIC (Standard Industrial Classification) code. This gave her an understanding of not just the big market, but the many sectors within that market on an international basis. Demonstrating is great to get a student started, but it does not help the student learn. They have to have the hands on experience, in order to learn. So after I have demonstrated, I ask them to sit and do the actual search.

I teach a workshop on how to use the library for several course related classes. I actually go to the class room and pull up the library's home page on the computer. From there I show the different places to go to get what kinds of information. I thought this would be helpful to the students. However, checking feedback revealed several problems. The students could not see the demonstration because the screen was too small and they were too far away. Many of the students were turned off by the lecture method. So the professors decided to have the students come to the library after my one hour lecture. When they got to the library, they were assigned a computer and a worksheet. To my dismay, it was like they had not heard a word I had said in the lecture. They were given one hour to complete the assignment. I was running around showing them which databases to go to in order to answer which questions. From this I learned just how important hands-on practice was in the learning process. Success is in the details. How could they get started? Where was this information buried? You have to click on "Research Databases" to get to the research databases. You have to go to *Business Source Premier* and then you have to click on this button to get to the SWOT analysis. You have to click on this button to browse a publication. You have to go to *Factiva* to get headlines of today's *Wall Street Journal.* Patrons do not know this stuff by osmosis. We must teach our patrons how to use all the services we are providing or those services will just sit there unused because they do not know we have the services.

We recently started offering a Bloomberg Certification Program. One of the graduate students was in charge of organizing it. He handed out a set of instructions on how to get signed up for the program. There were four simple steps. I do not think so. There turned out to be about twenty steps to successfully register. Since the only Bloomberg terminal resides in the library, I was inundated with questions about how to sign up. The instructors went through the material as if there was a fire. There were questions on the exam that were not covered in the class.

There were three modules which covered a lot of ground. This is usually the way it goes when you are doing something for the first time. I can show them some short cuts, like how to get the ticker symbol, EE for Earnings Estimates, FA for Financial Analysis, MGMT for Management, DES for Description, etc. Once they have learned how to use the Bloomberg, it is fairly easy to remember the commands.

Practice Patience

The majority of your international clientele are not in a big hurry like we Americans. They expect things to take time. They want to do the job well and thoroughly. It amazes me how much time they spend on their studies or on their recreation. I have a friend from South Korea who was a student here. She also lived in my apartment complex. She would check out 10 video movies and stay up all night watching them. How could anyone have that much patience to sit in front of a television for that long? I can barely sit for one hour in front of the television. Another friend of mine from Saudi Arabia went to three movies in one day. Where does this kind of patience come from? I guess it comes from a philosophy that life is very long instead of life is very short. When negotiating with people from Asia, it can take months, even years. That person standing in front of you would really like to form a lasting relationship with you. This takes time, lots of it. Asking open questions will help build that relationship. What is your assignment? What are you hoping to prove? Are you just getting started? Are you limited by a certain time? This get the conversation started. By gathering some information like this, you can get a better picture of what is really involved in helping the individual to successfully accomplish his task at hand.

When someone walks into your library, unless he is a regular patron, you have no idea of the level of experience that person has in your library. Most of the time the answer is none. Signage helps, but most libraries lack good signage. The next best thing is the librarian. However, the librarian may not feel comfortable in dealing with visitors who do not speak English well. This is one reason to slow down, be methodical in the approach and patiently wait for the visitor to express his information need. I hate it when someone comes into my office and says. "I have a quick question." The answer is invariably anything but quick. One such question was about finding how much money investors lost in the Worldcom scandal. The question might be quick, but the answer will probably take quite a while to answer. This is a real research question and research takes much time and energy. I am not sure there is a definitive answer to the question.

International visitors must be able to sense your patience. They can feel it or the lack of it. Besides, what is the big rush. You are going to be there 8 hours. If at all possible, it is best to ask the visitor to have a seat so that both you and he is comfortable. Then you can proceed with the reference interview. When someone comes in with an impossible request, you cannot just say, "That's impossible." You need to ask a lot of questions, you need to explain the situation, and eventually show them how much effort the research is going to take. At the end of maybe an hour or even an hour and a half, they have a full understanding of what is required. I have had several of these requests. One was to find a list of all manufacturing companies in the four surrounding states to Ohio that had between 500 and 5,000 employees. He wanted to do this simultaneously on all four states. The count was so high that I suggested he do one state at a time. Even then he could not download what he wanted because the download capability was not large enough. Even if he sorted them in ascending order and then in descending order it would not work. If he broke them down by SIC code it might work, but that would mean weeks of work. This would not be worth his time. I finally suggested he contact the vendor and get a price quote. Of course, that was too expensive. I have had Ph.D. students find the money they needed to accomplish their mission. These kinds of request can extend over weeks and even months. They require a lot of patience and negotiating.

On Being User Friendly

I am going to end on the same note I began. Learn to become a "user friendly" librarian. This is so important. Barbara Pachter in book, *When the Little Things Count . . . and They Always Count,* Barbara has few rules that make a world of difference in how we interact with others.

Rule number 1. When you arrive at work, greet others with "hello" or "good morning." She says, "It's amazing that I have to give this simple guideline, but it's clear to me that I do. One of the complaints I hear the most often from employees about their managers and their co-workers is that many people don't bother so say "hello" or otherwise offer a simple greeting. I hear: "It's like I don't exist" or "she thinks she's so important . . ."

Rule number 2. Don't assume you are greeting people. People think they do it, but often don't! You need to pay attention to your own greeting behavior for a few days and *really* discover whether you're greeting people or not.

Rule number 3. Use the 10–5 rule. If you see someone at 10 feet, you must acknowledge him or her. At 5 feet, you must say something: "hello," "good afternoon," etc. It's a good rule.

Rule number 4. Say goodbye. Make sure you say "goodbye" or "have a good evening," to your co-workers before leaving for the day. Don't simply sneak out. (Pachter p. 10).

Barbara is just talking about your co-workers. What about your customers, visitors, patrons, clientele, whatever you wish to call them. She was talking about the simplest of simple etiquette. We must use the same etiquette with whomever we have interaction. She goes on to talk about proper handshakes, attentive listening, taking people seriously. People come to your library to get things, service, help. If they are newcomers to the community, they need a lot of help. Libraries should give workshops about their communities. They should take the place of the welcome wagon if there is not one in their community. They would build up the businesses in the community and make people aware of all that the community has to offer. Reach out your hand and say, "Buenos Dias" to the next Hispanic you see in you library.

Chapter Nine

Cultures of the World, A–I

According to the Encyclopedia Britannica (1989), culture is defined as "the integrated pattern of human knowledge, beliefs, behavior, language, ideas, customs, taboos, codes, institutions, tools, techniques, works of art, rituals, ceremonies, and other related components." In other words, culture is not one of life's luxuries rather it is life itself. As the world becomes smaller through international trade and the development of communication devices, cultures move from one country to another. During this transferring of culture, people change their cultural values in order to adjust to another country. Because of this transition, we also need to make a transition in our cultural awareness.

In *Global Brains* Gary Ferraro outlines four specific sets of skills we will need in the 21st century. The very first is the ability to communicate effectively with people from a number of different cultural backgrounds and beliefs. This means maintaining an open mind on the various religious customs of the world; maybe not accepting them, but at the very least understanding them. Secondly, we must develop a type of "systems thinking" or a macro view of our organizations and operations across functional areas and cultural borders. Third, the global thinker needs to develop certain perceptual skills that will facilitate learning about different cultures. These include, but are not limited to, being open minded, flexible, and patient; tolerating ambiguity; learning from new situations; and adopting good, relevant ideas from wherever they might come. Fourth, having global brains involves developing those skills and attributes that enhance one's emotional and mental well-being, such as meditation, regular exercise regimens, and other ways of reducing stress levels. In conclusion, he recommends that we must develop a broad knowledge base, including knowledge of one's own culture, other cultures, corporate cultures, as well as the global economic and geopolitical forces affecting the conduct of business. (Ferraro p. 10)

Cultural Differences

According to Ferraro, culture is shared, learned, and adapted by a group of people. Cultures are always changing. When cultural diffusion happens there is a transfer of ideas, things and behaviors from one culture to another culture. An example would be the explosion of Chinese cuisine in the United States over the last decade or two. Many Americans have learned to eat with chop sticks. This one example of cultural differences hits the nail on the head:

> The concept of ethnocentrism can be illustrated by the following example. While waiting to cross the street in Bombay, India, an American tourist stood next to a local resident, who proceeded to blow his nose in the street. The tourist's reaction was instantaneous and unequivocal: "How disgusting!" he thought to himself. He responded to this cross-cultural encounter by evaluating the Indian man's behavior on the basis of standards of etiquette established by his own culture. According to those standards, it would be considered proper to use a handkerchief in such a situation. But if the man from Bombay saw the American tourist blowing his nose into a handkerchief, he would be equally repulsed. The Indian would think it strange for the man to blow his nose into a handkerchief and then put the handkerchief back into his pocket and carry it around for the rest of the day. Both the American and the Indian would be evaluating each other's behavior based on the standards of their own cultural assumptions and practices. In other words, both would be viewing the rest of the world through the narrow lens of their own culture.
>
> (Ferraro p. 21)

There are two basic kinds of cultures which are diametrically opposed to each other. In the American and British cultures time is of the essence or, as the saying goes, "Time is Money". This is also known as a Monochromic culture in which people tend to perform one task at a time, take their schedules seriously, and are very impatient. This type of person is easily irritated with a Polychromic person who perceives time as very flexible, allowing him to do several things at the same time such as taking a phone call while talking to someone in his office and polishing his shoes all at the same time.

The following discusses important cultural factors which will help the "global" librarian effectively with an international clientele. The following entries are in part from the *Columbia Encyclopedia, Culturgrams, Encyclopaedia Britannica Online, Passports* by the World Trade Press and *Worldmark Encyclopedia of Cultures and Daily Life*.

Americans

The Landscape

The United States covers the central part of North America, including Alaska and Hawaii. It is the fourth largest country in the world. The northeastern coast called New England is rocky. The Atlantic Coastal Plain extends from Maine along the rest of the eastern seaboard until it mergers with the Gulf Coastal Plain in Georgia. To the west is a plateau bound by the Appalachian Mountains which extends from southeastern Main into central Alabama. Between the Appalachians and the Rocky Mountains is a vast plain known as the Midwest where major farming areas, particularly for grain crops such as corn and wheat, takes place. The Rockies and the ranges to the west are parts of a larger mountain system that extends down through the western part of Central and South America. The coastal plains along the Pacific Ocean are narrow; mountains plunge directly into the sea in many places. Alaska lies in the extreme northwest portion of North America and Hawaii is a group of islands west of southern California.

The Economy

The United States of America is a democratic federal republic and a nation of immigrants with a population of approximately 265 million people. There are fifty individual states who hold sovereignty over their territories and have rights that are not reserved by the federal government. Each state is responsible for its own governance and educational system. The literacy rate is 99 percent. It has the largest, most diverse, and technically advanced economy in the world. Economic growth is strong. The currency is the U. S. Dollar. The United States is a key world financial center and its economy affects global markets and international economic growth. It is an open market with thousands of miles of paved highways and super highways, mass transit systems in the large cities, and an unsurpassed airline industry. The communications network is extensive and modern, with instant communications via television broadcast and cellular telephone networks. Most households have at least one telephone and one television, many more than one. It is a world leader in medical research and training. Infant mortality rate is 7 in 1,000 and life expectancy ranges from 73 to 80 years of age. A sedentary lifestyle and risky physical behavior are the greatest causes of health problems. Casual sexual relationships and high fat content diets are common. Americans often pig out on hamburgers, french fries, pizzas, and sweets of all kinds. Smoking cigarettes has become increasingly taboo in the United States. Often one can smoke only in designated areas. New York city has banned all smoking in the city. This is a very sensitive issue as it touches on both personal choice and government intrusion. (Passport p. 79)

The People

The first Americans are thought to have been prehistoric Asian peoples who first arrived before 10,000 BC. From these first settlers evolved the cultures of the North American Indian Tribes. When the people of European, Latin American, and Middle Eastern origin first immigrated to the United States, they brought with them advanced industrial, military, communications, transportation, and construction technologies that enabled them to dominate the native peoples. Today less than one percent of America's population is comprised of the first Native Americans. During the 18th and 19th centuries the European Americans imported African slaves to work on Southern Plantations. By the outbreak of the Civil War in 1861, the slave population had reached four million. European immigration to the United States peaked between 1880 and 1920 when over 20 million Europeans came to America mostly from Great Britain, Germany, Ireland and Italy. They were escaping from starvation, poverty, war and religious domination. America has always been the land of hope and freedom with equal rights and equal opportunities for all. Although she is called a "melting pot", Europeans were reluctant to welcome non-Europeans into this "melting pot" as equals. Today there is still discrimination and racism against certain minorities. However, demographers predict the immigration pattern will peak at similar levels as in 1880 and 1920, but will shift to Asians and Hispanics and by the 1990's. Asians will comprise 38 percent of all immigrants and Hispanics will comprise 48 percent of all immigrants with Europeans comprising only 9.6 percent. (Worldmark p. 32)

Religion and Holidays

The United States is primarily a Christian nation with 26 percent being Roman Catholic and 63 percent being Protestant. The remainder are Jewish or Muslim or members of one of the other twenty some major religions of the world. Some of the major holidays are New Year's day, Easter, July 4th (Independence day), Thanksgiving and Christmas. Some of the rites of passage are births, deaths, marriages, high school and college graduations, and retirement from work. Americans have one of the highest per capita incomes in the world, the average income is over $26,000. Nearly sixty four percent of Americans own their own home which is usually a single unit structure. Americans are in love with their automobiles. Almost every household owns at least one or in many instances two. Some households have a car for every member of the household. America has been termed a consumer society. They buy clothes from department stores, they buy food in "fast food" restaurants, they spend a great deal of money at sporting events, movie pictures, amusement parks, and home entertaining. About forty percent participate in sports of one kind or another including golf, tennis, swimming, skiing, walking, and jogging. America is becoming a nation of gamblers. They spend more on gambling than movies, theater, opera and concerts combined. Americans spend six times as much money on gambling as on all spectator sports combined. America is not a country without social problems. Her society struggles with crime, violence, drug abuse, poverty, racism, and sexism. These problems are reflected in American movies, American television, and American song and literature (Worldmark p. 38).

Americans are frank and outspoken. They are free to voice their opinions and share their views on very controversial issues even to the point of protesting without being afraid of adverse consequences. Freedom of the press is guaranteed. As has been shown in recent years, they consider their country to be the guardian of democracy and freedom and the promoter of peace worldwide. The country was founded on the cornerstones of freedom and independence, both as a nation and as individuals. Even when working as a team, they think in terms of several distinct individuals combining their uniqueness to attain a united solution. This is different from forming a consensus which assumes compromise or giving up some of one's ideals.

The Family

The face of the American family has drastically changed over the last couple of decades. In the fifties and sixties, the family unit was comprised of a husband, the bread winner, and a wife who stayed home and raised her two or more children while running the household. Today, only about one-fourth of all households consist of a mother, father, and one or two or more children. Other family units consist of single parent families (30 percent), unmarried couples with or without children, same sex couples with or without children, and extended families consisting of parents, children, and grandparents. One-third of all children are born out of wedlock and in poverty. Many grandparents are raising their grand children so the children's parents can both work in order to bring home enough money for all to survive. Nearly half the workforce is now comprised of women. With the population increase of African Americans and Latin Americans, whose origins are more collective than individual, the family unit is becoming more extended. By this I mean the elderly will be cared for in the home rather than in nursing homes.

Customs and Courtesies

For most Americans, owning their own home and automobile is no longer a luxury but a necessity. This is partly due to the size of the country and the fact that traveling by car is more affordable than other means of transportation. Americans are a very mobile group of people. Because they spend so much of their time in their car, their cars now come equipped with car phones, televisions, VCRs, DVDs, radios, CD players and OnStar

Communications Systems for emergency situations. Trends come and go fairly quickly in America. Health foods and exercise are the latest trends as well as gourmet coffee and capri pants. The United States is a self-serve nation from self-help books to pumping one's own gas at the gas station. This is a difficult concept for many visitors to understand. With the proliferation of Asian and Middle Eastern visitors one is beginning to see Oriental and Middle Eastern grocery stores, Chinese video rental stores, and a boom in the American film and theater business. These visitors think nothing of watching two movies on the same day or checking out 10 video rentals at the same time. They might not be getting enough exercise, but they are certainly learning as much as they can about American culture as it is portrayed in our movies and songs.

African Americans

African Americans are not considered to be immigrants because they came against their own free will. Beginning in 1619 they were captured in their West African homelands and sold as slaves mostly to work the fields of the Southern plantations. Slavery lasted until the end of 1865 when the Thirteenth Amendment to the U. S. Constitution was passed abolishing all slavery in the United States. At that time there were about four million African Americans, or about fourteen percent of the American population. Despite their newly found freedom, they remained a repressed and impoverished people. The National Association for the Advancement of Colored People was formed in the beginning of the twentieth century. This association together with the migration of about 1.6 million Southern blacks to the northern newly industrialized cities improved their lot over the next couple of decades. In 1963, the Reverend Martin Luther King, Jr. delivered his famous "I Have a Dream" speech at the Lincoln Memorial. During the sixties the country saw the black nationalist movement take off. However, it was not until the middle of the twentieth century that the black man attained his legal and human rights as well as equal educational opportunities from the Civil Rights movements. By the seventies, African Americans had been elected as mayors of several major cities, black representatives in the state and local legislatures were beginning to be seen, and affirmative action programs had created new opportunities in employment and education. By 1990 African American achievement in American society had been remarkable.

The People

Still there was great discrimination, a large majority of that population was living in poverty, and only a precious few seemed to be really making progress in their standard of living. African Americans speak standard

American English, but there has been a movement to adopt a variant known as Black English Vernacular (BEV). The grammar and syntax of Black English, as it is now being called, are traceable to West African and Niger-Congo languages combined with improvisation from disparate languages united under isolated bondage. They include such omissions as "to be" in "He nice"; replacement of a final "th" sound in a word by an "f" as in "I going wif you", and such words as cat, bad, rap, jive, hip, tote, awesome. In late 1996, Black English Vernacular, newly labeled Ebonics, was the subject of nationwide debate when the Oakland, California, school board passed a resolution declaring it a separate language distinct from standard English in order to institute programs aimed at educating teachers in this dialect and inculcating respect for its African linguistic roots. It is interesting to note here that especially in California, a bilingual requirement is surfacing as part of a job requirement, meaning English and Spanish since there are so many Latinos in that state. Some of the common greetings one will hear are "Yo Brother" or "Yo Man" or "Word Up" for What's Up. Another is "man" for two men or "girlfriend" for two girls. A common nonverbal greeting consists of slapping another's outstretched palm. When done above the head it is called a "high five" and when done at the knee level is it called a "low five." The women's version of this greeting consists of sliding one's forefinger across the forefinger of the other women. One expression of farewell is "Word to the Mother" referring to the motherland of Africa. Many young African Americans still observe the West African custom of addressing their elders as "Aunt" or "Uncle" whether or not it is a true aunt or uncle. Like people from many Asian and Latin American cultures, African Americans, especially those from the South, often avoid eye contact as a sign of respect. They may often live in an extended family environment, including not just grandparents, but aunts, uncles, cousins, and other relatives either temporarily or on a long-term basis. The life expectancy of an African American in 1900 was 33 years as compared to 73.3 years in 1990. They have come a long way in better living standards, but still have a long way to go to reach true equality.

The black culture has evolved from folklore dating back to the time of black slavery. Much of it has been imported from Western Africa folklore. Certain beliefs in spells, charms, folktale, and other superstitions have been passed from one generation to the next. These beliefs are quite firm. The "soul food" of the African American is the tradition stemming from the mingling of the West African culinary heritage of black slaves with the cooking style and available foods of the American South. The custom of using all edible parts of both plants and animals including hocks, snout, ears, feet, and tail -everything it is said, "but the oink"- is from the great need to sustain the life of those who had to make do with leftovers much of the time. Collard greens, sweet potatoes, pork and chicken are survival foods. Fish, especially catfish, is very popular as is watermelon which was brought to the New World from Africa. There is an old saying, and not just by the blacks but by the Asians as well, that if you eat watermelon in the summer, you will be healthy and survive the winter.

On June 15, 2003, I watched a segment on CBS Sixty Minutes on the plight of the African American. It was hardly about the plight. It was more about how some have arrived. A large number of blacks are moving from the North back to the suburbs of Southern cities such as Atlanta, Georgia from the North. They are going back to their roots. Black buying power has doubled in the last decade. They are black, not African Americans and they have college degrees. They have white collar jobs, are among the Upper and Middle class, and live in all black neighborhoods in homes costing between $500,000 and $3 million. They live in these segregated neighborhoods with their own schools, recreational facilities, and their own communities. There were three and a half million who attained this status in the 1990's. When you see an older black person wearing braces, they are wearing their "badge of courage." One of the interviewees said that her father had always raised her by saying, "Stop asking for a piece of the pie. Make your own damn pie!" Ten years ago, one in two were still living in poverty. Today it is one in five still living in poverty.

Religion and Holidays

The National Baptist Convention of the U. S. A., Inc., with over 7.5 million members in 1990 is the largest black denomination. The Church of God in Christ, a Pentecostal sect, is second with a membership of over 5.5 million. Roman Catholicism with 2.2 million and the Nation of Islam both claim a large following. Other religious affiliations include the African Methodist Episcopal Church, the African Orthodox Church, Judaism and Rastafarianism. Significant holidays are the birthday of Martin Luther King on January 15 and Malcolm X on May 19, and Juneteenth, which commemorates the date on which black slaves in Texas learned they were free on June 19, 1865. Their rites of passage are birth, marriage, and death. Unlike the Jewish religion, they have no religious ceremony for a boy passing into his manhood. However, the Urban League and PUSH (People United to Save Humanity) have developed a rite-of-passage program that focuses on responsibility, values, character, and discipline. The blacks are well known for their love of music including spirituals, gospel, rhythm and blues (R&B), ragtime, jazz, soul, Motown, funk, and rap.

Chinese Americans

It is thought that the Chinese came to America long before the Native American Indians and that the Indians are a mix of Chinese and South Americans. However the official historical version is that the Chinese first immigrated to the United States in 1820 and continued coming for the next thirty years. Many immigrated during the gold rush years in search of the "Gold Mountain" in California, just like other prospectors. Between 1850 and 1852 approximately 23,000 entered the country. Most of them were men because a respectable Chinese woman did not leave her parents' or in-laws' home. As a result there were very few Chinese woman in the United States. Local societies known as "tongs" began the business of importing young Chinese women and girls to act as sexual slaves and Chinese prostitution became big business.

If African Americans think they have been down trodden, they should look at the history of the Chinese Americans. That which was happening to the Blacks in the South, was happening to the Chinese in the West. They were only allowed jobs with low wages, they were robbed, beaten, and even killed by European Americans, and laws were passed discriminating against them giving them no rights. White Americans were beginning to feel threatened by what they termed "Yellow Peril" and an anti-Chinese movement began to develop. Racist organizations initiated boycotts of Chinese-American goods and services. Anti-Chinese gangs stormed Chinatowns destroying homes and property and physically attacking the residents. These Chinese fled to larger Chinatowns for protection. By 1876, San Francisco's Chinatown housed over 30,000 people in an area of nine city blocks.

The California state government joined the anti-Chinese movement by passing acts like the Foreign Miners Tax and Alien Poll Tax. Each miner of Chinese descent was charged $2.50 monthly until it was declared unconstitutional in 1862. California in 1850 passed the Criminal Act of 1850 which stated that no person of Chinese descent could testify in court. This gave the white Americans free rein to beat or kill any Chinese because the Chinese could not testify against them in a court of law. By 1882 the federal government decided the situation had gotten out of hand and passed the Chinese Exclusion Law barring any new Chinese laborers into the United States for the next decade. Other Chinese immigrants were admitted under very severe restrictions and all were denied US citizenship. A new Immigration Act was passed in 1924 barring any foreigners not eligible for US citizenship from entering the country period. The Act also prohibited future Chinese immigration, including Chinese women married to men who were already US citizens. Further discrimination laws forbad Chinese Americans from owning land, having certain jobs, attending certain schools, or marrying European-American women. In 1943 the Chinese Exclusion Acts were repealed by Congress, but there was still a limit of only 105 persons admitted per year. In 1965 a new immigration Act eliminated the national origins quota system and enabled up to 20,000 Chinese to immigrate to the United States each year.

Ultimately, more than 12,000 Chinese carved tunnels and laid track across the Sierra, Nevada and were a large part of building the

Transcontinental Railroad system. An estimated 1,200 of them were killed in the process from accidents, being buried in avalanches during the sever winters, or being blown apart while handling explosives. The work required both skill and daring. They worked extremely fast and could lay ten miles of track in one day. Without Chinese labor, the West would have developed much more slowly in all branches of industry, farming, mining, reclaiming lands, etc. They converted swamps into rich farmland, showed their remarkable skills in planting, cultivating, and harvesting many crops, orchards, and vineyards. Most of their contributions have gone undocumented, but some of them became highly successful and influential business men in trade, industry, fishing, and farming.

They brought with them the strong traditions of their country. Family is central. Confucian values which emphasize respect for elders and a clear hierarchy of authority among extended family members are an integral part of their life. Food and its preparation is also very important to their culture. Rituals and etiquette surrounding the purchase, cooking, serving and consumption are passed from one generation to the next. Along with this goes the beliefs and rich folklore that many have brought with them. As an example, I recall a friend telling me that if I eat watermelon in the summer, I will make it through the next winter without any illness! The Chinese have always placed a high value on education and the arts. The parents will spend large amounts of time, energy and money on their children's schooling. This is evident at all levels of the educational process. Today many Chinese Americans own family businesses where all members of the extended family, including children, work long hours and are very successful.

Mexican Americans

When Texas became a state in 1845 many Mexicans living there suddenly found themselves living in the United States. They were not offered US citizenship, so they were not even considered Mexican Americans. After the Mexican-American War ended in 1848, Mexico ceded the northern part of its territory to the United States. Those living there were given a choice to become American citizens or relocate back into Mexico. About eighty percent or 80,000 chose to become American citizens comprising the first large group of official Mexican Americans. This land had been in their families for generations. Suddenly it became the property of new European American settlers who assumed authority over it and relegated the Mexican Americans to second-class status. This is precisely why many Mexicans in Southern California consider that land to be owned by them and not California. The original promise to the Mexican Americans that they would retain all rights to their lands was broken and the United States courts awarded numerous land claims to European Americans instead. Does this scenario sound familiar? To add insult to injury, the Mexican Americans could only get jobs with low pay and menial work. Stores, saloons, and schools were segregated. The white man tried to wipe out their entire heritage. English was declared the official language and Mexican fiestas were outlawed. Thus Mexican Americans became impoverished, lower-class citizens in what had once been their own country.

The Mexican American population rose from 75,000 in 1890 to 562,000 in 1900 and the majority of them were poor and illiterate. They became unskilled laborers working mostly on farms, in mines, or on the railroad. Eventually, some seventy percent of track-layers and ninety percent of maintenance crews on US railroads were Mexican. The US mining industry, particularly in Colorado, Arizona, and California, was built on the backs of Mexican immigrants, and much of US agriculture for the past 100 years or more has been accomplished through the contributions of Mexican migrant workers. During the "Great Migration" in the 1920s, as many as 600,000 Mexicans legally crossed the border and were given permanent visas which allowed them to do contract work, but they were not allowed to become American citizens. The undocumented ones were easily exploited because they were illegal. Some employers made a practice of hiring undocumented migrants and then turned them in to the Immigration and Naturalization Service (INS) as soon as the job was done but before they had paid the workers their wages.

Now come the World Wars. With the onset of World War I in 1914, President Woodrow Wilson removed the restrictions on Mexican workers that had formerly limited them to agriculture labor. American men were going off to fight and Mexicans were needed to fill those jobs. Because they could now work in other industries, these contract workers moved to cities such as Chicago, Detroit, Cleveland, and Pittsburgh where industrial jobs were plentiful. By 1929, the Mexican American population had reach approximately one million. However, when America entered the Great Depression and many people were losing their jobs, an anti-Mexican sentiment developed. The American and Mexican governments instituted a program that encouraged Mexican Americans to be relocated to Mexico. Some 500,000 Mexican Americans took advantage of this program. Then along comes World War II. Again the United States requested Mexican workers to fill the jobs of American workers going off to fight the war. Only this time they were granted temporary visas; the workers were called *braceros* and mostly worked in the agriculture industry. They displaced Mexican Americans workers. Some 350,000 to 500,000 Mexican Americans fought in the US Armed Services during the war, receiving 39 Congressional Medals of Honor. Many of these soldiers used the GI Bill after the war to pursue higher education and vocational training, allowing them to move into skilled jobs and professional positions. Overall, about five millions Mexicans came to the United States as seasonal workers with this program between 1942 and 1964. Although it was hoped this program would discourage illegal immigration, it actually encouraged illegal immigration. The *braceros* were limited on the place they could work and on the pay, the illegal ones could work wherever they choose and for lower pay. In 1954 the INS instituted Operation Wetback which allowed them to deport illegal aliens. Through this program approximately 3.8 million were deported back to Mexico.

Most undocumented migrants today work at unskilled jobs in fast-food and other restaurants, hotels, motels, hospitals and nursing homes, small manufacturing jobs, on assembly lines, in sweatshops in the garment industry, gardening and landscaping businesses, and still in agriculture. Those who are legal and have become US citizens are beginning to make inroads into mainstream America.

Mexican Americans are nearly all Catholic, but their brand of Catholicism is different from the traditional religion in that it is a blend of Christianity and magic. I recently attended a Spanish mass on Easter Sunday. What an experience. Never expect a Spanish mass to begin on time. Usually it starts about 15 minutes late. This one, however, scheduled for 12:30 pm, actually began at 1 pm. The Spanish mass I usually attend has about 50 participants. On Easter Sunday there were about three hundred and fifty people. The children were dressed to the hilt. As the mass progressed, I observed that we were going to have first, about seventeen baptisms, numerous first communicants and some confirmations. The children participating in all these ceremonies were dressed in the most beautiful outfits I had ever seen in my life. Needless to say it was a very long mass which I finally left after receiving communion and the mass still was not finished. That was 2 hours after the mass started. Many elements of Mexican folk have been retained. I saw lots of gold being worn by the men, even the young boys, in the form of bracelets, necklaces, and rings. The children got up and walked around whenever they felt like it. Infants were totally covered by blankets, even their heads. People talked out loud whenever they felt like it. There was chaos within the ceremony and no more than a handful received communion. This was all very strange for an American onlooker. The two things that did impress me were their total patience with the whole thing and the beauty of their music. Mexican Americans celebrate tradition Christian holidays and countless fiestas. Two primary ones are *Diez y Seis* ("Sixteen") and *Cinco de Mayo* ("Fifth of May"). The first one celebrates the El Grito de Dolores speech delivered by Father Miguel Hidalgo on 16 September 1810, which marked the beginning of Mexico's struggle for independence from Spain. The second one celebrates Benito Juarez's defeat of French forces at the city of Pueblo on 5 May 1862. Both are celebrated with parades, floats, traditional dress, music, and other festivities.

The Mexican culture has begun to have a lot of influence on today's American culture. Mexican cuisine is very popular. Many signs now have both English and Spanish. There is now a Spanish mass at many Catholic churches. Latino music is played everywhere, even in Burger King. Ricky Martin and Jennifer Lopez are immensely popular. Mexican Americans have begun to make inroads into United States politics. Joseph Montoya became the first Mexican American US senator and several have become governors of states and mayors of cities. Astronaut Ellen Ochoa became the first Hispanic woman in space in 1993. American sports have their Mexican American heros like Pancho Gonzales in tennis, Lee Trevino and Nancy Lopez in golf, and Tommy Nunez in baseball. Although we have seen a few successful Mexican Americans, most are still living at the poverty level, are illiterate, hard workers taking low paying jobs. There needs to be a real effort to better educate these people and understand and accept their rich culture.

Argentines

The Landscape

Approximately 60 percent of the land is used for agriculture and 20 percent is covered by forests. Cool ocean breezes help keep Buenos Aires relatively smog free. The seasons are opposite those in the Northern Hemisphere: the warmest month is January, the coolest is July. Here too, as the European settlers moved out across the country the native Indian populations were ousted from their lands and literally disappeared. Argentina, once one of the wealthiest nations in the world from exporting meat and corn to Europe, now has an economy badly affected by soaring inflation and a series of complex political conflicts. The country is divided into four provinces: the Andes; the lowland North; the Pampas, home of the famous gaucho (the Argentine cowboy); and Patagonia. Approximately eighty percent of its population lives in urban areas despite its rich rural forests and farmlands.

The Economy

Argentina's economy has been traditionally based on agriculture which employs twelve percent of the population. Livestock, cattle and sheep, and grains have long been the bulwark of its wealth. In fact its cattle herds are among the world's finest. As an exporter of wheat, corn, flax, oats, beef, mutton, hides, and wool it rivals the United States, Canada, and Australia. It also exports oilseeds, sorghum, soybeans, and sugar beets. It is the largest producer of tannin and linseed oil. Important industries include food processing, textiles, chemicals, printing, and metallurgy. Domestic oil and gas production has made the country self-sufficient in energy and its pipelines connect the oil and gas fields to Buenos Aires and other refining centers. The real gross domestic product per capita is

$8,937 one of the highest in South America. However, in certain regions there remains a gap between the wealthy and the poor. Argentina also exploits its ample hydroelectric resources. This industry, long protected by a strong nationalistic policy, has made the country virtually self-sufficient in the production of consumer goods and many types of machinery. The economy was hurt by Brazil's recession and currency devaluation in the late 1990's, but the pegging of the peso to the dollar combined with Argentina's own economic problems resulted in economic collapse in 2001. Unemployment has doubled as the government has laid off employees in preparation for privatizing industries.

The People

Argentina in Latin America is a country of approximately 36 million people whose origins come from many European countries including Spain, Italy, the Basques, Wales, England and the Ukraine. With more than 12 million people, the capital of Buenos Aires is one of the most populated metropolitan areas in the world. The Mestizos Indians (a Spanish and Indian mix) comprise 15 percent of the people while 85 percent are European immigrants. It has the eighth largest Jewish community in the world comprised of 400,000 plus Jews. More than 45 percent of the population is younger than age 15. The official language is Spanish, but a number of the European-descended communities still maintain their own languages such as Italian. English is widely understood because it represents one of the larger immigrant communities. Argentina regards itself as extremely cultured and European.

Religion and Holidays

The official religion is Roman Catholicism, but Protestant movements are converting these believers in Argentina as well as other Latin American counties. It is a very spiritual country where many worship the dead and the saints. Religious freedom is guaranteed, as church and state are officially separate.The rites of passage such as Baptism, Holy Communion, saint's days, and funerals are highly celebrated with family get-togethers due to their strong Spanish and Italian heritages and the influence of the Roman Catholic church. Major holidays celebrated are Christmas and New Year's Day which are celebrated with fireworks, Good Friday, Easter, Labor Day (1 May), Anniversary of the May Revolution (25 May), Flag Day (20 June), and Independence Day (9 July) among others. Argentines are proud of their nation. Prosperity, home ownership, strong and personal relationships and education are important to Argentines. Urban Argentines tend to be cosmopolitan, progressive and outgoing. They are extremely gregarious and eagerly invite visitors to participate in their activities.

One year we had a group of MBA's (Masters in Business Administration) who went to Argentina for a field trip. Everyone was a bit anxious about the trip at the time because of Argentina's poor economy. They thought they would be hated. This was certainly not the case. The Argentines knew that these Americans had nothing to do with their own economic and political upheaval. However, on the surface, they are quite formal and very aware of the proper civilities. Even when asking a stranger for directions, one is expected to approach the person with a greeting such as *buenos dias* or *buenas tardes*, "good day" or "good afternoon." The Argentine diet is very meat oriented and family get-togethers can be very elaborate and take a lot of time. This is because they love to socialize. The literacy rate is about 94 percent which makes it one of the most literate countries in Latin America. From the age of five to the age of twelve education is free and compulsory. The comprehensive secondary education system is based on the French model which means it is very difficult to get accepted. Having achieved this goal, the Universities are traditionally free and open.

Customs and Courtesies

Cafes are very popular in Argentina. Like the French cafes, they are very popular with the country's great writers. The center of Argentina's social life, cafes offer a meeting ground for everyone from liberal intellectuals, to politicians, business people, even taxi drivers who want to discuss the state of the country and the world. Mate is the drink of the country. It is a Paraguayan tea. Its preparation and consumption follow strict social norms that transcend class and ethnicity. A hollowed-out gourd is packed two-thirds full with the chopped yerba mate leaf. Warm, but not boiled, water is poured to the top of the gourd, producing a slight froth. The liquid is drunk through a steel straw, known as a bombilla. The first few sips are spit out. Often shared among a group, one person is charged with emptying out the gourd before it is refilled and passed on to the next person. Argentines consume an average of 5 kilograms of the leaves per person per year, more than four times the average intake of coffee. One might liken its consumption to a national addiction. As one domestic worker claimed, "Mate is my relaxation. When I am drinking mate I cannot do anything else." (Passport p. 72)

One of the most noticeable sights upon visiting Argentina are her shrines, soccer players, picnickers, and sunbathers. Like some other countries, this country is soccer crazy. There are more first-division soccer teams in Buenos Aires than any where else in the world. The upper-middle- class leave Buenos Aires by the droves on the weekends to go to the country where they enjoy getting away from the city to go horseback riding, playing soccer, and relaxing by their swimming pools. The Tango song sums up the fears and anxieties of everyday life for the Argentines. Its themes are about love, jealousy, working, coping with one's neighbors and is often full of sad nostalgia about a way of life that is fast disappearing. They love music, dance and movies. Many of the dances and their music, such as the Gato, Chacarera, and Escondida, are accompanied by a guitar and a drum that follow the cadence of a cantering horse.

Brazilians

The Landscape

Imagine a county big enough to represent 30 European Countries within its borders. Fill it with natural and geologic wonders. Color it with exquisite hues of exotic colors of birds and flowers, set against a background of lush green vegetation. Etch it with thousands of miles of tumbling rivers. Embellish it with mountains, forests, beaches, and islands. Burnish this paradise with the orange and yellow hues of the southern sun. Blend in hues of multitudes of races and cultures and glaze them with the warmth and hospitality of a single united people. Link the five regions of this country, each a gem of inimitable brilliance and give this glittering tropical tiara a name – Brazil. (International Video . . .)

Brazil is the fifth largest country in the world and the sixth most populous, home to more than 175 million people. It is the largest country in South America, comprising half of that continent's landmass. This country is extremely rich in rain forests, water ways, and agricultural land. Nearly one third of its land is taken up by the world's largest tropical rain forest in the Amazon River Basin, which is being threatened as a result of logging and deforestation. Ten thousand acres are lost every day.

The Economy

In colonial times, Brazil played an important role in the world economy, providing nearly 75 percent of the world's supply of coffee. After achieving independence from Portugal, Brazil underwent a period of economic growth and relative prosperity. Rubber led this economic growth as well as the exportation of sugar and gold. The major industries are agriculture, mining, manufacturing, and services. The real gross domestic product per capita is $5,362, which has more than tripled in the last generation. However, vast disparities remain in the country's distribution of land and wealth. Nearly half of all private lands are owned by only one percent of the people and there is a serious poverty problem in both the rural and urban areas affecting a third of the population. It is the world's largest producer of coffee, oranges, and bananas. Roughly one third of the workforce is involved in the agriculture sector. Other agriculture products are soybeans, sugarcane, rice, corn, cocoa, cotton, cattle, pigs, and sheep. Timber is also important, although much of it is harvested illegally. Brazil is self-sufficient in food and consumer goods.

Much of its sugarcane is used to produce ethyl alcohol, a fuel used in more than one and a half million Brazilian cars. It has a vast mineral and gemstone wealth.

Today Brazil is the world's greatest provider of gemstones, diamonds, and emeralds. She has since developed a significant industrial sector and currently has the world's eleventh largest economy. Due to a series of uprisings and coups, the country faced incredible inflation and corruption. Cardoso, as finance minister, introduced a new currency, the real ®$) as part of an anti-inflation program that cut annual inflation from 5,000 percent in 1994 to 10 percent in 1996. Brazil's economy has great potential for the future. It is a member of the Southern Cone Common Market (Mercosur), a regional free trade pact that includes Argentina, Paraguay, and Uruguay. Most trade is with the European Union nations, the United States, Argentina, and Japan.

The People

Brazil is an ethnically diverse country. Its population comprises European migrants, descendants of African slaves, and a variety of indigenous ethnic groups. Many of the indigenous tribes are facing cultural extinction. Ninety percent of the people live on 10 percent of the land. Brazil was colonized by the Portuguese. This is why it is the only Latin American country whose official language is Portuguese. Seventy percent of its population is under the age of 30. This makes it a very energetic, friendly, warm, and free spirited population. They love to party with their magnificent street festivals and the carnivals.

Brazilians consider themselves highly cultured. European culture has had a great influence on them, especially Portuguese, Italian, and French cultures. Some of their educational system is based on the French. They eat in the continental style with the knife in the right hand and the fork in the left hand. They wash their hands before eating and refrain from touching the food while eating. This reminds me of an incident I experienced while growing up with my aunt. I had just returned from a long stay in France and my aunt wanted to reacquaint me with some of my peers in the region. We lived in a very rural part of the state. So she invited some of the people about my age to a dinner party. Since I had just recently started living with her, and did not know these people well, I was on my best behavior. As the "hostess with the mostest", I began to cut into my breast of chicken which was fried. In France one would never think of eating it with one's hands. After several bites, one of the guests asked if he could eat his chicken with his hands. I had totally forgotten that Americans eat fried chicken with their hands! In Brazil, one wipes the mouth *before* drinking, not afterwards. After dinner one continues conversation over a strong cup of coffee. When invited to someone's house for dinner, a two-hour visit is expected and being on time is not expected. People from Brazil see time as a sequence of events, not in hours and minutes as is done in the U.S. Therefore, most of the people have an extremely casual attitude about time except in San Paulo. The American gesture for "OK" is very offensive in Brazil, and in general, should never be used in the international arena.

Religion and Holidays

The traditional religion is Roman Catholic. Since there is a separation between church and state, religious freedom is guaranteed. The church continues to have a strong hold over politics. However, when the Africans were brought over as slaves, they brought with them many of their own religions and beliefs in gods and goddesses. Over the years, membership in the Roman Catholic church has steadily declined from ninety-five percent to seventy percent. Although they consider themselves quite religious, most just attend church on special occasions. Many of the religions have combined Catholic practices with other African and non-African practices which include worshiping gods and goddesses such as Iemanja, the goddess of the sea. This religion is known as *Condomble* and is characterized by pulsating drums and rhythmic music that encourages followers to reach a trance-like state. In this state the good spirits are asked to enter the body and heal it. Many physical ailments have been healed by this ritual and the person comes out of the trance both healed and with renewed energy. On February 2 the residents of Salvador celebrate the major religious festival called *Condomble*. Some gifts and offerings are made to Iemanja, the goddess of the sea, and floated out to sea in small handmade sailboats. These offerings are usually made by the wives of fisherman in hope that the goddess will protect the fishermen and ensure calm waters. Another religious sect is known as *Umbanda*. It is common for these religious services to be conducted by a female priestess. Followers invite spirits into their bodies and, when they are possessed, they traditionally light a cigar. Umbanda services account for the majority of cigar sales in Brazil.

Tiradentes Day (21 April) celebrates the death of Joaquim Jose da Silva Xavier a nationalist who died in the struggle for independence. June festivals coincide with the feasts of St. John and St. Peter and are celebrated with local fair-like activities. Other holidays are Easter, Labor Day (1 May), Independence Day (7 September), Memorial Day (2 November), and Republic Day (15 November). On Christmas Eve people eat a large meal and exchange gifts. Only those gifts from *Papai Noel* (Father Noel) arrive on Christmas day. New Year's Eve is a time for large parties.

Customs and Courtesies

Carnival is one of the world's most famous festivals, equivalent to Madi Gras in the United States. It is celebrated the five days preceding Ash

Wednesday. The country literally comes to a halt as Brazilians take off work to join in street parades, dance contests, and other festive activities. Preparation begins six months prior to the event. The citizens wear elaborate costumes made of sequins and feathers, paint their bodies, and don exquisite masks. Some of the costumes are very brief. It is not unusual for women to remove their tops as the evening progresses. The festivities begin at sunset and go well into the morning hours. This is a celebration by the common poor where there is much drinking and debauchery. The upper and middle class leave the cities to go to their country retreats. It is the one week in which the poor can escape their mundane life, with dancing and song. Brazil is famous for the samba. It is thought to have origins from Africa. Although it is only one of many Brazilian rhythms and musical traditions, it is certainly the most famous internationally. It speaks of a sadness so overwhelming, inclusive of everything from homesickness to man's essential solitude to man's lost dreams, much like the blues and jazz in the United States. Samba schools are an important source of recreation in the favelas, the urban slums that surround Brazil's large cities. These schools work all year long to teach dancing, create elaborate costumes, and the writing of songs that will be in competition during the Carnival.

Canada

The Landscape

Canada is the second largest country in the world in land mass, second only to Russia. It covers nearly 4 million square miles, much of which is sparsely inhabited because of the arctic climate and permanently frozen ground. It spans six time zones and borders three oceans, the Atlantic, the Pacific, and the Arctic. Despite this huge area, most of its people live in a narrow strip of land along its long southern border with the United States and inland about 100 miles. The Capital of Canada is Ottawa. Canada shares four of the Great Lakes with the United States – Lakes Superior, Huron, Erie, and Ontario. Canada has several natural regions, the largest being the Canadian Shield, which is centered on the Hudson Bay and extends over eastern, central, and northwestern Canada. It covers about one half of the entire country. This region consists of rolling hills, vast fields of grain, many lakes and mineral deposits. East of this region are the Great Lakes-Saint Lawrence lowlands. This region extends along the Saint Lawrence River to the Atlantic Ocean. This is a rich farming area and the most heavily populated part of the country. The eastern part of Canada is known as the Atlantic Provinces and three of the four – New Brunswick, Prince Edward Island, and Nova Scotia are also known as the Maritime Provinces, alluding to the livelihood of their inhabitants which is fishing. Whereas the Rocky Mountains extend into western Canada, the Appalachian Mountains cover much of the lower Atlantic Provinces. It is awesome to realize that a mountain range extends from Tennessee to Northern Canada.

The Economy

Canada has one of the strongest economies in the world. Real gross domestic product per capita is $21,459 reflecting the country's economic prosperity. The economy once depended heavily on developing the country's natural resources. Today, however, it is based mainly on services and manufacturing. Among the large service industries are finance, real estate, insurance, health care, education, and tourism. One third of all U.S. international travel is to Canada. Mining is a major primary industry in Quebec. Canada ranks second in the world in gold and uranium production, third in silver, and fourth in copper. It is also a world leader in production of wood pulp and other timber-related products. Many U. S. Newspapers are printed on Canadian paper. The most valuable manufactured goods include automobiles and other transportation equipment, electronic products, processed foods, chemicals, and metal products. Agriculture accounts for only a small percentage of the national income. However, it is known for its grains and oilseeds. Wheat is the main export crop. Cattle, pigs, and dairy cows are important livestock. Fish are caught in both Canada's rivers and many lakes, as well as in the three oceans surrounding it.

Canada is also one of the world's leading mineral producers. Minerals and mineral products are among the country's major exports. Petroleum and natural gas account for over half of the dollar value of mining production. Other valuable minerals include gold, zinc, copper, nickle, iron ore, potash, and cement. In 1993 Canada became a member of the NAFTA (North American Free Trade Agreement) together with the United States and Mexico which provides for freer movement of capital and goods, more cross-national investment, and a large market for many goods in each country. British Columbia serves as the gateway to Pacific Rim markets. The currency is the Canadian dollar. Canadians refer to it as the *loonie*, after the image of the waterbird (the loon) mounted on the gold-colored coin.

The People

When Europeans came to what is now Canada, many American Indian people lived in the south and the Inuit (Eskimo) lived in the north. Together the Indians and the Inuit numbered only about 200,000. Today there are many more due to better health care. The French were the first to establish permanent settlements in the eastern territory around the first half of the 17th century. Next, the English began moving in the area. Several power struggles ensued. In 1763 the English were successful in driving the French out of North America. The largest ethnic groups in

Canada today are people of French and British descent. During the twentieth century many people from all around the world immigrated to Canada. They came from Germany, Italy, the Ukraine, China, Holland, and they make up significant minority groups. More recently people from South and Southeast Asia, Latin America, Africa, and the Middle East have immigrated to Canada.

Canada's population is approximately 29 million people. The combined population of the Atlantic Provinces is about 8 percent of the total. The French are concentrated in New Brunswick. The people of Newfoundland are ninety-five percent of British descent. Quebec's 7.3 million people account for one fourth of Canada's total population. About 83 percent are of French origin and French is the official language. In fact very few speak English and Quebec has maintained its old, quaint European atmosphere. Those with a British heritage are called *Anglophones* and those with a French heritage are call *Francophones*. In all of Canada, both French and English are official languages. Approximately 37 percent of the Canadian population reside in Ontario providence. Not only people of French and English descent reside here, but there are also sizeable communities of Germans, Italians, Ukrainians, Chinese, and Japanese. Canada's strongly egalitarian society affords its people excellent access to health care, education, and economic prosperity. The people of Ontario are fairly reserved and formal whereas the people of the Prairie Provinces and British Columbia are more open and friendly. Canadians often see U. S. Americans as more aggressive and materialistic than themselves. They also feel they are more tolerant and community oriented, as well as more polite. Canadians respond to *Thank you* with *You're welcome* rather than with silence or some other phrase.

Religion and Holidays

There are two major religious groups; the French descendants are Roman Catholic and the British descendants are Protestant. Official Canadian holidays include New Year's Day, Easter, Victoria Day (third Monday in May), Canada Day (July 1), Labour Day (first Monday in September), Thanksgiving Day (second Monday in October), Remembrance Day (11 November), Christmas, and Boxing Day (26 December). Boxing Day comes from the old British tradition of presenting small boxed gifts to service employees and is a day of visiting and shopping. Holidays unique to Quebec include the *Carnaval de Quebec,* a two week period in February filled with activities, and St. Jean-Baptiste Day (24 June), which is celebrated as Quebec's national holiday (different from Canada Day).

Customs and Courtesies

Although Canadians often get together among themselves unannounced, it is considered polite to visit only when invited or to at least call ahead.

Guests remove their shoes when entering a home to avoid tracking in dirt. Guests arriving in the morning will be offered coffee or tea and fruit or light sweets. The same foods may be offered to the afternoon visitor, but a heavier selection of sweets is the fare. Evening guests will be offered an alcoholic drink, usually wine, and cheese and crackers. If one has been invited for dinner, it is polite to offer to bring a part of the meal and help in the preparation of the meal. Never reach for food. Always ask if a dish could be passed to you. Resting hands in the lap during the meal is considered impolite as is leaving food on one's plate. Asking for second helpings is a compliment to the hostess. During a meal, it is polite to wipe one's mouth before drinking from a glass. Children are taught not to place elbows on the table, to sit still while eating, and to say *Please* and *Thank you*. Children are also taught to be silent and listen and talk only when spoken to by their elders. Canadians eat in the continental style, with the fork in the left hand and the knife in the right hand. Food is a reflection of the region, fish on either coast and an abundance of grains in the middle section. Promptness is showing gratitude and is important and a smile is always welcome.

Ice hockey is a very popular sport, but so is fishing, swimming, and an array of other sports in particular curling. In curling, two four-person teams slide a large stone (with a gooseneck handle) over ice toward a target. Because Atlantic Canadians are a people of the sea, lobster cook-outs and beach parties are common social events.

The People's Republic of China and Her National Minorities

The Landscape

Although China is just a little larger than the United States, she is the home of 1.2 billion people, the largest population in the world. Much of the country is covered by mountains and desert, so the majority of the people live in the fertile east where rivers and plains allow for productive agriculture. China's climate is much like that of the United States, but the summers are warmer and the winters are colder. Monsoons cause frequent summer floods. Some of her geographic wonders are the Himalaya Mountains, the Great Wall of China which stretches 1,500 miles, and the Great Yangtze River which is 3,900 miles long. Under great controversy, this river is soon to be damned for its potential hydroelectric power. Two thirds of China's territory is inhabited by national minorities. The northern frontier is formed by the Inner Mongolia Autonomous Region, (some 500,000 square miles), the northwestern frontier by the Uighur Autonomous Region (some 617,000 square miles), the southwestern frontier by the Tibet Autonomous Region (some 471,000 square miles), and by Yunnan Providence (some 168,000 square miles), whose population is comprised of twenty-two national minorities. These autonomous regions control the most important timber, hydroelectric power, petroleum, and mineral resources all of which are vital to China's economic development. Distance, weather, altitude, and lack of infrastructure are additional obstacles to the development of these resources. Furthermore, according to China's constitution, all nationalities are equal under the law so one cannot just invade these territories.

The Economy

China is a developing country with a potentially huge economy. However, its large population offsets this economy. The real gross domestic product per capita is only $2,064. In 1976 Deng Xiaoping came to power and vowed to move the country away from Maoism. His more modern policies in the eighties led to foreign tourism, a more liberal economy, private enterprise, growth, trade, and educational exchanges with Western countries. In 1992, following the Tiananmen Square massacre, Deng and his supporters won a quiet power struggle to bring China back on track in economic reform. China then became one of the world's fastest growing economies. By 2000 it surpassed the economy of the United States, but its per capita is far less. After Deng's death, President Jiang Zemin proclaimed that Deng's ideals would continue to direct Chinese policy of economic freedom, but within the framework of a strong central government control. In a country accustomed to equal wages for all, the people and government alike are struggling with the economic freedom in which wealth is not distributed equally. Successful and honest entrepreneurs are well respected, even in the rural areas, and the government applauds the vibrant and growing private sector even as it struggles to control it. With the growing economy, urban areas are experiencing a strong growth in the middle class and villagers are gaining better diets and health. With the continuation of rural immigration to the big cities to gain work, agriculture is experiencing a decrease in production. About sixty-one percent of the population is employed in the agriculture sector. Since China is a world leader in the production of rice, tobacco, corn, barley, soybeans, peanuts, eggs, and pork this could have ramifications on the feeding of other parts of the world. Other important products that come from China are wheat, fish, and potatoes. In the manufacturing sector China produces much of the microchips in an international chip industry which is being devastated from the recent outbreak of SARS (Severe Acute Respiratory Syndrome). Other manufactured goods, oil, minerals, coal and steel are also large factors in the economy.

The People

The Chinese population consists of hundreds of tribes and groups and is one of the oldest populations of the world. According to Chinese historical records dating back to the Zhou Dynasty, 1121–222 BC, there were four groups of Barbarians, a term covering large groups of tribes who inhabited the Chinese Middle Kingdoms of the Yellow River Valley. These nationalities exercised full sovereignty over their kingdom and principalities. All through Chinese dynastic history, the relationship between the Chinese (Huaxia in ancient times, Han since the Third Century AD and the Barbarians oscillated between hostility and friendly cooperation. There has been uninterrupted intermarriage between the Han (92 percent of the population) and the other ethnic groups, as well as within the ethnic groups themselves, so there are no "pure" ethnicities in China. In 1912 Sun Yatsen established the Republic of China and defined it as the Five Nationalities: the Han (Chinese), Manchus, Mongols, Hui, and Tibetans. In 1949 Mao Zedong established the People's Republic of China and invited the various groups to manifest themselves in order to enjoy their newly won equal rights. By 1955 more than 400 groups had registered. Later these groups were reduced to 56 nationalities. Han formed the national majority comprised of more than one billion people, with the remaining 55 nationalities accounting for ninety million people or approximately eight percent of the total. There are many different dialects spoken throughout China, Mandarin being the largest. The four major dialects are Han spoken by some 1.04 billion, Altaic, Southwest, and Indo-European. There are several subsets within these dialects but most speak Mandarin even if it is spoken as a second language.

The Religion and Holidays

There are three major religious traditions in China: Taoism, Confucianism, and Buddhism. Taoism, perhaps the unofficial religion of the Chinese people, is the only religion; the other two are schools of philosophy. Taoism is a religion developed from the Taoist philosophy and Buddhism. It origins come from many ancient popular religions linked to shamanism and nature worship although its historical evolution has been lost. In the second century AD, a Taoist preacher named Zhang Daoling established a formal Taoist Church, the blueprint for which he claimed had been revealed directly to him by the divinized Lao zu who became the god of his church, called the "Heavenly Masters." This church was closely linked to the ancient cults, beliefs, and magical practices of popular religions and quickly spread throughout China. Despite the efforts of the government to proclaim Communism or atheism, the Taoist Church prevailed. While Taoism refers to an ineffable being, Confucianism refers to the teaching of a very wise man by the name of Confucius. He felt that although man should respect divine beings, they should keep them at a distance. He felt that man was innately good and wise and did not need to seek inspiration from outside but only from within. Confucius, the father of Chinese philosophy insisted that the quality of human relations within the family circle was the foundation of an orderly society and of a prosperous state. He was a profound reformer who tactfully demythologized ancient Chinese religious beliefs and practices and sought to establish universal humanistic value based on reason and human nature. Buddhism originated in India by a prince named Siddharta Gautama. The term Buddhism means enlightened and is based on meditation rather than ritual. The essential teaching was the "Four Holy Truths": 1) Life is suffering; 2) suffering comes from desire; 3) to overcome suffering, one must extinguish desire; 4) to extinguish the desire, one must follow the "Eightfold Path" which is right views, intentions, speech, conduct, livelihood, effort, mindfulness, and concentration in order to attain the state of perfect bliss or nirvana. Each of these three main religions emphasized one aspect of three important concerns of religious consciousness: man's relation to nature (Taoism), to society (Confucianism), and to the absolute (Buddhism).

The Chinese lunar calendar, based on the solstices and equinoxes, dictates days on which holidays will fall. The biggest of all holidays is the Spring Festival, better known as the Chinese New Year. It lasts a week and falls between January 21 and February 20. It is celebrated with lavish banquets, family gatherings, carnivals, and dragon dances. The government provides extra food which includes fish, a symbol of abundance. Other holidays are the Lantern Festival on the 15th of the first lunar month, the Dragon Boat Festival on the fifth of the fifth lunar month, and Tibet's Fruit-Expecting Festival in August. One should be aware of the most common meeting phrase which translated means, "Did you eat?" If the answer is no, or not yet, some small form of food will be offered or one may be taken to a restaurant. So be forewarned.

Customs and Courtesies

The Chinese nod politely or bow slightly when greeting anyone even Westerners. A handshake is acceptable especially in a formal setting. Titles are used and the order of introduction is very important because the elderly and the one in charge are to be introduced first. This is not always easy to ascertain and asking is certainly accepted. Their clothing is less formal than in the past, but women are still seen in long skirts made of light material due to the temperatures. College students are forbidden from marrying until after graduation. Their customs stress moral purity and the longer one waits to marry the better are the benefits that come with waiting. The bride keeps her maiden name, but her children carry the name of the father. Tipping in a restaurants is considered an insult, something a superior does for an inferior.

Gifts are not readily accepted so several attempts is the norm. Colors and numbers are very important. Red is lucky, pink and yellow represent happiness and prosperity, and white, gray, and black are funeral colors.

Present gifts with both hands. Be very careful when giving or sending flowers. White and yellow, especially chrysanthemums, are used for funerals. Pears sounds like their word meaning to be separated and is considered bad luck. Red ink symbolizes the ending of a relationship and NEVER give a clock as a gift. It sounds like their word meaning death. Numbers also have very strong connotations especially the number four which sounds like death in the Chinese language. People from the United States need to be very conscious of this as many things are packaged by the fours in the U. S. This number is so significant that many buildings have a 3A or a 3B floor in place of the fourth floor. The number thirteen symbolizes bad luck just as it does in the West, but the numbers six represents luck, eight sounds like prosperity, and nine stands for longevity.

England

The Landscape

England is located in the British Isles, which include Great Britain, Ireland, the Isle of Man, and the Channel Islands, in the English Channel. England, Scotland and Wales are all located on the island of Great Britain. Politically, Great Britain and Northern Ireland make up the county known as the United Kingdom. England is the largest country in the British Isles. It covers 50,363 square miles, roughly the size of New York state. It has a long jagged coastline. The terrain consists of rugged highlands in the north, flat plains to the east, lowlands and hills in the south, and moors, famous for their prevailing winds, in the southwest. Nearly 30 percent of the land is cultivated and almost half is meadow and pasture. The climate is temperate, but the clouds and often rainy days make the temperatures feel cooler than they are. The surrounding seas have given England a certain sense of security and isolation that other European nations have not experienced. By the mid 19th century England had become the center of an empire that was eventually to cover a quarter of the entire globe. At the height of the empire England controlled so many colonies overseas that its population worldwide was nearly 100 times larger than its own. In fact the saying "the sun never sets on the British empire" meant just that because it was always daytime in some part of it.

Britain established itself as a great naval power by defeating the Spanish Armada in 1588. It became the world's most powerful economy during the Industrial Revolution. She acquired colonies around the world including Canada, the American colonies, and lands in the Mediterranean, the Caribbean, Africa, and Asia. Only in 1997 did Hong Kong gain its independence from Britain. The country established itself as a modern welfare state after World War II and is known for its socialist health care and educational systems.

The Economy

The United Kingdom is a global economic power and one of the largest in the European Union. Like other industrialized countries, its major industries have shifted from manufacturing to financial and other service industries. While agriculture as an industry has diminished, farmers still supply about 60 percent of the country's agricultural needs. The country does the bulk of its trading within the European Union. Natural resources are oil, coal, natural gas, tin, iron ore, and salt. Important exports include crude oil, manufactured goods, and consumer items. The service sector is now more important than the manufacturing sector. The U.K. has a vibrant, fast growing service sector led by world class banks, insurance companies, and emerging technology companies. London is one of the world's most important financial centers. The gross domestic product per capita is $18,620 and the literacy rate is 99 percent. Most of the people have a good standard of living, although there is a large gap between the wealthy and the lower classes. The richest fifth of the population receives more than fifty percent of the nation's income. The National Health Service provides free medical treatment and many other social services. Only prescriptions and some dental services are paid for by the individual. Also, financial services which track the economies of the world is a large part of the economy.

The People

In general, the English are a curious breed known for their dry wit and sarcasm which allows them to be self-critical. Although the majority of them are Caucasian, Britain's colonial heritage has brought cultures from India, Africa, and Asia together. The nation is highly urbanized. Ninety percent live in cities. The English have a class system and one does not easily move from one class to another. That was the whole theme of the musical *My Fair Lady*. They are very conservative, prideful, reserved, and have a great respect for law and order. They are a very polite society and patiently stand in line, keeping the proper distance from one another, and would never think of pushing their way through a crowd. They love their royalty and all the pomp and circumstance that goes with them and take great pride in the royalties' proper behavior.

After the death of Princess Di, Ferggie made a statement that it behooves one to stay within their own circle. I think that is the epitome of English thought. One is often judged by the way in which one speaks, the school one attended, one's parents' occupation, and many other things that all speak to one's stature in life. They do not touch and do not approve of loud or demonstrative behavior. Manners are important and are an indication of one's station in life. Tea is England's national beverage and they consume about one third of the world's tea exports. Tea is an afternoon snack which is either "high" or "low". Low tea is taken around 4 o'clock in the afternoon and consists of hot tea and cookies. High tea can be served at the same time, but it involves hot tea and little sandwiches such as cucumber or watercress finger sandwiches and chocolates and is much fancier. Their food is very bland but often rich in cream and dairy products. Rice and bread puddings come from the English as well as Shepard's pie and steak and kidney pie.

Religion and Holidays

The Church of England or the Anglican Church is the established church in England and its head is the reigning monarch. About sixty percent claim membership although only about twenty percent attend church on a regular basis. Other Protestant sects are the Methodists and Baptists and are called free churches. The Roman Catholic Church still has a very strong presence mainly due to a large number of Irish immigrants and Polish and Italian refugees who have settled in England. The country has a large number of Jews (about 400,000) making it one of the largest Jewish communities in Europe. Recently many cities have become home to large Sikh, Hindu, and Muslim immigration populations.

Most of England's holidays are those found in the Christian calendar. New Year's Day, May Day, and August Bank Holiday are some of the other holidays, but by far the largest are Guy Fawkes Day (November 5), April Fools Day (April 1), and Fat Tuesday, the day before Lent starts when Britain is awash in pancakes. Guy Fawkes Day commemorates the foiling of the 1605 Gunpowder plot to blow up Parliament. This day is celebrated with bonfires, fireworks, and the burning of "guys" (cloth dummies made from old clothes). Children stand in the street and shout, "Penny for the Guy!" hoping that passerby will drop coins in a hat or box. That night they throw the dummies into a huge bonfire and set off fireworks displays. Chestnuts are roasted in the same bonfire in which the guy is burning. April Fool's Day is taken quite seriously by the British. Even the BBC (British Broadcasting Corporation) and the national news-papers carry outlandish spoofs disguised as straightforward reporting like the government plans to move Trafalgar Square. All joking is supposed to end at Noon, but is usually carried out through the entire day. Remembrance Sunday (the Sunday closest to November 11) celebrates all the soldiers who died in both World Wars. Other holidays revolve around the royalty and Parliament.

Customs and Courtesies

English families are small and tight-knit. Because so many people live in the cities, there has been a trend to move to the country and develop more rapport with the land. The British are fanatical gardeners. Today, programs about gardening are among the highest rated on the main tele-vision channels and are routinely shown during prime time. Even if they just have a window box and a small plot of ground in their apartment complex, they will spend hours cultivating it for just the right look. A popular weekend activity is to visit one of the 3,600 public gardens or the manicured grounds of a private estate. In the 19th century flower seeds and cuttings began arriving from around the world such as dahlias from Mexico and tea-scented roses from China. Knot gardens and labyrinthine maze gardens were carefully clipped into elaborate geometric shapes. Ferdinand de Rothschild had parrots placed on stands on his Mentmore estate, which had been planted so that the flowers matched the bird's feathers. (Passport P 72)

Another trend is the Do-It-Yourself industry which is becoming very popular in view of high labor costs for plumbers, electricians, and heating. Just the service call has become exorbitant. Because of the slump in the world economy, making your own home repairs is more affordable if one does them oneself. DIY magazines show examples of " how to" with designs and complete instructions. When someone is asked what they did over the weekend, often the reply is, "A spot of DIY.". It is also a matter of British pride to be able to do these things such as papering walls, stripping furniture, or paving garden paths.

I would be remiss if I did not mention an old tradition of Briton's genteel heritage which is that of hunting fowl or riding to the hounds. The Fox Hunt and Polo have long been the sports of the kings. The horse has played a very significant part in British entertainment from horse racing to polo. Of course, soccer (called football), cricket, and rugby are very popular as well as local pubs with dart games. Angling is the most popular pastime in the country where they fish for trout, carp, bream, and roach. Half of the population owns a pet, the most popular being the dog.

France

The Landscape

The largest country in Europe, France is located on the extreme west coast of the continent. It and Spain are the only countries that both have Atlantic and Mediterranean coasts as well as direct access to the North Sea. France is slightly smaller than Texas. The terrain is varied, from plains to mountains and forests to farmland. Mountains stretch along the border with Spain, called the Pyrenees, and the mountain range along Italy, and Switzerland is called the Alps. France boasts Europe's highest peak, Mont Blanc. Its major rivers are the Rhine that forms part of the border with Germany, the Seine which runs through Paris, and the Rhone. The northern border with Belgium is a flat plain with rolling hills. The north is temperate and prone to rain. The south climate is Mediterranean with warm, moist winters and hot, dry summers. The Loire valley and the

Bordeaux regions are world famous for their vineyards. The Payee Basques borders Spain where one can still see farmers tilling their land with oxen. The Atlantic Ocean and the Bay of Biscay lie to the west, the English Channel to the northwest, and, indeed, France's sovereignty extends to the island of Corsica as well as ten overseas territories.

A favorite destination for tourists, France offers many historical and cultural sites, artistic and architectural treasures, and recreational facilities. The capital city is Paris, home to such world renown structures as the Eiffel Tower, the Louvre, and the Cathedral of Notre Dame. Throughout the country one will find centuries-old cathedrals and castles that are sure to boggle the mind. In addition, the palaces of Versailles, Vincennes, and Fontainebleau are ranked among the world's leading architectural master-pieces. The Mediterranean coast boasts the celebrated French Riviera and the Alps mountain region attracts the rich and famous and skiers from around the world.

The Economy

France is one of the major economic powers of the world. The real gross domestic product per capita is $20,510 which has tripled in a single gener-ation. The economy is based largely on manufacturing and services. Major industries include iron and steel, motor vehicles, aircraft, machinery, elec-tronics, textiles, chemicals, and food processing. As one of Europe's leading agricultural producers, France is self sufficient in most foods. The agricultural sector employs only about seven percent of the workforce, but is a world leader in wine, milk, butter, cheese, barley, and wheat production. Exports include machinery, transport equipment, steel prod-ucts, and agricultural goods. Tourism and finance are important service industries and employ two thirds of the workforce. More than half of France's power is generated by nuclear power plants. The currency is the French *franc.*

The People

France has a population of over 59 million people, growing annually at 0.3 percent. Three-fourths of the people live in urban areas. Greater Paris claims some eight million people. Ethnically, the French have a Celtic her-itage that has mixed with other European groups – Latin, Nordic, Teutonic, Slavic, and others over the centuries. Immigrants and descendants of immi-grants from France's colonial possessions also inhabit France. Recently, growing immigration from Asia, Turkey, and North Africa has brought to France a large Muslim population of about 3 to 5 million. Although they have integrated into French society, the various ethnic groups do not mix with one another. French is the nation's language as well as an import-ant international language and the official language of the United Nations. Some 300 million people around the world speak French. It is the second language of 23 African countries, six in Asia and the Asian Pacific, and five in Europe. The French believe success is judged by educational level, family reputation, and financial status. They are extremely proud of their culture, heritage, and way of life. They are a very patriotic people who expect visitors to have some knowledge of French and to show appreciation for French culture. Politeness is a valued human interaction as is the phrase Please – *s'il vous plait*.

Religion and Holidays

Roman Catholicism is by far the largest religion in France with only five percent being practicing Catholics and the remainder being just nominal Catholics. Most practice their faith by celebrating various religious holidays and attending mass once or twice a year especially on Christmas and Easter. North Africans remain the most notable separate community because of their Islamic religion.

The French celebrate several holidays each year such as New Year's (*Etrennes*) during which flowers are presented to the older family members and some exchange gifts; Mardi Gras (Shrove Tuesday) is celebrated with parades and parties, Easter Sunday and Monday are legal holidays; Labor Day (1 May) is marked by parades and celebrates the coming of Spring; and Noel (Christmas). On Christmas Eve the tree is decorated, followed by a big meal and midnight mass. Wooden shoes are left by the fireplace for Santa Claus to fill. Bastille Day, the 14 of July is the *La Fete Nationale* where there is great celebrating commemorating the storming of the Bastille prison in Paris during the French Revolution. Other holidays are Ascension, Pentecost, Assumption (15 August), All Saints' Day (1 November), and World War I Armistice day (11 November).

Customs and Courtesies

The French are formal in their visiting customs. People do not visit unannounced. Punctuality is a sign of courtesy so one should never be late except at social events when it is polite to arrive a few minutes late, allowing the hosts extra time for final preparations. Guests should wait to be invited in and should sit where the host directs them to sit. In international circles, it is still polite to bring a small token of appreciation such as candy, wine, or flowers. Be very careful with flowers as red roses connote romanticism, chrysanthemums are used at cemeteries, carnations symbolize bad luck, and yellow roses signify adultery. If in doubt, ask the florist what would be appropriate. The French are very knowledgeable about the quality of wines so unless you have a fine recommendation by the wine shop keeper, it is better to stick to bon bons. It is considered quite rude to eat and run as we would say in the states. When ending a visit, a guest waits for a polite silence before rising and even then it takes a while to say your good-byes. As in many countries there is no hurry in visiting, maybe in business, but never when one has been invited for tea or dinner. One should follow up with a short thank you note the next day. People remember the small gestures which can make or break a relationship.

The French are a very private people and such intimate subjects as politics, religion, and money should never be discussed. They are also very proud of their cuisine and its presentation. Always compliment the host on the meal and the good cooking as well as one's fine home. Etiquette is very important in most European countries as well as those countries influenced by the Europeans.

Both hands remain above the table at all times. A man may rest his wrists and a woman her forearms on the table edge. One does not place the elbows on the table and it is very impolite to speak with food in the mouth. Lunches and dinners may last up to two hours or more. Be prepared to be patient.

The family is still the most important unit of society. Although the closeness is not what it was, many children still remain at home until they finish their education before leaving to find work elsewhere. As in Great Britain, children are outnumbered by pets who receive very special attention at times. The French are enthusiastic spectators especially when it comes to soccer and rugby. A famous national event is the *Tour de France,* a cycling marathon, which is two thousand miles long and runs through the entire country. People line the streets to cheer on their favorites. Lance Armstrong, an American, has won it six times. Fishing, cycling, and hiking are also popular sports. People of all ages enjoy *petanque,* a form of bowling that originated in southern France. Cafes are very popular and many a literary artist has produced their work at a café.

Germany

The Landscape

On October 3, 1990 the two separate countries known as East Germany and West Germany became one with the collapse of Communism in Eastern Europe. Geographically it can be divided into three regions: the low-lying North German plain, the central German uplands, and to the south the ranges of the Cental Alps and other uplands. The capital of Germany is Berlin. The country is surrounded by nine countries: Denmark to the north; the Czech Republic and Poland to the east; Switzerland and Austria to the south; and France, Luxembourg, Belgium, and the Netherlands to the west. About 40 percent of Germany is forest. There are three main rivers: The Rhine that runs through the southwest and the vast Black Forest; the Elbe, located in the east, runs along the industrial centers; and the famous Danube that originates in the Black Forest running west to east and empties into the Black Sea.

The Economy

Germany is one of the top five economic powers in the world. The real gross domestic product per capita is $19,675, but the figure in East Germany is about half that of West Germany. Since unification, the east has made substantial progress in its shift to a market economy, but is still far away from being equal to the western states. The region still relies heavily on the subsidies from the west (to the tune of about 100 billion per year). The government has undertaken large projects to retrain workers, rebuild roads, railways, public transportation and communication facilities. Construction is currently the largest economic sector in the east. Many western companies have bought eastern factories and upgraded them, but much more private investment is needed to revitalize eastern industries and relieve the west of heavy tax burdens. For years West Germany has benefitted from a highly skilled population that enjoys a high standard of living and an extensive social welfare program. Now it must share its wealth with those in the east in order to bring a balance to the whole country. Germany is one of the world's largest exporters of cars, steel, aluminum, iron, machinery, other manufactured goods, food, beverages and textiles. Agriculture accounts for only one percent of the GNP, but it is a very important sector. The main crops are potatoes, wheat, barley, rye, sugar beets, cabbage, fruits, and dairy products. It is a major producer of hops, which are used in the country's world-renowned beer industry. Grape production supports the notable wine industry in the Rhine and Moselle valleys. It conducts fifty percent of its trade with other European Union countries.

Tourism is a well developed industry in Germany. People from West Germany love to travel. Most of this industry centers on winter sports in Bavaria, numerous historical sites, art galleries, museums, and cultural events. Most visitors are Europeans, followed by North Americans. Many Germans living in the United States will make an annual visit back to their homeland. The economy is gradually recovering from several years of stagnant growth and will in time regain its global competitiveness.

The People

More than 90 percent of the people are ethnic Germans descended from Germanic tribes, Slavs, and other groups. Reunified Germany has the second largest population of any European country, approximately 86 million. The rest of the people are mainly other Europeans, the Turkish being the largest group. In western states, numerous political refugees from the Middle East, India, Africa, and Asia receive room and board until their applications for asylum are processed. Many ethnic Germans from eastern Europe nations have emigrated to Germany to find work. However, new laws restrict the definition of a valid asylum seeker and limit other forms of immigration. Germans are industrious, thrifty, and orderly. They appreciate punctuality, privacy, and skill. They have a strong sense of regional pride and spend about ten percent of their income on home furnishings and decoration. Their humor tends to be of the farcical and slapstick kind. The Rhine landers of the north are easy-going and good-natured while the Bavarian to the south are lively and excitable.

Germans have a strong classical education because of the nation's rich heritage in music, literature, history and art. They expect others to have an appreciation as well. Education is a source of pride, especially in technology and craftsmanship. The literacy rate is 99 percent. German is the official language. English is a required school subject and is widely understood. Many Germans in eastern states know Russian as well. Education is free at all levels although entry into the universities can be very difficult. Preschool begins at age four and full time school is mandatory until age 16. Then part time or full time schooling continues on a chosen track until one reaches the age of 18. Students may choose from several educational paths, job training programs, specific professional careers, or college preparatory. Nearly ever occupation, from mechanic to accountant to waiter has a school or program designed specifically for it. For example, waiters and waitresses might attend school for up to four years before certifying as servers. Because of this rigorous schooling, wages are high, making the German labor force one of the best paid in the world. Nearly half of all German workers belong to labor unions. Two of Germany's largest employers are the auto manufacturers Daimler Benz and Volkswagen, each employing about 320,000 worldwide.

Religion and Holidays

Germany is essentially a Christian society with about 35 percent of the population belonging to the Roman Catholic Church and 36 percent belonging to Protestant (mostly Lutheran) churches. Two percent is Muslim.

Fasching (Carnival) is perhaps the most famous custom in Germany which is a pre-Lent carnival that lasts from November through March. It is actually more of a season than a holiday. There are three main days during this season: *Weiber Fasnacht* when women are allowed to cut in half any man's tie they see; *Rose Monday* a day of big parades; and *Fastnacht* which means a night of fasting in which people eat, drink, and carouse wholeheartedly day and night. Another celebration is known as *Oktoberfest*, more familiar to Americans, but in Germany it is celebrated for two weeks when people eat, drink and listen to Bavarian band music. St. Nicholas' Day, *Nikolaus,* is celebrated on December 6. On this day adults, children, and coworkers receive bags of candies. In Germany, Advent is celebrated much like Lent in the United States. The front door is decorated with a wreath. A second wreath is placed on the mantelpiece or on the dining table with four candles. On each of the four Sundays before Christmas a candle is lit. Advent calendars are also a tradition given to children who open one window per day until Christmas arrives. Everyone, including non-Christians, are expected to greet each other with *Frohe Weihnachten* meaning Merry Christmas on Christmas Eve and Christmas Day. From then until December 31st, the greeting is *Guten Rutsch ins Neue Jahr* which means literally "Good slide into the New Year." The tradition of decorating an evergreen tree is a German one. On their trees they have real lighted candles. The song "Silent Night, Holy Night" was composed near Salzburg, Austria in 1818.

Customs and Courtesies

German culture has made a great contribution to Europe and the world, especially in the area of music and literature. The country's renowned composers include Johann Sebastian Bach, Ludwig van Beethoven, Johannes Brahms, Robert Schumann, and Richard Wagner. Some of the greatest German poets are Johann Wolfgang von Goethe and Heinrich Heine. Notable German writers include Friedrich von Schiller, Nobel Prize winners Thomas Mann and Heinrich Böll.

When invited to dinner in a German home always bring a small gift. A bottle of wine, not from Germany, is always acceptable as well as flowers which should consist of an uneven number except thirteen, red roses, white lilies (used in funerals) or heather (placed on graves). Always unwrap the flowers before giving them to the hostess. American wine or candy is always a safe bet. Germans eat in the continental style keeping knife and fork in their hands while eating. It is considered bad manners to place a hand under the table, wrists should rest on the table's edge. They love their beer and they prefer their drinks without ice as they consider cold drinks to be unhealthy. Their main meal is in the middle of the day, with a light supper in the evening. However, dinner parties are elaborate and may last well into the evening. Leaving food on one's plate is regarded as wasteful, something Germans do not appreciate.

Hong Kong

Landscape

Hong Kong is a part of China, but it has special status within the country. Formerly a British colony, it is now called a Special Autonomous Region. Britain agreed to return all of Hong Kong to China with the stipulation that the people would continue to govern themselves and to trade freely. Hong Kong is located in the southeast coast of China and is surrounded on three sides by the South China sea. The area contains a natural harbor that is very deep and large. The land is around 421 square miles, about half the size of Rhode Island. It covers a small portion of the mainland adjacent to Guangdong Province, the Kowloon Peninsula, the two large islands of Hong Kong and Lantau, and two hundred smaller islands. The Guangdong Province connects to the New Territories which in turn connects to the Kowloon Peninsula which in turn connects to Victoria, the center of business and government in Hong Kong which connects the huge harbors in the South China Sea. This entrepot is a gateway to the manufacturing and financial centers and a vital agent in international trade and the modernization of China. It has become an important center for global commerce.

The Economy

Hong Kong is a free port, which, means there are no tariffs on imports or exports. However, duties are placed on tobacco, liquors, cosmetics, and a few other items. It has a bustling trade center and a shipping and banking emporium. It is one of the greatest trading and transhipment centers in East Asia. The textile and garment industry is one of the largest industries, but electrical and electronic equipment are also very large as is the toy industry. This region has very limited natural resources, thus it depends heavily on imported goods for virtually all of its requirements, including raw materials, food and other consumer goods, capital goods, and fuel. More than 35 percent of the population is employed in manufacturing and the tertiary sector now makes up four-fifths of the gross domestic product which employees those in the services industries namely shipping, aviation, tourism, and finance. The average salary of a working person in Hong Kong is one of the highest in Asia. The Real gross domestic product per capita is $22,310, the world's fifth largest.

The People

About 98 percent of the people are ethnic Chinese while the other two percent constitute large communities of Americans and British. British, Americans, Australians, Canadians, and New Zealanders make up the non-Asian group while Japanese, Indians, Pakistanis, and Singaporeans make up the Asian group. Its total population is about 6.3 million with a growth rate of 1.7 percent per annum with a large influx of Chinese immigrating from the mainland. It is one of the most densely populated areas in the world with more than 14,000 people per square mile. The government has not been able to provide adequate housing for the people which has resulted in poverty, drug abuse, and the worst possible scenario for the elderly because they are forced to live alone in their apartments until they die. It is bad karma for an elderly to die in his home. The passage from this life into the next is a most important ritual and large amounts of money are spent on the funeral. Cantonese and English are both official languages. English is the language of business. Hong Kong is referred to as the "Pearl of the Orient." The name not only describes its scenic beauty, impressive modern structures, and magnificent natural harbor, but also the energetic, hardworking people who have built Hong Kong into a major trade center. The Chinese value modesty and patience over aggressive behavior. They prefer a slower interaction, with contemplation on what is happening and how it is happening. "Saving face" is of utmost importance so it is better to introduce several concepts rather than just one and certainly the negative is never acceptable. *If they say the photocopier is broken, it is better to explain that the machine is in an energy saver mode than to say outright 'it is not broken'.* Modesty and personal cleanliness are important in public. If they seem to be in a rush try to slow them down even to the point of asking them to return when you both have more time to devote to the situation.

Customs and Courtesies

Chinese religions, superstitions, and myths date back thousands of years. Strong elements of Taoism and Confucianism, both of which originated in China, and Buddhism, with roots in India, form part of the religious life of many Hong Kong residents. Folk religious practices and ancestor veneration are also widespread. The people celebrate the festivals and holidays of both the East and the West such as the Dragon Boat Festival, the Mid-Autumn Festival, the Lunar (Chinese) New Year, and Christmas. Other holidays include Easter and Liberation Day (last Monday in August). Gift giving and receiving are a very important part of Chinese culture. To give gifts means an expression of friendship, a hope for a good future relationship, concluding a successful enterprise, showing appreciation for a favor, or to celebrate Chinese New Year. One could equate it with the "Thank you" in the West. Keep in mind that the gift might be a very small one, but it symbolizes something of great important in the mind of the giver. A gift is tangible evidence of sincerity. They should be presented in red or gold paper and such things as clocks, flowers, or sharp objects are never acceptable. To bring toys for the children shows concern for the entire family. Present the gift with both hands and expect a few refusals before an actual acceptance. A quick acceptance indicates greed. I invited some visiting business people over to my house for dinner one day. They showed up *each* with a small gift, but the sum made a very nice gift. One was a set of wooden Panda bears, one was an exquisite cut paper picture, and one was a beautiful fan. It was summertime. When American business men are giving gifts it is important to give a gift to every member of the team with the nicest going to the leader. This is very important to get a relationship started and to keep it going. Do not open in front of the givers unless they insist and if they do open it *very slowly*. When giving stay away from sets of two, four, or anything divisible by two. It means bad luck.

India

The Landscape

India is about one-third the size of the United States. It has three major regions: the northern mountains, the northern plain, and a southern region of both highlands and plains. The northern mountains are dominated by the Himalayas. The most important river is the Ganges which begins in the Himalayas and flows to the Bay of Bengal. This river is considered sacred. Half of the country is under cultivation and one fourth is in forest. Much of India is a peninsula that extends into the Indian Ocean. To the west is the Arabian Sea and to the east is the Bay of Bengal. India's climate is controlled by monsoons, or winds that change direction according to the season. Most of the country has three seasons: hot and dry (March to May), hot and wet (June to September), and cool and dry (October to February). In a sense, India seems to have two separate countries: village India, supported by primitive agriculture where tens of millions live below the poverty line and urban India, one of the most heavily industrialized areas in the world.

The Economy

India is largely an agriculture country in which two thirds of the population work in farming. It is self-sufficient in food production. It is a leading world producer of peanuts, rice, cheese, tobacco, wheat, cotton, milk, sugar cane, and rubber. Some of its leading exports are tea, coffee, textiles, and manufactured goods. India has more cattle, water buffalo, and goats than any other country in the world, but their economic value is severely limited by the Hindu prohibition against the slaughter of cattle (since the cow is sacred). Since the Green Revolution of the 1970's, significant progress has been made by government agricultural modernization efforts and several reclamation and irrigation projects. Industry is becoming increasingly important to the Indian economy. Among the most valuable industries are the manufacturing of textiles, fertilizers and chemicals, processed foods, iron and steel, automobiles, and cement. Today it is a leader in software development and other high technology industries. India's middle class, of which there are 150 million, is rapidly expanding. Half of the population is under 20 years of age. Companies have been sending students to the United States to get a college education in computer and accounting skills and then bringing them home to develop worldwide software systems. Farmers plow the fields in southern India while steel is cast at a Tata truck factory in northeastern India. Despite its booming economy, serious gaps remain between the rich and the poor. The real domestic product per capita is $1,348. The currency is the *rupee* (Re).

The People

India has the second largest population in the world, 952 million strong with an annual growth rate of 1.6 percent. It is one of the most ethically diverse countries in the world, but such factors as rural versus urbanization, religious, and socioeconomic differences are more likely to separate than bring people together. The Indo-Aryans in the north make up 70 percent of the population while the Dravidians in the south make up 25 percent of the population. The rest is made up of a myriad of other groups including Mongoloids. Although 80 percent of the population is Hindu and speak Hindi in the north, English is the official language of politics and commerce. There are more than 1,500 languages and dialects spoken in the various villages. Fourteen percent are Muslim while other significant religions are Christian, Sikh, and Buddhist. Hinduism is extremely diverse, polytheistic, and rich in ceremony, and is associated with the caste system. There is no supreme authority, but the caste system provides structure for the Hindu doctrine that dictates individuals must work their way via reincarnation from the lowest *Shudra* (laborer) through the *Vaishya* (farmer and merchant) and *Kshatriya* (warrior) castes to the highest *Brahmin* (intellectual and leader) before they can exit life on earth to a better existence. (Culturgrams p. 118) People are born into these groups each of which has its own traditional occupations, diet, and customs. The caste system has organized Indian society for many thousands of years.

Customs and Courtesies

Indians are religious, family oriented, and philosophical. The culture of India is one of the oldest and richest in the world. The country's traditional music, dance, and drama go back nearly 2,000 years. It is probably best known for its architectural masterpieces such as the Taj Mahal and the Buddhist remains at Sarnath, Sanchi, and Bodh Gaya. The film industry is one of the largest in the world producing about one thousand films per year far out pacing Hollywood. Film stars are esteemed as cultural icons and its cultural influence reaches throughout the Arab world.

Indians see the left hand as unclean and never use it when eating. Many eat with their fingers and use the banana leaf as a plate. Since the cow is sacred, water buffalo meat passes for meat although many are vegetarians. There is a strong taboo against eating or drinking from another's plate or glass. Out of respect for a woman's privacy, men do not touch women in public even when greeting her. The married woman wears a red dot on her forehead to indicate that she is taken.

Two national holidays mark the recent emergence of India as an independent nation. Independence Day on August 15 commemorates the day in 1947 when India achieved its freedom from colonial rule and Republic Day on the 26th of January marks the inauguration of India as a Republic in 1950. Hindu festivals are observed as holidays. Some of these are Shivrati dedicated to the god Shiva, Holi, the Spring Festival, Janamashtami the birthday of the god Krishna, Dasahara the festival of the goddess of Durga, and Divali the Festival of the Lights. The Muslim festivals of Id-ul-Fitr and Bakr-Id and Muharram are holidays. The Christian holy days of Good Friday and Christmas are also observed as are the birthdays of the founders of Buddhism, Jainism, and Sikhism.

Indonesia

The Landscape

Indonesia's 17,000 islands stretch 3,200 miles along the equator south, east, and west of Malaysia and is the world's largest island nation. It previously known as the Dutch East Indies. Only 6,000 islands are actually inhabited. The country's only land boundaries are with Malaysia in northern Borneo and with Papua New Guinea on the island of New Guinea. The largest unshared islands are Sumatra, Java, and Sulawesi. The islands total about one fifth of the United States. Vast tracks of rainforests in Sumatra and Kalimantan are being destroyed by loggers and developers. Hundreds of acres are being destroyed on a daily basis thus making many birds, plants, and animals extinct or displaced. Indonesia is home to tigers, elephants, monkeys, tropical birds, small deer, giant clams, Komodo dragon lizards, and abundant marine life. The climate is tropical with heavy monsoons from November to March. As one moves outward from the national capital, Jakarta, into the rural areas where 70 percent of Indonesians live, an individual's ethnic group determines more and more his or her identity and way of life. There are more than 250 distinct cultural groups speaking as many as 700 unintelligible languages. This archipelago is crossed by the world's prime trade routes and is the source of one of the world's most coveted commodities – spices. The tropical climate, abundant rainfall, and remarkably fertile volcanic soils allow for a rich agricultural yield.

The Economy

The Indonesian economy is dominated by agriculture which accounts for a third of the gross domestic product and employs nearly sixty percent of the workforce. Only twelve percent of the land is cultivated with thirty-three percent of the land being suitable for agriculture. The most important islands, both culturally and economically, are Java, Bali, and Sumatra. Rice is the major crop. The majority of the people are self sufficient in food. Indonesia is rich in natural resources, but many of them remain undeveloped. Crude oil and natural gas are the most valuable natural resources and are a major source of export revenues. Indonesia is also one of the world's major rubber and palm oil producers. The government controls the large plantation crop farms which produce sugarcane, coffee, tea, palm oil, cinchona, cloves, cocoa, and spices. Fish is also a major industry along the costal regions. Indonesia accounts for nearly one half of the world's tropical hardwood trade with its vast timberlands and vast rain forests of giant trees. The manufacturing sector has been strengthened and many cottage industries have sprung up that produce consumer items such as clothing and shoes for the global market. The real gross domestic product per capita is $3,740 which is rising as the growing middle class becomes more established. However, wealth is still highly concentrated among the elite. The economy is growing at seven percent. Indonesia is called an "emerging Asian tiger." The currency is the Indonesian rupiah (Rp)

The People

Indonesia's population of 200 million is the fourth largest in the world with a growth rate of 1.5 percent. Most Indonesians share a Malay racial heritage even though there are more than 300 distinct cultural groups, known as sukus, speaking as many as 700 mutually unintelligible languages. The national motto, "Unity in Diversity" expresses the desire to develop a national identity that transcends the purely ethnic and regional loyalties. The official language is Bahasa Indonesia, a dialect of Malay; it is used in government, commerce, education, and mass media. However, a regional language is used by the ethnic groups for private, family and local communities. Some of the major ethnic group regions with their own language are Java (100 million); Sumatra (25.4 million); Kalimantan (1.8 million); Sulawesi (4 million); the Lesser Sundas (4.5 million); the Moluccas, Irian Jaya, and the Chinese (4 million). Java is the most densely populated island. Although it comprises only seven percent of the land, it holds 60 percent of the population. English is taught as a third language in the schools after the main ethnic language and Indonesian.

Indonesians value loyalty to family and friends. They rarely disagree in public and prefer to say *belum* meaning "not yet" instead of "no." They appreciate a quiet voice, an unassuming attitude, patience, and discretion. The vast majority, about 90 percent, are Muslims and adhere to the Islam religion.

Ireland

The Landscape

Ireland is known as the "Emerald Isle" because of its famous green countryside. The Republic of Ireland occupies most of the island of Ireland. Northern Ireland occupies only one sixth of the island and is part of the

United Kingdom. The island lies off the western coast of Great Britain, separated by the Irish Sea. The highlands of the north, west, and south are generally barren, but the central plain is very fertile and the climate is temperate and moist. The rains are heaviest in the west which results in brilliant green grass and large stretches of peat bog, a source of valuable fuel. The famous Shannon River is the longest of the Irish rivers and drains the western plains. The irregular coastline provides many natural harbors. Dublin is the capital. Other famous cities are Waterford (known for its crystal), Killarney (known for its lakes), Galway (Jim Galway, the famous flutist), and Cork (5 miles from the village of Blarney). The famous Blarney Stone attracts thousands of tourists every year. It is believed that if you kiss the Blarney Stone, you will receive the gift of persuasive eloquence or the gift of blarney, i.e. the ability to talk your way out of any situation. Now who would not want that gift?

The Economy

Ireland was rural and agricultural for much of the twentieth century, but industry has steadily grown in importance. Agriculture accounts for about five percent of its economic production and employs about nine percent of the population. The service industries, combined with trade, finance, transportation, and public administration, account for more than 50 percent of total economic production. Tourism is one of the largest service industries. During the nineties, Ireland experienced great economic growth partly through the development of an extensive technology industry. About 40 percent of economic output comes from manufacturing, mining, and construction. The major manufactured goods are office equipment and computers, chemicals, recorded media, pharmaceuticals, and, of course, alcoholic beverages. When we think of Ireland, we think of Scotch Whiskey, woolen sweaters, and Waterford crystal. Ireland is generally self-sufficient in food and fishing provides a major source of food. The economy is growing about six percent per annum. The real gross domestic product per capita is $16,061. The currency is the *euro*.

The People

Ireland's population of about 3.6 million is mainly composed of ethnic Irish, with a small group of English. The Irish are descended primarily from ancient Celtic tribes, but there is also a strong Norman influence as well as some Anglo influence. Both English and Irish are official languages. The Irish language is also known as Gaelic and is the historic language of Ireland. When I think of the Irish I think of the fighting Irish and some of them do seem to have quite a temper. For the most part they are a lighthearted, cheerful, and optimistic group with a very warm and hospitable nature. They usually have a quick wit, a twinkle in their eye, and a hearty laugh. They are also known for their stubborn-ness, and for their love of the Roman Catholic Church and God. The Irish have given the world wonderful music and dance as in The Lord of the Dance. They are also known to be great storytellers. They often socialize in neighborhood pubs for a brew and a game of darts. About 93 percent of the population is Roman Catholic. The Church has played a significant part in the values of the people and the laws of the land. It has also greatly influenced the educational system. Adult literacy is nearly 100 percent. All children must attend school from ages 6 until 15 and they attend single-sex schools instead of coeducational ones. The National School is the primary school and both English and Gaelic are taught at this level. Secondary school students receive an Intermediate Certificate at 15 or 16 and a Leaving Certificate after completing another two addi-tional years of schooling. This last certificate is required for entry into one of Ireland's three universities which are free. Ever since the great potato famine in 1845, Ireland has lost a large percentage of its population to emigration mostly into the United States.

Customs and Courtesies

Ireland's legal holidays are New Year's Day, St. Patrick's Day (March 17), Good Friday, Easter Sunday and Easter Monday, bank holidays on the first Mondays of June and August, Christmas, and St. Stephen's Day (December 26). Also a variety of customs and celebrations are associated with certain saint's days. One of these is St. John's Day (June 24), tradi-tionally the time to dig up and eat the first new potatoes. On the night before, bonfires are lit on hilltops throughout the west of Ireland. On Halloween a traditional dish called *calcannon* is served consisting of cabbage, potatoes, and milk. A ring, coin, thimble, and button are inserted into the dish. The person finding the ring is supposed to be married within the year. The coin symbolizes wealth, the button, bachelorhood, and the thimble, spinsterhood. Ireland has much folklore and stories with magical qualities such as the leprechauns and the legend of St. Patrick which together with folk songs and dances are celebrated at many folk festivals. Ireland is also famous for its writers who include James Joyce, Oscar Wilde, George Bernard Shaw, Samuel Beckett, and the poet William Butler Yeats. Winners of the Nobel prize for literature are Yeats, Shaw, Beckett, and recently modern poet Seamus Heaney in 1995.

Israel

The Landscape

Israel is an elongated strip of land about 3,020 square miles or about the size of New Jersey. Despite the country's size, the land and climate vary substantially by region. The terrain ranges from fertile valleys and flower-covered hills to unique deserts and the Dead Sea, which at 1,300 feet below sea level is the lowest point on earth. Israel has a tremendous variety of plants and animals for its small size. The rainy season from November to March does not provide enough moisture to last through the dry season, from April to October, so lack of water is always a problem. Sophisticated irrigation and water-transportation and water-conservation techniques have been developed, highlighted by the National Water Carrier, a huge system of pipes, aqueducts, canals, reservoirs, and dams, designed to carry water from the fertile north to the drier south. Through these sophisticated techniques, Israel has managed to create enough arable land to grow almost all the food needed by its people. The most important river is the Jordan. The largest cities are Jerusalem, a mixture of ancient and modern, Tel Aviv-Yafo, the commercial and financial center, located on the Mediterranean coast, and Haifa, a busy Mediterranean port city.

The Economy

The economy of Israel is based on both state and private ownership and operation. It is well developed and modern despite a lack of natural resources. Agriculture employs about five percent of the labor force and produces fruits, vegetables, cut flowers, cotton, wheat, barley, peanuts, sunflowers, and olives. It produces about five percent of the gross national product which is about $16,023 per capita. This figure has tripled in the last generation. The strong industrial sector includes high technology, diamonds, and machinery. Tourism is another vital part of the economy and is one of Israel's largest sources of revenues. The major exports are processed diamonds; high technologies including computers, software, telecommunications, biotechnology, and medical electronics; military products; and agriculture products. Most of the land, apart from the land that belongs to non-Jews, is held in trust for the people of Israel by the state and the Jewish National Fund. The fund was set up in 1901 to buy land in Palestine for Jews to cultivate, and now implements a wide range of forest and land development activities. The Israel Land Authority leases the land to kibbutzim, which are communal agricultural settlements; to moshavim, which are cooperative agricultural communities; and to other agricultural or rural villages. Growth, unemployment and inflation fluctuate with immigration and the peace process as well as global market trends. Taxes are very high. The currency is the new shekel (NIS).

The People

Israel's population of 5.4 million includes about 300,000 Israeli settlers in the West Bank, Gaza, the Golan Heights, and East Jerusalem. Nearly 90 percent of the people live in cities. While the Jewish population once consisted mostly of those from central and Eastern Europe, not including Russia, increasing numbers of Jews from African and Asian countries have immigrated and now constitute a majority of the Jewish population. About 500,000 Russian Jews have recently immigrated. The Arab population of only sixteen percent primarily are Sunni Arabs. By law, all Jews in the world have the right to emigrate to Israel as long as they can prove their identity (inherited through the mother) or are recognized converts. The word *Jewish* does not describe an ethnic group or population. Rather it is a religion, a culture, and a nation. There are three identities in Israel: religion, citizenship, and nationality. A Jew is Jewish by religion and nationality, but Israeli by citizenship. Hebrew is Israel's official language. Arabic has official status, is spoken by the Arab minority, and is taught from the fifth grade on in school. English, frequently used in commerce, is spoken by most Israelis and is also taught from the fifth grade on.

The city of Jerusalem and the surrounding areas have played an important role in the development of several of the world's major religions, including Judaism, Christianity, and Islam. Jerusalem therefore is holy to all three religions and is a source of conflict between them. Religious freedom is guaranteed by the state, but there is little separation between church and state as the Jewish faith and rabbinical law are intricately entwined with the political and public sectors. Jews, Muslims, and Christians all view the land of Israel as their birthplace and the first five books of the Bible as holy scripture. Despite this common foundation, they developed in very different ways, some of which are very contradictory and have led to constant conflict. One small difference is an example of much larger issues. The Muslim day of rest is on Friday, the Jewish on Saturday, and the Christian of Sunday. Muslim men and women pray separately, Jewish men and women sit separately while praying, and Christian men and women sit and pray together. Jewish holidays are state holidays in Israel. During the Jewish Sabbath, from sunset Friday to sunset Saturday each week, almost all public and commercial enterprise stops. On *Yom Kippur*, the Day of Atonement, which occurs ten days after the *Rosh Hashana*, the Jewish New Year, the whole country comes to a standstill while observant Jews complete 25 hours of total fasting and prayer. No Jewish hotels or restaurants will serve bread or fermented foods during the week of *Pesach* or Passover which commemorates the exodus of the Jews from Egypt during Biblical times. Independence Day is observed on May 15 because the founding of the state of Israel was first declared on May 15, 1948.

Customs and Courtesies

Israel is a land of informality as seen by their casual dress habits and custom of addressing each other by their first names. Even school children call their teacher by their first name. Respect is shown through courtesy and neighborly help. They are civic minded and involved in their communities. They value determination, hard work, frankness, and humor. They are also very inquisitive to an extent that may seem rude at times. The family is central to Israeli life. Children are given a great deal of care and attention and their education is paramount. Jews believe God is everywhere. In deference to God, men cover their head with an embroidered *kippah* cap or yarmulke. Married Orthodox women cover the head with scarves, hats, or wigs. All synagogues have a Holy Ark which faces to Temple Mount in Jerusalem that contains at least one handwritten *Torah* scroll. The *Torah* contains the first five books of Moses: *Genesis, Exodus, Leviticus, Numbers,* and *Deuteronomy.* Services are led by a rabbi, meaning teacher of traditions, or a learned layperson. *Very Orthodox Jews, when greeting, are not allowed to touch people of the opposite sex.* Unless one is a Muslim, one must ask permission to enter a Mosque and may not enter during sermons or prayers.

The laws of Kashrut dictate which foods Jews may eat and how they should be prepared. Many Israeli Jewish families eat only foods that are *kosher,* meaning which are fit and proper, and avoid foods that are *trafe,* or forbidden. Only animals that chew their cud and have cloven hooves are kosher. Sheep, cattle, oxen, goats, antelope, and deer are acceptable, but pigs, horses, camels, and donkeys are not. Only fish with both fins and scales are permitted. Therefore, shrimp, lobster, clams, crabs, mussels, or oysters are not. Meat and dairy products are not to be consumed at the same meal or from the same utensils. In fact kosher kitchens have two separate sets of utensils and dishware for dairy and meat meals. Most families will eat meat during the mid-day and a dairy meal at night. All kosher meat and poultry must come from animals killed in a traditional way – swiftly, with a minimum of suffering to the animal, and in a manner that all blood is drained. This must be done by a licensed *shochet,* kosher slaughterer.

Italy

The Landscape

Italy is a peninsula that extends into the Mediterranean Sea from Southern Europe and is subject to numerous earthquakes. Its shape is often compared to that of a boot. It is a mountainous country. The Italian Alps run along the northern border and the Apennines form a spine down the entire peninsula. Northern Italy is made up of a vast plain. It is the richest part of the country with the best farmland, the chief port of Genoa, and the largest industrial centers. It has a flourishing tourist trade based on the Italian Riviera, the Alps, its three beautiful lakes – Lago Maggiore, Lake Como, Lake Garda, and, of course, Milan, Florence and Venice. Central Italy contains great historic and cultural centers such as Rome, and the Vatican. Southern Italy is the poorest and least-developed part of the country yet can boast of Naples and the islands of Sardinia and Sicily. The weather is temperate for the most part although winters can be cold in the north and Sicily has subtropical temperatures.

The Economy

Italy's economy which was bad before World War II, was devastated afterward, but with the help of other countries, the country experienced an "economic miracle". Prior to this "economic miracle" life in the South was often miserable and there had been continuous massive emigration to the United States, Argentina, etc. Now largely over, this emigration had a dominating impact on Italy's memories. Since 1950 it has held an important place in the world economy. Although only eight percent of the workforce is involved in agriculture, this industry is a very important part of the economy. It produces wheat for pasta and bread, olives for olive oil, and grapes for wine. Italy is nearly self-sufficient in food production. It is one of the world's largest producers of wine and cheese. Manufacturing employs about one third of the workforce and contributes 35 percent of the gross domestic product. The main products include machinery, automobiles, electrical appliances, textiles, clothing, cement, chemicals, glass, and ceramics. Real gross domestic product per capita is $19,363 which has more than tripled in the last generation. The service sector has growing importance in Italy; by the early 1990's it employed well over half of the workforce. Italy has a large foreign trade, facilitated by its sizable commercial shipping fleet. Small- and medium-sized businesses in the north are a strong driving force in the economy. Today, Italy earns more money from clothing, textiles, and footwear than from any other of its exports and these industries are Italy's largest employers. The Mafia in the south of Italy, especially in Sicily, and other criminal groups, have been able to siphon off into their own pockets a substantial portion of the huge amount of money invested by the government into large projects aimed at improving the Southern economy. This has caused major drug and economic problems for the Southern part of the country and for the country as a whole. Italy is a very bureaucratic country with many of the bureaucrats coming from the South. The country has a long Bourbon heritage. The unsatisfactory political experience is a major factor in Italy. A long period of political dominance by the D. C. party developed a corrupt relationship with the Mafia. Today, this has been overthrown by a remarkable clean-hands campaign, but progress is slow. Italy has had serious problems with terrorist political gangs know as Red brigades.

The People

Italy's population is about 60 million mostly ethnic Italians with a very small percentage of Germans, French, and other Europeans. There is a sharp division in temperament, traditions, and socio-economic conditions between Italians living in the north and central regions and those living in the south. In the north the people are more formal and prosperous. As one travels down the country, one can see the people become less prosperous and poorer as one reaches the south. Italian is the official language and is spoken by the vast majority. However, there are certain dialects spoken in various regions as well as French and German along those countries' borders. Ninety-nine percent declare the Roman Catholic religion as their religion, but for a vast majority, it is more cultural than religious in observance. They take great pride in their personal appearance and tend to dress up even for an informal stroll in the evening. After all, Italy is a major center of the European fashion industry. They also take great pride in art, food, and celebration. They still refer to one another by their city of origin such as Milanese or Roman. There exists a real disdain of Southerners by Northerners.

The family is certainly the critical social group in Italy. However, there is something called "Mamismo" which is an exaggerated cult of motherhood both in religion and family life. The children are spoiled rotten and take a long time to grow up. Young men find it difficult to become self-sufficient and often live at home for years and are subsidized by the parents. Catholicism is closely intertwined with many aspects of Italian life from education to family life, yet Italy has an extraordinarily low birth rate. Respect for elders is extremely important. Italians are characteristically open, friendly, outgoing, and very expressive in their conversation. Social life and interaction are very important, so social events such as parties and celebrations are often and elaborate. A good reputation and approval from their peers is an absolute necessity. Their self-worth is measured by their family, education, financial security, and social status. People in the industrialized north value punctuality, reliability, organization, and economic success. Southerners, on the other hand, are valued for their warm character and friendliness. They enjoy a leisurely life and take time doing business. Italians pride themselves on their cuisine. Pasta is the national food and wine is considered a food in Italy. Most meals are accompanied by a carefully selected wine that is consumed by children as well as adults. Lunch is the main meal of the day and can take several hours in midday. There is also the "Siesto" when shops and museums, etc close for two to three hours at midday. A formal dinner will include antipasto, or soup, a small portion of pasta, main entree, salad, cheese, dessert, fruit, espresso and an after-dinner drink. Different wines accompany different courses.

Italians celebrate both religious and national holidays. Included are New Year's Day, Epiphany (January 6), Easter including Easter Monday, Liberation Day (April 25) which commemorates Italy's liberation in World War II, Labor Day (May 1), the Anniversary of the Republic (June 2), the Assumption of the Virgin Mary (August 15), All Saints Day (November 1), the Immaculate Conception (December 8), Christmas, and St. Stephen's Day (December 26). Every Italian city, village, and town celebrates it own saint's day or feast day such as St. Peter for Rome. As in many countries, the days preceding Ash Wednesday are devoted to Carnival which is lavishly celebrated and culminates on Martedi Grasso. Saint Francis of Assisi began the tradition of the Nativity scene when he asked a Greccio villager to prepare the likeness of a manger for a Christmas Mass.

Italians all seem to take holiday at the same time from August 15 until September 15. There is a mad dash to the coast or to the mountains with huge traffic snarl-ups. Families stay for the month while husbands commute at the weekend. Offices and government virtually shut down for the month.

Customs and Courtesies

Cafes are found everywhere in Italy, usually at the center of town or a neighborhood. They are places to go to socialize, to read, or to write. The tables are tiny and usually crammed close together. One goes there to have a cup of coffee or an aperitif or a snack. One does not go there to eat a meal. One thing that is never done in Italy is to eat while strolling down the street. It simply is not done. Although one will see many strolling down the street eating an ice cream cone called a gelato. Whom one knows is critical and it is imperative to maintain a *bella figura* meaning to "cut a fine figure." Italians are other-dependent, primarily, but with a significant sense of individual and personal responsibility. They have great respect for age and power. There are correct and incorrect ways to get things done and behaviors are ruled by proper etiquette and protocol. The U.S. "Okay" sign is considered vulgar and obscene as is the *corno* – making the sign of goat horns by raising the pinky and index finger up while the middle two fingers remain curled. It implies that a man cannot satisfy his wife. Gestures are so numerous that there is actually a dictionary of Italian gestures. Never chew gum at a restaurant or on the street nor be last in line. These are two things that just are not done. Also putting thumb and forefinger together and pulling down like holding a balloon is considered quite vulgar. Italians talk a lot with their hands and stand very close when conversing. When seated for a meal one never gets up until the meal if finished. Wrists may rest on top of the table, not elbows, and one never puts their hands in their lap. Dishes are passed to the left and never cut lettuce in your salad. Fold it with your knife and fork into a little bundle that can easily be picked up with your fork. In Italy one does not use a spoon while eating pastas. One uses the side of the bowl or plate to assist in twirling the pasta onto the fork.

Gift giving is an important part of Italian culture. Italians are more impressed with thoughtful and creative gifts, wrapped very nicely and tailored to the recipient than with expensive ones. Gifts are expected for social events, especially as a thank you for a private dinner party. The best gift to send is a bouquet of flowers, (odd number of stems), ahead of time on the day of the dinner. Simple floral arrangements are not appreciated. Never send chrysanthemums (funerals) or red roses (romantic) and when presenting flowers yourself be sure to unwrap them first. Do not bring gifts with your company's logo. It is in poor taste. Also avoid cutlery, handkerchiefs, embroidered linens, or a brooch all which indicate the severing of a relationship. Baskets of fruit, chocolates, and fine pastries as well as fine American wines will be appreciated. If you receive a gift from an Italian always reciprocate. And finally, Italians are the first to spot an American who lacks style, especially if his shoes are ugly.

Chapter Ten

Cultures of the World, J–W

Japan

The Landscape

Japan is an archipelago located off the east coast of Asia. It consists of a string of four large islands and more than 3,900 smaller islands. From north to south, the main islands are Hokkaido, Honshu, Shikoku, and Kyushu. The largest is Honshu, which is considered the Japanese mainland. Tokyo, on Honshu, is the capital and one of the world's largest cities. Mountains cover more than 80 percent of the land surface. The largest and highest mountain mass lies in central Honshu, part of which is known as the Japanese Alps. Mount Fuji, Japan's highest mountain, is a volcano that has been inactive since 1707. The islands form an arc stretching about 1,500 miles. Most of the plains lie along the seacoast. The country has many earthquakes and volcanoes. Japan experiences hundreds of earthquakes a year, but most are mild. A destructive earthquake hits the country every few years. In 1995, a quake in and around Kobe killed more than five thousand people. The country is also subject to typhoons in September. To the north the winters can be bitterly cold; to the south a more tropical climate prevails.

The Economy

After World War II, Japan's economy was devastated, yet it has emerged as one of the most advanced economic powers in the world. Its economy grew incredibly during the 1960s, 70s, and 80s. It is also one of the most productive industrialized nations in the world. What is so amazing is that it has very few natural resources of its own and relies heavily on imported raw materials for its industrial success. The economy revolves around manufacturing and trade. It is a leader in the manufacture of ships, automobiles, and advanced electronics equipment such as televisions, VCRs, computers, cameras, microwave ovens, watches, photocopiers, and robots. It is also a major producer of crude, steel, synthetic rubber, aluminum, chemicals, plastics, cement, pulp, and paper. Japan must import nearly half of its food supply including grains except rice. Other main crops include sugar, vegetables, tea, and various fruits. It is also a leading producer of fish, accounting for 15 percent of the total world catch. Rice and fish are the main staples of its people. However, the economy slowed greatly in the early 1990s and has never quite recovered. Despite this, the real GDP per capita is $21,581 with low inflation and unemployment rates. Japan's *yen* is still one of the world's strongest currencies.

The People

Japan's population is about 125 million people. Although its population is about half that of the United States, its people live on less than 5 percent of the total land of the United States. Nearly 80 percent of the people live in urban areas. About 45 percent are concentrated in three major metropolitan areas: Tokyo, Osaka, and Nagoya. Practically all Japanese speakers live in Japan. It is an Altaic language and its nearest relative is Korean. It is not related to Chinese. *San* is a universal title of respect equal to Mr., Miss., and Mrs. Thus one would say Tanaka-san which would mean Mr. Tanaka, Miss Tanaka, Ms. Tanaka, or Mrs. Tanaka. Shinto, Buddhism, and Confucianism are the main religions. Shinto deals with issues of this world such as crops, social relations, and clan ancestors. Buddhism is concentrated more on ethical and metaphysical issues. This division still works for the Japanese. Confucianism is a social ethnic imported from China. There is little institutional evidence of Confucianism but its values have powerfully influenced Japanese society.

Japanese society is group oriented. Loyalty to the group and to one's superiors are essential and takes precedence over personal feelings. Companies expect workers to put company interests before personal concerns. The "lifetime employment" ideal extends to only about one third of the Japanese workers. Many younger workers question the lack of mobility required for lifetime employment and are opting for more risky and potentially rewarding career paths. The family is the foundation of Japanese society and is bound together by a strong sense of reputation, obligation, and responsibility. A person's actions reflect on the family. The wife is in charge of the money and education of the children. Japanese schooling treats boys and girls equally, guaranteeing well-educated women. Japan claims a 100 percent literacy rate. Compulsory education covers only elementary and middle schools, but 94 percent go on to high school. One third of high school graduates enter college or a university and most of those graduate. University entry requires a very competitive examination and most students face serious burnout in the first year of college.

Customs and Courtesies

A bow is the traditional greeting between Japanese, but they prefer the hand shake with Westerners. While some appreciate it when Westerners bow, others do not, especially when two people are not acquainted. This can be very tricky. My rule of thumb is to follow what the other person does. If they extend their hand, I do the same. If they make a slight bow, I do the same. It is important for them not to be embarrassed and for me this "saves face" for both of us. When entering the home of a person from Japan, one should remove one's shoes at the door, just like they do. So always wear socks or hosiery that you will be happy to be seen in. The Japanese are enthusiastic gift givers. Gifts often have more symbolic than monetary value. Here are a few rules. Gifts should never be wrapped in black, grey, or *white* paper (funeral colors) and elaborate ribbon bows should be avoided. It is the thought that counts, not the monetary value. A gift of sweets, fruit, or small items from your native country are best. Avoid giving combs as the Japanese word for comb is *kushi* meaning suffering, *ku*, and *shi* means death. Also avoid sets of items in fours or nines. These are unlucky numbers. Flowers are expensive and are probably not a good idea as they are considered a bit ostentatious, but if you must give flowers at least avoid camellias, lotus blossoms and lilies as they all are associated with funerals. Also pens or paperweights with a company logo are acceptable and a high quality Scotch is a particular favorite.

At the New Year, Japanese take an extended holiday from the last day or two in December to about the third of January. Businesses and government offices close. Buddhist temple bells are rung 108 times at midnight. The New Year is celebrated with an array of symbolic foods. Beans are eaten for good health, fish roe for prosperity, dried squid for happiness, as well as a midnight New Year's supper of long *soba* noodles which symbolizes carrying the previous year's good fortunes into the new one. Another traditional dish is *ozouni*, a soup that contains a soft rice cake so sticky that the choking deaths of senior citizens are regularly reported in the next day's newspapers. *Toso*, a special mixture of sake and vegetable extracts sweetened with herbs, is also consumed. Other important holidays include Adults' Day (January 15) when those who will turn 20 during the year are honored as coming of age; National Foundation Day (February 11); Vernal Equinox (in March); *Midori No hi* (Greenery Day – April 29); Constitution Day (May 3); Children's day (May 5); Bon Festival (August 15); Respect for the Aged Day (September 15); Autumnal Equinox (in September); Sports Day (October 10); Culture Day (November 3); Labor Thanksgiving Day (November 23); and Emperor Akihito's Birthday (December 23).

Japan has a rich and complex culture. Native Japanese traditions have been mixed with cultural styles adapted from China and, later, from the

West. Japanese culture and art emphasize understated simplicity, elegance, and grace. Such examples as the traditional Japanese tea ceremony, flower arranging, and garden design are highly stylized and refined. They are also great sport enthusiasts. The most popular professional sport is baseball and the native sport of Sumo wrestling. They are avid fans of television and have more television set per capita than the United States! When being invited to a restaurant, be prepared to participate in karaoke. They are addicted to this form of singing.

Mexico

The Landscape

Mexico lies between the Pacific Ocean and the Gulf of Mexico and Caribbean Sea, south of the United States and west of Guatemala and Belize. Most of the country is a highland plateau with very little rainfall most of the year. This plateau is enclosed by two mountain chains running the length of the country. They are the Sierra Madre Oriental to the east and the Sierra Madre Occidental to the west. Only about 15 percent of the land is arable with about 25 percent in forests. Much of the north is hot and dry while humidity is high in the south where tropical jungles are found. The Gulf of Mexico's coastal plain extends about 900 miles from the Texas border to the Yucatan Peninsula. The Pacific coastal plain is more than 800 miles long and contains good natural harbors. West of the Pacific lowlands is the peninsula called Baja California. This dry, mountainous strip of land is nearly 800 miles in length, but only around 100 miles wide. The Gulf of California separates the peninsula from the rest of Mexico. It has few major rivers and lakes. The Rio Bravo del Norte, called the Rio Grande in the United States, forms part of the border between Mexico and the United States. In comparison, Mexico is about one fifth the size of the United States.

The Economy

Mexico is slowly recovering from its worst recession in more than 50 years. With the signing of the North American Free Trade Agreement with the United States and Canada, Mexico has enjoyed a strong growth in its export industries. NAFTA lowered trade barriers and led to a dramatic increase in the number of *maquiladoras,* or manufacturing plants, where U.S. investment employs Mexican labor. Manufactured goods account for about 90 percent of the value of Mexico's exports. The *maquiladoras* became a means of providing employment and significant foreign exchange earnings for Mexico's developing economy. That employment increased from 200,000 in the mid 1980s to more than one million by the late 1990s. It also stimulated rapid population migration to the border region, particularly at its eastern and western extremities. The *maquila* plant imports and assembles duty free components for export. The arrangement allows plant owners to take advantage of low-cost labor and to pay duty only on the "value added" – that is, on the value of the finished product minus the total cost of the components that had been imported to make it. The vast majority of *maquiladoras* are owned and operated by Mexican, Asian, and American companies.

The Mexican government plays a major role in planning the economy and owns and operates some of the basic industries including petroleum, its major export. However, the number of state-owned enterprises fell from more than 1,000 in 1982 to fewer than 200 in 1998. Agriculture is no longer a leading source of income for Mexico, but it still employs about twenty percent of the workforce. The two most important industries, mining and petroleum, employ less than 2 percent of the workforce. Tourism provides employment for many. Manufactured goods include machinery, metal products, chemicals, food, beverages, tobacco, textiles, paper and paper products, and mineral products. Mexico has large deposits of oil and natural gas. The country is the world's largest producer of silver and a major supplier of sand and gravel, salt, zinc, lead, cadmium, copper and other minerals. The major crops exported to other countries are coffee, cotton, fruits and vegetables. Corn, wheat, rice, and beans are the leading food crops while cattle and pigs are the major livestock. Some of the major tourist resorts are Acapulco, Cancun, and Puerto Vallarta. Colonial towns of central Mexico and the Mayan ruins of the Yucatan Peninsula are also major attractions.

The People

Mexico has approximately 96 million people, 60 percent of whom are Mestizo, a mix of Spanish and Indian. Another 30 percent belong to various Amerindian groups. Most of these are descendants of the Maya and Aztec Indians. About nine percent have European ancestry. Most Mexicans tend to identify with their Amerindian or Spanish heritage. More than 70 percent live in cities. The largest is the capital, Mexico City. Every year more than 350,000 people move into the capital and surrounding areas. They traditionally have had a relaxed attitude toward time which is very evident here in the United States. If a mass in Spanish is scheduled for 1 PM, it is likely to get underway by 1:15 if one is lucky, but they are still streaming in at 1:30. Arriving on time when invited to dinner or a party is considered rude. In fact, it is not considered unusual for invited guests not to arrive at all with no explanation given later. *Manana*, although literally meaning "tomorrow", may refer to any indefinite future time. Generally, they believe individuals are more important than schedules. If a person drops by unexpectedly, most Mexicans will stop to talk, regardless of other commitments. They value friendship, good humor, honesty, hard work, and personal honor. Machismo, the ideal strong, forceful man, is still prevalent. Carried to extremes, this can result in difficulties in communicating with women on an equal basis.

Family values are alive and well in Mexico. The family unity and responsibilities are high priorities. The right to a dignified home is in the constitution, but two thirds of the people are poorly housed so the household in many cases includes grandparents, aunts, uncles, as well as parents and children. The godparents play a very important part in Mexican life. Among middle class and well-to-do Mexicans, even the servants form a part of the family unit. Married children and their spouses also remain part of the unit until they can afford to set up their own households. Respect for the elderly is paramount and one would never think of abandoning them. Education is compulsory and free between ages six and fourteen. However, many of them, especially in the rural regions, do not complete the required years; one in ten Mexicans cannot read or write. Because of inadequate funding, public schooling is often of poor quality. Private schools at every level, often run by the Catholic Church, now educate most children and youth from the middle class and well-to-do families.

Mexican cuisine is anything but the fast-food most people in the United States are familiar with; it is a complex and rich cuisine, with variations reflecting the traditions of each individual section of the country. Many foods are wrapped in corn husks, plantain skins, or other coverings which are not eaten. The staple of Mexican food is corn, supplemented by beans, squash, and chili peppers. Cornmeal or flour *tortillas* are eaten everywhere. Cornmeal is patted into a thin pancake called a *tortilla* which encloses a great variety of fillings to form a soft sandwich-like *taco*. The crisply fried U.S. taco is really a *tostado*. If made with wheat flour, it is called a *burrito*. Fried in chili sauce, the taco becomes an *enchilada*. Hot, spicy food is called picante, while hot (temperature wise) is called caliente. Picante foods are often eaten with bland foods such as bread, tortillas, or rice to relieve the burning sensation. *It is inappropriate for adults to eat while walking on the street.*

Customs and Courtesies

Mexican folk customs derive from beliefs and practices dating back well before the European discovery of America. One of these is herbal medicine. In certain Indian communities, *curanderos* function as healers and diviners who communicate with nature gods and spirits. Among them are persons seen as sorcerers or witches credited with great healing and magical powers that dispel evil spirits. There are many feasts commemorating Christian saints as well as the worship of Indian gods dating back to the pre-European past. During the festivals, the people wear bright costumes and ornaments and perform traditional dances and music.

Traditional masks represent animals, spirits, and religious or mythical figures. Alcohol, and sometimes hallucinogenic drugs, play a role in these observances, as they do in healing and divining.

Between 90 and 95 percent of the Mexican people are Roman Catholic. However, just as early Christianity retained many beliefs and customs of pagan Greece and Rome, Mexican Catholicism includes folklore and practices of the pre-European period. The Virgin of Guadalupe is the patron saint of Mexico and accredited with an appearance on December 12, 1531. Businesses and government close on this day and many pilgrims come to the Basilica of Guadalupe in Mexico City in honor of this day. Other religious holidays include St. Anthony's Day, when children bring their pets to church to be blessed; *Semana Santa* (Palm Sunday through Easter Sunday); Corpus Christi in May or June; and Assumption (August 15). On *Dia de los Muertos,* the Day of the Dead, November 1–2, families gather to celebrate life while they honor the dead. Graves are cleaned up and fruits and flowers are placed on them. At the evening meal a table is traditionally set with food and drink for the departed.

National public holidays include New Year's Day; Constitution Day (February 5), which marks the beginning of Carnaval, the week of parties and parades before Lent; Labor Day (May 1); *Cinco de Mayo* (May 5) which celebrates an 1867 victory over the French; Independence Day; Columbus Day (October 12); Revolution Day (November 20); and Christmas Day. Many offices close for half a day on Mother's Day when schools sponsor special festivities. *El Festival Cervanino,* named after Miguel de Cervantes, the author of *Don Quixote,* draws an international gathering of theater groups, musicians, artists and craftspeople every autumn.

Philippines

The Landscape

The Republic of the Philippines is an archipelago consisting of over 7,000 islands and islets situated off the Southeastern Asian mainland. It has a unique heritage of Malay, Spanish, and American cultures and is the only predominantly Christian nation in Asia. The Philippines are surrounded by the Pacific Ocean on the north, the Philippine Sea on the east, the Celebes Sea on the south, and the South China Sea on the west. The two largest islands, Luzon and Mindanao, comprise more than 70 percent of the land area and contain more than 70 percent of the population. The islands are very mountainous, which means the terrain is very rugged. There is a very limited amount of land suitable for agriculture, but rice is grown on the sides of the mountains and in the plains. The country has an extensive coastline stretching 21,500 miles with 60 natural harbors of which about half have been developed and are heavily used. The islands are in the typhoon belt and have a tropical and humid climate. Because the islands are so close to the equator warm, temperatures prevail throughout the year. Manila is the largest city and the national capital. It is located on Luzon, the largest island in the north. Mindanao is the second largest island and is located in the south.

The Economy

The Philippines is one of the five founding members of the Association of Southeast Asian Nations (ASEAN), an economic common market that was formed on August 8, 1967. The other founding nations are Indonesia, Thailand, Malaysia, and Singapore. These are generally free-market economies that are closely tied to the United States, Japan, and the nations of Western Europe by political alliances and trade and aid relationships. Private enterprise is predominant in the Philippines, as it is in other ASEAN countries. The islands are largely agricultural with two thirds of the work force living in rural areas and half of them in farm-related work.

During the long colonial period the Philippine economy was dominated first by Spain, then by the United States,. Since Philippine independence, foreign economic control has remained significant. Japan and the United States in particular exercise control in the form of investment and aid, which have been vital to Philippine economic development. The Philippine government is now looking to increase local ownership of business and industry. Rice, corn, and coconuts take up about 80 percent of all crop land. Sugarcane, sweet potatoes, manioc, bananas, hemp, tobacco and coffee are also important crops. Caribou (water buffalo) are used to plow the fields. Fishing is also an important occupation. In addition to agricultural products, electronics, clothing, minerals, and chemicals are exported. Manufacturing is concentrated in metropolitan Manila, near the country's primary port. However, recently there has been considerable industrial growth on Cebu, Negros, and Mindanao. The real gross domestic product per capita is $2,681. The currency is the Philippine *peso* (P).

The People

According to the 1990 census, well over 66 million people inhabit the Philippines, representing a tenfold increase since the beginning of the century. This figure varies according to different sources and is placed anywhere from 62 to 74 million people, which indicates the difficulty in obtaining an accurate count. The islands are homogeneous in that about 90 percent of the population is Filipino of Malay origin and 83 percent of the population is Roman Catholic, although regional variations exist. The Philippines are heterogeneous in that about five percent is Muslim and another five percent is composed of indigenous peoples, including the Negritos (the first inhabitants of the islands) and several other groups collectively labeled uplanders, hill tribes, and highlanders. Approximately

50 percent of the population lives below the official poverty line. Sharing of resources by more affluent family members and relatives working overseas mitigates somewhat the hardships of many of the poor. While recent economic growth has benefitted a growing portion of the population, most of the nation's wealth remains in the hands of a small fraction of the population – elite families (once largely of Spanish mestizo origin but now increasingly Chinese-Filipino) who own plantations and other large enterprises (Worldmark p. 208).

English and Filipino, also known as Tagalog, are the official languages. English is the main language for government, business, and higher education. About 70 other languages are spoken as mother tongues in the Philippines. When the United States took over the Philippines, it introduced mass education in the English language and improvements in public health and communications. Education is highly valued in the Philippines, where the elite (the native intelligentsia or *ilustrados*) send their sons to Europe for an education. Literacy rate is about 95 percent. Elementary school lasts for six years beginning at age seven. While many of the poor children do not go on to high school, those that do, go on to college, either to the very prestigious University of the Philippines or to low-quality "diploma mills."

The family is Filipino society's central institution. Individuals forego their own interests for the benefit of the family and other social groups to which they belong (including the workplace). Filipino children learn at an early age to depend on their families for their basic needs. They learn that they must, in turn, fulfill obligations to their families. As children, their responsibilities include respect for elders, care of younger siblings, performance of household chores, and behavior that will bring honor to the family. Filipino women have approached equality with men more closely than in most Asian countries. They wield considerable power in that they manage family finances, dispensing pocket money to their husbands as well as their children. They are well represented in the professions of medicine, law, teaching, government and business. Many own or run their own businesses. Unlike in Western societies marriage strengthens the obligations of both the bride and groom to their respective parents. A typical meal in the Philippines consists of boiled rice or rice noodles, fish, stewed vegetables and fruits. Corn is the staple for about one fifth of the population who live in areas not suitable for rice production or who cannot afford rice. Diets may include root crops such as sweet potatoes and an array of tropical fruits such as mangoes. A traditional garment for men is the *barong tagalog*, an embroidered shirt. Women wear a heavily starched, butterfly-sleeved *terno* on formal occasions.

Customs and Courtesies

Christian holidays are the most widely celebrated as a majority of the population is Roman Catholic. Christmas festivities begin on December 16 with masses held before sunrise every morning until Christmas itself. After Midnight Mass on Christmas Eve, kindred families gather at one of the homes for a feast, the *Noche Buena*. On Christmas day more parties are held, with children making the rounds of relatives and godparents to pay respect to them and receive presents. Godparents are part of the extended family. Another important holiday is Holy Week. Many towns hold a *sanakulo*, a traditional sung drama, staged over several nights, occupying many hours per segment, focusing on the sufferings of Christ but often including scenes from the Old Testament all the way back to Genesis. Mass on the night before Easter is followed by a re-enactment of the meeting of the resurrected Christ and his grieving mother. Another nation-wide festival is the *Santacruzan* in May, commemorating the discovery of Christ's cross by Helen, mother of Constantine the Great, the first Christian Roman emperor. These celebrations feature processions in which the daughters of prominent families are splendidly dressed as *Reina Elena* (Queen Helen) and promenade with a male escort and a cortege of other couples. As in many other countries predominately Roman Catholic, on All Souls' Day (November 2), people gather at the graves of family members for a 24-hour vigil during which, in addition to praying, they clean the graves, decorate them with candles and wreaths, eat, drink, and play cards. Widows will wear black for a full year.

The most prominent types of traditional group music making are the *rondalla*, an ensemble of Hispanic plucked and bowed string instruments to accompany social dancing. The Philippines were ruled by Spain for over three hundred years, which resulted in the adaptation of much Spanish culture and tradition. A famous folk dance is the *tinikling*, where a couple executes intricate figures while skipping through two bamboo poles being clapped together at an accelerating pace. "Ouch" is what first comes to mind when watching this dance! *Sipa* is an indigenous game in which two teams of one to four players each hit a wickerwork ball with their knees, legs, or feet over a net or across a circle. Baseball and basket-ball, introduced by the Americans, are also popular. But by far the most popular sport is cockfighting, which commands a fanatical following. Held during Sundays, public holidays, and fiestas in mini-stadiums, cockfights are the occasion for intense gambling. People will bet thousands of dollars hoping to win their fortune, much like people in the United States play the lottery. Cocks are highly bred for this sport and can be very costly, similar to race horses in the U.S., but the poorer people breed and keep cocks in their back yards.

There are several superstitions of which one should be aware. Taking care to bury the placenta in a place where it will not be stepped on is one of the many folk customs which to some extent ensures the well-being and good fortune of a newborn child. *Kapre* are gorilla-like creatures that live in trees, smoking giant cigars that glow in the dark. Those who neglect to ask permission to pass by, risk fever or death.

Aswang can take the form of various animals. They like to sit on the roofs of houses; from there, their long spiny tongues slip down to suck on the fetuses of sleeping pregnant women via their navels. Though such primitive fears flourish in the provinces, many supernatural beliefs are harbored by sophisticated urban dwellers as well. Owners of a newly built house or just-occupied office will have a priest come to the premises to bless them to foil mischievous spirits from occupying them. Also it is not uncommon to see business executives or politicians wearing *anting-anting* around their necks–amulets that feature Christ or a saint to ward off bad spirits. (Francia P 76)

Poland

The Landscape

Located in the east central region, Poland is one of the largest countries of Eastern Europe. It extends 403 miles from north to south and 428 miles from west to east. The most extensive physical feature is a great plain that covers the northern two thirds of the country. The southern third of the country consists of hills and mountains, home to the country's skiing and resort areas. The longest river in Poland is the Vistula, which rises in the Beskids, a major range of mountains, and flows for 664 miles in a wide S-shaped curve across Poland until it reaches the Baltic Sea. In the southwest, the Sudetic Mountains form part of the border with the Czech Republic. Farther east several ranges of the western Carpathian Mountains continue along the border of Slovakia. To the north of the Carpathians there are areas of hills, the most notable of which are the Holy Cross Mountains which reach more than 2,000 feet. Warsaw is the capital city. About one quarter of the country is forested. The quality of soils for farming varies considerably from one region to another. Many areas in northern and central Poland have sandy soils mixed in places with clay. These soils are not very fertile. Areas of former marshland and along rivers are more fertile. The best soils are found in the south, where dust created by retreating glaciers was blown southward, creating thick deposits of fertile loess soils. Deer and wild boar are found in the forests while bears and wildcats are found in the Carpathian Mountains. Some of the fish found in the area are trout, perch and pike. Poland's main mineral wealth is coal; it has some of the richest reserves in Europe. Other important natural resources are copper, zinc, lead, and aluminum.

The Economy

Poland was the first communist country to begin the transition from socialism to a free market economy in the early 1990's. It continues to make progress in its transition, though it has been a very slow and difficult process. Reforms initially resulted in high unemployment, hyper-inflation, shortages of consumer goods, a large external debt, and a drop in the standard of living. The situation later stabilized; by 1996 the economy was growing at 6 percent with a real gross domestic product of $5,002 per capita. Today it is generally self-sufficient in food production. Agriculture is mostly privately run and was so even during the Communist years. It accounts for 15 percent of the gross national product and employs more than 25 percent of the workforce. About 50 percent of the land area is cultivated. The major crops are rye, potatoes, beets, wheat, oats, barley, and fodder for livestock. Pigs and sheep are the main livestock. Polish ham is a major export product.

The privatization of the country's large coal, steel, and chemical industries has been a major factor in the successful transition of its economy. Poland exports a large amount of coal and ranks fourth in the world in coal production. About 80 percent of electric power production comes from coal. Production of metals includes zinc, copper, and aluminum. The chemical industry is significant with sulfuric acid, salts, and fertilizers being major products. Manufacturing industries produce ships, transport equipment, agricultural machinery, machine tools, and other equipment. The leading products for export are locomotives, freight wagons, automobiles, trucks, tractors, and ships. A large factory in Warsaw produces Polish Fiat automobiles. Textile production of linen and cotton is a traditional branch of Polish industry. Important trading partners are Germany, Russia, Italy, France, and the Netherlands. The currency is the *zloty* (Zl).

The People

The population of Poland is approximately 38 million; it grows at about 0.14 percent yearly. During World War II, 6 million people died, half of them in the Nazi death camps. Today more than 98 percent of the people are of Polish origin. The official language is Polish, a Slavic language. Religion plays a major role in Polish life; about 75 percent are practicing Catholics, with another 15 percent belonging to the church. Pope John Paul II was the first pope of Polish origin; his visits have helped the Polish people remain faithful. About 60 percent of the people live in urban areas. Warsaw, the capital, is the largest city.

The Polish people value self-reliance and individualism, and they place great emphasis on family and education. Outspoken and straightforward, they value generosity. Those not willing to share their time, resources, or power are not highly regarded. They are very proud of their cultural heritage and pride themselves on their ability to survive during adverse times. One of the major cultural contributions of Poland to the world has been its literature. The earliest known writers appeared in the 15th century and continue through each century, culminating in Czeslaw Milosz's the Nobel prize for literature in 1980. Frederic Chopin was one of Poland's greatest composers. Music is very much a part of Polish culture. Folk music, with its dancers and singers in costumes, is evident at the many carnivals. Poland has 10 symphony orchestras, 17 conservatories, 100 music schools, and over 1,000 music centers.

Poland has a 98 percent literacy rate and a 97 percent attendance rate in its schools. Education is considered very important; Polish parents want their children to have the finest education they can afford. Education is compulsory from ages 7 through 15 and free through high school. The students decide on the type of secondary school they wish to attend and take the appropriate entrance exams. Choices include four- and five-year technical and professional schools, three- year vocational schools, or university prep schools. Entrance to a university is also determined by exam and about 5 percent of students are accepted into the best schools. Higher education is also free. A university degree takes about five or six years to complete. Today, the emphasis is on foreign language and computer skills. Two thirds of the dental and medical students are women.

Customs and Courtesies

The Poles are known for their hospitality. In fact there is a famous Polish saying, "Every day is good for celebration." They love to entertain. When invited to their home for dinner, it is unthinkable not to bring a bouquet of flowers (an odd number as even numbers are used for sad occasions and not red roses or white chrysanthemums, reserved for wakes and funerals), or a bottle of wine or vodka. The Polish good luck gesture is a thumb tucked into the palm of one's hand and covered with the other four fingers. Conservative modern Western-style clothing is wore by most although, even today, women do not wear pants, opting for long skirts instead. In rural areas one will still see older women wearing full skirts, thick stockings, and headscarfs.

Important public holidays are New Year's Day, Good Friday, All Saints Day, Corpus Christi Day, and Worker's Day, which commemorates Solidarity's triumph over Communism. Adults celebrate their name day rather than their birthday. This is the day assigned to the Catholic saint after whom the person is named. Christmas is the most important holiday. On December 6, children receive small gifts from St. Nicholas. Another important feast day is the *Wigilia* (vigil) or Christmas Eve festival. It is a huge meal consisting of 12 traditional Christmas Eve dishes – herring, potato and apple salad, mushroom soup (dried mushrooms, beet-root, and three kinds of carp – jellied, fried, and boiled), cabbage or other *pierorgies* with poppy seed, a fruit compote, tea, and poppy-seed cake. The next day they eat the traditional Christmas goose or duck! One tradition, is to place some hay under the tablecloth (to remind us of the manger in which Christ was born) and to set a place at the table for the Christ child. In Krakow, there is a famous annual competition over the making of the Christmas creches. Easter, with much celebration and festivities, is the second most important holiday. Carnivals are enjoyed throughout the country the week before Lent begins. On Easter, food is brought to the church to be blessed; egg rolling contests and hard boiled egg matches are all part of the fun. Easter Monday is Wet Monday, a day for young people to squirt or dump water on each other.

Russia

The Landscape

Russia, the former Soviet Socialist Republic and the world's largest country, is almost twice the size of China or the United States. It covers much of Eastern Europe and all of Northern Asia. It extends almost halfway around the Northern Hemisphere. Russia has the longest border of any country on Earth. In the west it borders Norway, Finland, the Gulf of Finland, Estonia, Latvia, and Belarus. In the southwest Russia borders the Ukraine. In the south it touches the Sea of Azov, the Black Sea, Georgia, Azerbaijan, the Caspian Sea, Kazakhstan, Mongolia, China, and North Korea. In the east and north it borders various branches of the Pacific and Arctic oceans, respectively. It contains four of the world's largest rivers and Baikal, the world's deepest freshwater lake. Much of Russia is covered by great plains. Two such plains are divided by the Ural Mountains that form the boundary between the small European region and the larger Asian region. Eastern Siberia is mostly hilly to mountainous, and can be freezing nine months out of the year. Much of western Russia is covered by forests. The chief cities are St. Petersburg, Novosibirsk, Nizhni Novgorod, and the capital, Moscow, which was also the capital of both the Russian Federation and the Soviet Union.

The Economy

Russia's economic growth and development has enormous potential because of her great natural resources. Natural gas, coal, gold, oil, diamonds, copper, silver and lead are all abundant. It is one of the world's leading producers of petroleum and natural gas. Extensive pipelines link producing districts to all parts of Russia and across the borders to many European countries. Yet, Russia's economy is weak and unstable. Most agricultural land is not fertile, timber is being produced inefficiently, and fishing is on the decline. Its industrial base was energy intensive and technologically backward. It is such a vast country that nearly 30 percent of its people live without running water or electricity. It had been in a recession for a decade with high unemployment, high inflation, and high prices. Russia's burdensome and complicated tax system has been one of the main impediments to investment and growth. Regional authorities impose additional taxes and levies which are often illegal, sending businesses underground into organized crime and corruption. There is increasing disparity between the rich and the poor. According to official data, by 1999 household incomes were at around 40 percent of their 1991 levels. Relatively little is being spent on healthcare, education or basic physical infrastructure. The attitude of both officials and business towards strategic foreign investors remains ambiguous, with the result that Western companies still play a very limited role in Russia. Nearly all transactions are made in cash. Small- and medium-sized enterprises (SME's), which have acted as an important source of growth in other economies, are woefully underdeveloped in Russia. According to some estimates, 20 large conglomerates now account for up to 70 percent of the Russian GDP. Real gross domestic product per capita is $4,828. The currency is the *ruble* (®).

The People

Russia's population is approximately 150 million people, with about 80 percent being ethnic Russians. Although they are primarily eastern Slavs, many Russians have a Finnish, Siberian, or Baltic heritage. There are about 120 different ethnic groups in Russia, though most of them are small. During the Soviet years there was a massive mixing of Russians with Ukrainians, Belarusian, Jews, Finno-Ugric peoples and others. Russian is the official language. Modern Russian is an Eastern Slavic language. It uses the Cyrillic alphabet which consists of 33 letters, many of them unlike any letter in the Roman alphabet. During the 10th century, two Orthodox monks, Cyril and Methodius, wanted to translate the Bible into the native Russian language. This older language, which later came to be known as Old Slavonic, is still used today by the Russian Orthodox Church. Examples of everyday Russian words are *Kak delah?* (How is it going?), *da* (yes), *nyet* (no), *pozhaluistah* (please), *spaseebo* (thank you), and *do sveedanniya* (goodbye).

Generations of authoritarian influence have helped form a distinct division between public and private behavior in Russian society. In public, Russians are very reserved and formal; in private, they are very cordial and sincere. This is the result of a long regime of tyranny. However, when one Russian asks another, "How are you?" a courteous response is expected as without one would be considered rude. A lengthy conversation will ensue about what is really happening in the lives of each person. Americans should use some patience and listen attentively to the response. The family is the basic social unit in Russian society in which parenthood and large families are revered and children have a privileged role of honor. Because of the general lack of housing, often several generations will live in the same apartment or house. Russian adults do not hesitate to assist any child in need and will readily reprimand any child who is misbehaving regardless of the relationship. Parents will make tremendous personal sacrifices for their children. Children begin their schooling at 1 year old and attend a nursery school until they are 3, after which they attend kindergarten until they are 6. Elementary school consists of grades 1 through 4, middle school is 5 through 9, and high school is 10 through 12, but they must pass an exam in language and mathematics at the end of the 9th grade in order to get into high school. At this point they can choose vocational school, professional training, or two years preparation for university studies. It is extremely difficult to get into a university, which requires five years for a bachelor's degree or six for a medical degree.

Serious gaps between the rich and poor, skilled and unskilled, healthy and ill are widening and threatening Russia's future development. Women earn only one fifth of the nation's income. About 74 percent of the population live in urban areas. Although food is plentiful in the cities, many products are expensive and the average person cannot afford them. Russians prefer a large breakfast whenever possible. They consume a lot of *chai* (hot tea), sugar beets and cabbage, often in the form of *borsch* (cold beet soup), and potatoes. Bread is another staple. They like *zakuski* (appetizers), such as caviar, for lunch and dinner. Vodka is preferred to wine, but beer is also popular.

Customs and Courtesies

The Russian Orthodox Church, the dominant religion, is known for its elaborate rituals and long services in which everyone must stand for two or three hours as there are no pews or benches in the church. The gold incense burners and elaborate dress of the bearded priests stand in stark contrast to the relative poverty of the parishioners. For many Russians, the church is a symbol of the Russian national spirit and identity as it has survived the Soviet regime. Orthodox Christmas occurs on January 7 (because the church still follows the old Julian calendar which differs from the modern Gregorian calendar by 13 days). Epiphany, which occurs 12 days after Christmas, is a major holy day and is celebrated with much pageantry and symbolism. New Year's Day has emerged as the most important occasion on the Russian calendar, with much celebrating the week before including caroling, exchanging of gifts, and decorating of trees. Women's Day is celebrated on March 8. The first of May is celebrated as May Day, and is a day of parades. Victory Day on May 9 commemorates the end of World War II. Russia is famous for ancient folk tales which generally fall into three categories: fairy tales, animal tales, and tales of everyday life. The origin of one of the world's most famous Christmas traditions, Santa Claus, began with St. Nicholas of Myra, a patron saint of Russia. "Old wives tales" are popular too. Superstitious beliefs are widely held. Some of the more prominent ones are that it is bad luck to light a cigar from a candle on a restaurant table, Monday is a bad day to start a journey or business venture, a cat should be the first creature to cross the threshold of a new home, and spitting three times over one's shoulder prevents bad news. My uncle had a similar belief; every time a black cat crossed his path, he would make a circle over his head with his hand three times. We children got a big kick out of that one.

Scotland

The Landscape

Scotland occupies the northern third of the island of Great Britain. It is bordered by England to the south, the Atlantic Ocean to the west and north, and the North Sea to the east. The North Channel separates it from Northern Ireland to the southeast. A land of rugged cliffs and heather-covered hills, it is a place of wild natural beauty. It is divided into three geographic regions – the Highlands in the north, the Lowlands in the center, and the Southern Uplands. Numerous islands line the west coast. Two island clusters lie to the northeast. They are the Orkney Islands, and the Shetland Islands from whence comes the Shetland pony. The Highlands are famous for a long valley called Glen More which cuts through from southwest to northeast and for the many *lochs* or lakes. Among them is the Loch Ness, which is famous for myths that a monster lives in the lake. The great majority of the Scottish people live in the Lowlands in the center of Scotland. Though lower than surrounding areas, the Lowlands are not flat and contain many hills. Most of the farming is done in this area as it has very fertile soil. It is also the country's main industrial area. The Uplands are lower than the Highlands and have gentle hills and narrow flat valleys. Throughout the country one sees rugged mountains, green valleys, deep blue lakes, and offshore islands which provide breathtaking scenery. The climate is generally mild and cool due to the southwest winds which make it warmer than one would expect at these latitudes. The east is drier and sunnier with very fertile agricultural land.

The Economy

In the past, Scotland's economy relied on heavy industries such as coal mining, steel, and shipbuilding. Today the oil and natural gas industries in northeast Scotland on the North Sea coast have created ten of thousands of jobs. Industries that produce high technology goods such as computers, electronics, office equipment, and chemicals have also grown. Service industries such as tourism, finance, and retail trade have greatly expanded in the last decade. Around the Firth of Forth lies Scotland's richest agricultural area where farms produce wheat, oats, barley, vegetables, fruits, and disease-resistant seed potatoes highly prized in England. Sheep provide wool for the textile industry. Fishing has taken on an even more important role. More than 65 percent of the British fish and shellfish caught is handled by Scottish ports. Salmon and trout are raised on fish farms while haddock, herring, sole, mackerel, and other forms of seafood are caught in the many scattered fishing towns along the islands. Forestry is expanding in the rural areas where Sitka spruce, Norway spruce, Scotch pine, European larch, and Douglas fir are grown. A major export is, of course, the internationally famous Scotch whisky produced in the Highlands.

The People

Scotland has a population of over 5 million, about two thirds of whom live in the Lowlands. The Scottish people are mainly from two groups. The Scots of the Highlands have Celtic origins. The people of the rest of Scotland are mostly Anglo-Saxon. There are also small groups of Irish, Lithuanian, Italian, Polish, and South Asian descent. Most Scottish people are Christian. The national church is the Church of Scotland, which is Presbyterian. English is the official language, although some small groups speak Scottish Gaelic and Scots (Scottish English). The Scots have been stereotyped as being thrifty, cautious, and careful of detail. My aunt was of Scottish origin and we had a saying about Aunt Isabel, "She would hold onto a dollar bill until it squeaked." It has been argued that the Scottish culture is merely a regional variation of the dominant British culture, but Scottish culture is a vigorous one in its own right. Edinburgh's international festival of music and drama draws more than 250,000 people every year, making it one of the world's largest cultural events. There are over 100 gatherings of the clans in the Highlands which draw visitors from all over. In the early days the ruggedness of the land led to the separation of the Highlanders into small groups called clans. Each clan was ruled by a chief, and the members claimed descent from a common ancestor. The traditional garment of the Highland clansmen is the kilt, a knee-length pleated skirt, suitable for climbing the rough hills. Each clan had its own colorful pattern, called a tartan or plaid (a length of cloth worn over the shoulder). Today the kilt is a national costume, proudly worn for special occasions such as parades and other major occasions, while playing traditional music on bagpipes. Two famous Scottish writers are Robert Burns and Walter Scott, considered the inventor of the historical novel.

The Scots are well educated people; their history is full of people of humble beginnings who acquired university educations. Andrew Carnegie, the Scottish-born American Industrialist, set up the Carnegie Trust Fund in 1901 in the U.S. to help needy students and to foster research. Universal education has been an institution in their country for centuries. Scots read more newspapers than any other European people. Their educational system is operated separately from that of England. The literacy rate is about 99 percent. Children attend primary school for seven years and secondary school for six years. After that they can go on to a vocational school or one of the thirteen universities. The universities of St. Andrews, Edinburgh, Aberdeen, and Glasgow are especially prestigious.

Customs and Courtesies

Scots celebrate many of the Christian holidays and holidays celebrated in the UK. Interestingly enough, one of the most important celebrations of the Scottish year is Halloween on October 31. Scottish "guisers" go from door to door, dressed in costumes, asking for candy or money. However, they must perform a song or poem before receiving their treat. There are also parties with supernatural themes and decorations. New Year's Eve, the biggest holiday, is known as *Hogmanay*. This involves the ceremony of "first footing" a custom of visiting the homes of friends, neighbors, and even strangers in the "wee small" hours" of New Year's Day. On Boxing Day, celebrated on December 26, boxed gifts were given to servants; today it is just a day of visiting and relaxing. Banquets called *"Burns Suppers"* honor Robert Burns on his birthday on the 25th of January. Traditionally the Scottish national dish, haggis, is served as Burn's poem, "Address to a Haggis," is recited. Haggis is made from ground sheep entrails that are mixed with oats and spices, tied in a sheep's stomach, and cooked. St. Andrew's Day, patron saint of Scotland, is celebrated on November 30. Other holidays include May Day (May 1); the Queen's Birthday, celebrated the last Monday of May; and Remembrance Day held on the Sunday closest to November 11.

The Scottish are known for their taciturn and reserved manner. The showing of affection is not done in public. Their sense of humor is deadpan and ironic. However, they tend to have close relationships at home which include "inside jokes". Proper etiquette is important and admired. Afternoon tea, which was usually at 3 o'clock, is now mostly reserved for weekends as many men and women work during the week. Evening tea, often called dinner, is a formal meal. When one is invited to dinner it is proper to bring a small gift such as flowers, chocolates or a bottle of wine. A standard rule of thumb is to bring a gift equal to the cost of the meal. The present is presented when one arrives. Scots are open and candid in conversation and have a keen subtle sense of humor. Religion, salary and politics are subjects to be avoided. One indicates one is finished by placing the fork and knife together on the plate. Most socialization outside the home is done in pubs. Be forewarned that Scots smoke more and eat more sugar and fats than any other nationality in Europe.

Scots are fiercely independent and hard working and value the same virtues in others. Parents love their independence and will remain on their own for as long as possible.

Singapore

The Landscape

The Republic of Singapore is a city-state linked to the Malaysian mainland by a 1.1 kilometer causeway that carries a road and a railway. Known as the Lion City, Singapore is a modern metropolis with one of the world's busiest ports. It is also known as the Garden City for its many parks and tree-lined streets. The land area is 692.7 kilometers. The country is located in southeast Asia in the Indian Ocean and consist of a main island and 60 small islands. It is separated from Malaysia by the Johore Strait to the north, and from Indonesia by the Strait of Malacca and the Singapore Strait to the west and south. The Strait of Malacca is an important link between the Indian Ocean and the South China Sea. Much of the urban sprawl of Singapore occupies land that was reclaimed from the sea and low-lying areas through landfill operations. By 1985 land reclamation had increased the original size of the island by five percent. Within the city run the Singapore and Rochor rivers. The commercial center is located in the middle of the city with population nodes in the outlying areas. However, Singapore's traditional ethnic neighborhoods remain downtown. Chinatown, Little India are located near the downtown area and the Malay community, called Geylang Serai, located in the Northwest suburbs, and the Arab Muslim area of Kampong Glam reflect the city's diverse population. The land is mostly flat and low lying with several hills. Since it is near the equator, its climate is tropical; the weather is hot, humid, and often rainy. There are two monsoon seasons. The Northeastern monsoon season is from December to March and the Southwestern monsoon season is from June to September. The Jurong Bird Park is home to 139 species of birds. Other nature preserves contain various small forest animals, trees, and more than 700 plant species.

The Economy

Since the Republic of Singapore declared independence in 1965, it has worked hard to create and maintain a strong economy. The country is one of the wealthiest in the world. According to the World Bank, it is one of the newly industrialized Asian countries along with Hong Kong, Taiwan, and South Korea. The gross national income per capita is $20,690. Economic growth has been nearly nine percent since 1996. Manufacturing generates approximately 25 percent of the gross domestic product. Major industries are petroleum refining, machinery, appliances, electronics, metal engineering, and precision equipment. Most of the heavy industries are located in Jurong, an industrial estate. Agriculture contributes only one percent to the GDP. The nation is not self-sufficient in food production and must import rice, vegetables, and meat. Energy accounts for 40 percent of all imports. Singapore has long been a major center of transport and communications. Transshipment trade accounts for 40 percent of total trade, which means the majority of products are imported from one country and then exported to other countries. The container-handling facilities are among the most extensive and modern in the world. Air transport is also world class and one of the most modern in the world. There is high quality public transportation consisting of buses, taxis, and a mass-rapid-transit (MRT) system with routes linking major population centers in housing estates with industrial estates and the central business district. Financial services are also a major source of income for the country. Tourism is increasingly important to the country.

The People

Singapore has a population of 4.1 million, resulting in a population density of 13,753 persons per square mile, the highest of any nation. The multiethnic nature of the population provides for a rich and varied cultural, religious, and linguistic heritage. Singapore's citizens may be classified into three ethnic categories: Chinese numbering 2.6 million or 77 percent of the population; Malays numbering 510,000 or 14 percent of the population; Asian Indians numbering 221,000 or 8 percent of the population, and 1 percent others including Eurasians. The Chinese population represents seven different regional Chinese cultures: Hokkien and Techiu from southern China, Hakka and Three Rivers People from central China, people from Hainan Island off the south China coast, Cantonese and Malays long residents of Malaysia. Malays are the indigenous inhabitants although they are now in the minority. The unifying force for Muslim Malays is Islam. The Chinese share a common religious history which is a combination of Buddhism, Taoism, and Confucianism. The Asian Indians in Singapore refer to people from South Asia: Indians, Bangladeshis, Burmans, and Sri Lankans. The majority of Indians are Tamils from Tamil Nadu state in southeastern India. Most Indians are Hindus or Sikhs. Race relations are harmonious.

The official languages are Malay, Chinese (Mandarin), Tamil, and English. Many young people also speak Singlish, which is a combination of English, Chinese, and Malay. Malay is the national language, although English is the primary language of schools, businesses, and government. English is widely used to communicate among the different ethnic groups. Most Singaporeans are at least bilingual. The government encourages the use of all languages to sustain traditional cultures and values. They value discipline, self-control, education, honesty, and humility. Family and friends are highly valued and operate within a hierarchy based on age and sex. Etiquette is very important. This is a "collective" society in which values are shared and decisions are made by consensus. High moral and ethical values are stressed. A single and never married mother cannot purchase low-cost government housing nor receive public health benefits for her children. She has caused her family to "loose face" thus shaming her family. Singaporeans have a reputation as one of the world's best workforces. Every male Singaporean must serve for two years in the National Service (the military). If they do not, an extremely high fine is assessed.

Cooperation, loyalty, respect for elders, and unity are deeply valued by all Singaporean families. Children are expected to obey their parents and care for them in their old age. Financial incentives are given to young people to buy apartments near their parents so they can care for them in their old age. Young people are encouraged to finish their education prior to dating. Women have equal political, employment, and educational rights and men are encouraged to share household responsibilities. Since both the husband and wife work, grandparents often take care of the children. Members of the rising generation look to the five "Cs" as life time goals: career, condominium, car, cash, and credit card. They know that the quality of life coincides with the level of education. The national literacy rate is very high, over 90 percent, and among 15 to 19-year olds it approaches 100 percent. Primary education is free and the schooling period lasts over 12 years. Private schools account for more than one third of primary enrollment. In primary school children study in their mother tongue as well as in English. However, for Chinese children, Chinese is compulsory in primary education. English is the language of instruction. Higher education is provided by the National University of Singapore, Singamore Management University, and Nanyang Technological University, but many students study abroad because there is no room for them at the universities. There are several technical schools of higher education, some specializing in practical engineering courses.

Customs and Courtesies

Public holidays include International New Year on the first of January; Chinese New Year set by the Chinese lunar calendar; Easter including Good Friday; Vesak Day celebrating the birth, enlightenment, and nirvana of Buddha, celebrated in the fifth lunar month; Labor Day on May1; and Singapore National Day held on August 9. Other Chinese celebrations are held throughout the year. Muslims celebrate *Hari Raya Puasa,* which is the feast held at the end of the Islamic month of *Ramadan.* Another Muslim festival is *Hari Raya Haji,* which celebrates the pilgrimage to

Makkah, Saudi Arabia. *Deepavali*, the Festival of Lights, is celebrated by the Hindus and Sikhs for the triumph of light over darkness. Another Hindu celebration is *Thaipusam*. Thai is the tenth month of the Tamil calendar and Pusam is the brightest star in the constellation of Cancer. Usually observed between January and February, it is a celebration of purification. Christians celebrate Christmas.

The Chinese New Year is a huge celebration with 15 days of revelry. In preparation there is a thorough house cleaning, paying off old debts, buying new clothes, and preparing symbolic foods. New Year's Eve begins with a family dinner intended to reinforce family ties. Everyone shouts as they start to mix up the ingredients of the traditional raw fish salad, *lo hei*, a symbol of their call for future wealth. Other holiday foods include long noodles for longevity, sea moss for prosperity, shark's fin soup, and *nian gao*, a steamed or fried cake. Single people give married people oranges and married people give children, relatives, or friends; and regular service personnel gifts of money in red envelopes called *hung pao*. New Year superstitions include not using needles or scissors (symbols of bad luck), hiding all brooms on the first day so that good luck cannot be swept away, and not washing one's hair (again so that good luck will not be washed away). Rain is a sign of no drought and winning at gambling is a sign of good fortune for the next 12 months. Orange-colored citrus fruit brings good luck, so bring some in even numbers if you are invited to the celebration. Gifts should be given in pairs and black clothing is unlucky. Belief in numerology is very significant for the Chinese so let them decide on the time, date, or the month of any meetings. They also use it in deciding home and business addresses. If the gift recipient is Muslim or Hindu, do not give alcohol as their religion forbids it and avoid any gifts that have anything to do with turtles or dogs as both have negative connotations. A Muslim friend of mine told be that dogs are considered dirty and if you touch one, then you must wash your hands seven times. This is a far cry from the American perception that "A dog is man's best friend."

One of the outstanding offerings of Singapore is the array of local and international cuisine. The Chinese have one of the world's greatest and most varied cuisines. The Indian community brought with them Indian cuisine which is characterized by the use of spices and is usually very hot. The Malay and Indonesian elements add another dimension to the local cuisine. *Nonya* cuisine is a combination Malayan, Indonesian, and Chinese food. Rice is eaten on a daily basis with fish, seafood, or chicken. The Chinese eat rice with chopsticks, Malays and Indians eat with the fingers of the right hand. All groups use spoons and forks for certain types of foods. The food is placed in bowls in the middle of the table and the diners sit in a circle around the table. Each diner has his own bowl. Small portions are taken from the communal bowls during the course of the meal.

South Africa

The Landscape

South Africa is located in the southernmost part of the African continent, one of the oldest and most stable of the Earth's landmasses. It has long coastlines along the Atlantic Ocean in the southwest and the Indian Ocean in the southeast. Most of South Africa is a plateau, a raised but fairly flat area known as Highveld, with an elevation of 3,000 to 6,500 feet above sea level. A mountainous region known as the Great Escarpment separates the high plateau from the lower plains along the coast. The highest part of the escarpment is a mountain range known as Drakensberg. Parts of western South Africa are covered by the Kalahari and Namib deserts. The three most important rivers are the Orange, Vaal, and Limpopo. Since drought is a major problem, much capital has been spent to build some 360 dams on the major rivers that supply water to urban areas. The seasons are opposite those in the northern hemisphere. The climate is moderate with few extremes of heat or cold. At the time of the 1994 elections, Pretoria was made the sole capital of South Africa. However, Cape Town is the largest city and maintains the nation's legislature. Bloemfontein is the judicial center. Other major cities are Durban, Johannesburg, Soweto, and Port Elizabeth. South Africa is known for its long beaches, green forests, rugged mountains, and great canyons. Diverse foliage and colorful wildlife add to its scenic beauty.

The Economy

The Republic of South Africa combines an advanced first-world economy with a third-world culture within its boundaries. It has the most productive economy of all African countries. This economy is based largely on mining and manufacturing. It mines a major portion of the world's twelve main mineral resources; it has 77 percent of the world's chrome reserves, 94 percent of the world's platinum group metals, 62 percent of the world's gold, 72 percent of the world's vanadium, 92 percent of the world's manganese, and 11 percent of the world's fluorite. Other natural resources are asbestos, nickel, phosphate rock, copper, zinc, antimony, and lead. Both gem-quality and industrial diamonds are mined in large quantities and sold on world markets. It is the world's largest producer of platinum and gold. Only 15 percent of the country is suitable for farming. However, except for wheat and coffee, South Africa is not only self sufficient in its food production, but exports many crops such as cane sugar, corn, potatoes, fresh fruits, canned fruits and vegetables, and wine. Grapes are grown and used to make outstanding wines. Sheep and Angora goats provide wool and mohair, which are major exports. Since 1946, 2.4 million acres of trees have been planted. Such species as eucalyptus, pine for pulp paper and building materials, black wattle for leather tanning chemicals, poplar for softwood and safety matches are harvested. The abundance of minerals has made metalworking and iron and steel production into key industries. Other important manufactured goods include foods, beverages, machinery, textiles, and chemicals. Wine and tourism are fast growing sectors. The real gross domestic product per capita is $4,291. The currency is the *rand* (R).

The People

South Africa's people are usually categorized as belonging to one of four groups: blacks or Africans, whites and Afrikaners who speak Afrikaans, Coloreds, and Asians or Indians. Black Africans make up about three fourths of South Africa's population of 45 million. Africans are comprised of mostly nine ethnic groups: Zulus are the largest at about 21 percent followed by Xhosas, then North Sothos, South Sothos, Tswanas, Shangaan-Tsongas, Swazis, Ndebeles, and Vendas. Each has its own cultural heritage, language, and national identity. Whites (English speakers) are descended mainly from British, Irish, and Scottish settlers. Afrikaners are mainly descended from Dutch, French, and German settlers. Coloreds are descended from Africans, Indians, and other Asians who are descended from people brought to South Africa from India to work the sugar plantations in the 19th century. More than 95 percent of South Africans live in the eastern half of the country and along the southern coast.

For much of the 20th century South Africa's white minority dominated the government and passed laws that separated the population by race. This was known as *apartheid*. This system collapsed in the early 1990s. The election of the first black president, Nelson Mandela, in 1994 began a new non-racial democracy in South African history. During apartheid, groups were assigned to "homelands" or territories according to their race. Soweto, on the edge of Johannesburg, is an example of a black city, with an estimated 2 million or more inhabitants. It has many primary. secondary and technical schools. People commute to the cities by train, bus, taxi, and private automobile. The transition to equality for all has been a slow and difficult one. The Coloreds who were once aligned with the whites now feel they will be left behind because they are not totally black. During apartheid, education from ages 7 to 16 was compulsory for all white, Indian, and Colored children, but not for blacks (except in 300 primary schools where parent committees requested it). Education has long been seized upon as the road to self improvement among the members of South Africa's colored community. As a result, families will save and sacrifice to send their children to the best available schools and colleges. In 1994 the student-to-teacher ratio in white schools was 18 to 1; in colored schools it was 22 to 1; and in black schools it was 50 to 1. Today education is compulsory for all until the age of 16. It generally takes 12 years to obtain the high school diploma or senior certificate that is required to continue studies at a technical college or university. There are 19 universities; any child can attend any one of them. A high priority has been given to mechanical education for youth at all levels through institutions called *technikons* located in most cities. This enables the children to be well prepared for a future in which advanced technology will play a key role in everyday life. Also, most industrial companies offer their workers technical training during working hours. Medical services are socialized. Medical, dental, health services, including hospitals and clinics, are free (or have a nominal fee) to all people. Unfortunately these services are still inadequate, especially in rural areas. South Africa is facing a serious health crisis with the HIV virus. In the early 21st century it had more people infected with HIV than any other country in the world.

Customs and Courtesies

Official holidays in South Africa include New Year's Day, Easter including Good Friday and Family Day on Monday, Human Rights Day on March 21, Freedom Day on April 27, Workers' Day on May 1, Youth Day on June 16, National Women's Day on August 9, Inheritance Day on September 24, Reconciliation Day on December 16, Christmas, and Day of Goodwill on December 26. Each religion observes its important holidays. Christmas is the most important holiday for both blacks and whites and, although it falls in the summer, great effort is made to create a wintery environment with fake snow flakes and plastic reindeer. In an effort to integrate instead of segregate, the African National Congress (ANC) has adopted two national anthems: *Nikosi Sikelel iAfrika* (God Bless Africa), the anthem of the anti-apartheid liberation movement and *Die Stem* (The Call of South Africa), the Afrikaner-inspired anthem of apartheid days. Both are sung at official functions and sporting events. Another important change was to rename the holiday on December 16 from the "Day of Covenant" to the "Day of Reconciliation" to emphasize national racial harmony. It had always been the Afrikaner national holiday celebrating one of the greatest Afrikaans folk heroes, Andries Pretroious, and his victory over the Zulu in the Battle of Blood River in 1838. Music and dance have always been a very important part of South African culture. *Toi-toi* is the traditional liberation dance of the people. *Mapantsula* is a unique black South African music form which is a cross between traditional jazz and early rap.

Isicatamiya is a mournful type of music sung by a choir or choral group. Each tribe has its own traditions. When invited to the home of a Zulu, it is polite to shout from the gate that you have arrived, but when you walk into the home, it is rude to make yourself comfortable without first being seated by the host. In the Sotho culture, once invited into the home, you are expected to sit down immediately; the hosts will arrange themselves around you. In most cases, African cultures are more respectful of the individual than Western cultures. Sports is a national obsession and international competition is fierce. There are more than 15,000 registered soccer clubs and more than one million active players. Sports has proven to be a great unifier, one of the few areas in which races can compete with equality.

South Korea

The Landscape

The Republic of Korea is a nation of East Asia, commonly called South Korea. The country occupies the southern half of the Korean peninsula. North Korea occupies the northern half of the peninsula. Korea, once unified, has been split into two separate countries since the middle of the 20th century after the end of the Korean war. Since then, South and North Korea have faced each other across a heavily guarded border. North Korea is the country's only land border. The Sea of Japan borders it on the east, the Yellow Sea is to the west, and the East China Sea is to the south. South Korea's landmass is a little larger than Indiana. Seoul, the capital and largest city, lies near the border with North Korea. The east coast forms a long, smooth curve without many islands. The western and southern coasts are jagged and have many bays and small islands. Most of South Korea is covered by low mountains. The Taebaek Mountains run along the east coast. The Sobaek Mountains form an S shape across the southern part of the country. Mount Hen la, the highest peak, is found on Cheju Island off the southern coast. The country's main lowlands are found in the basins of the Naktong river in the southeast and the Han River in the northwest. Many people live on these lowlands, which provide the country's best farmland. Almost 70 percent of the land is forested; only 20 percent is suitable for cultivation. The climate is temperate. The greatest influence on the climate of the Korean peninsula is its proximity to the Asian landmass. This produces cold, dry winters and hot, humid summers as well as monsoons from June to August.

The Economy

Since the early 1960s, South Korea's economy has grown at a rapid pace. In 1962 business and government leaders formed a strategy to transform the country from a poor society into one of the world's most highly indus-trialized nations. The growth, fostered by strong government support, was driven primarily by the development of export-oriented industries. Textiles and light manufacturing were the first industries to be targeted. Heavy industries such as iron, steel, and chemicals were developed during the 1970s. Later, electronic and automobile industries were developed. Government-exercised strong controls on development encouraged giant corporate conglomerates known as *chaebol*. Small and medium companies became subcontractors to the *chaebol*. Some of the leading *chaebol* are Samsung, LG, and Hyundai. With preferential reinvestment in export industries, consumer products and spending were suppressed. South Korea is one of the four major newly industrialized Asian countries, the others are Singapore, Indonesia, and Taiwan. To give one an understanding of how much this economy has grown over the last forty years, in 1960 the real gross domestic product per capita was around $700, today it is around $20,000.

In 2000 agriculture accounted for about 5 percent of the GDP, industry about 52 percent, and services about 43 percent. Less than one fourth of the country is cultivated. Rice is the most important crop, constituting about two fifths of all farm production in value. Other important crops are barley, wheat, soybeans, and potatoes. Despite successful reforestation efforts, timber provides for only a small amount of the demand. Fishing has long been a chief source of protein in the Korean diet. The industry has emerged as one of the world's major deep sea fish sources, and seafood has become a significant export product. A seaweed product, agar, is also an important export item. Heavy industries including chemicals, metals, machinery, and petroleum refining, are highly developed. In the 1980s shipbuilding, motor vehicles, and electronics equipment grew in importance. In 1996 and 1997, South Korea suffered serious set backs from major labor disputes and strikes, large budget deficits, political scandals, *chaebol* bankruptcies and competition from other countries. In 1999 the country began to recover from the Asian financial crisis of 1997 and 1998 as economic reforms promoted sustained growth. Today such high technology industries as bioengineering, aerospace and services have shown remarkable growth. There has been major growth in the banking industry as well as in financial and investment services.

The People

The Republic of Korea's population is about 47 million. The people are all ethnic Korean, making Korea one of the most homogeneous countries in the world. All Koreans speak the Korean language which is classified as one of the Altaic languages. The South Korean script, known as *Hangul*, is composed of phonetic symbols for the 10 vowels and 14 consonants. Scholars estimate that about 70 percent of present day Korean vocabulary is of Chinese origin although there is a trend away from this. English, however, is spoken in the business world and is often taught in South Korean schools so many people have a good understanding of it. Confucianism permeates all aspects of Korean society and emphasizes being calm, obedient, and respectful. It is more an ethic than a religion that stresses many rituals of courtesy, behavioral formalities, customs, and harmony in social relationships.

Freedom of religion is constitutionally guaranteed and there is no national religion. Almost one in four are Buddhists. A large number are practicing Christians, with Protestants far outnumbering Catholics. Some Koreans follow the religion of *Chondogyo* which means "Teaching of the Heavenly Way." It began in 1860 and combines elements of Buddhism, Confucianism, and Christianity. However, there is little uniformity of religious belief, a situation that is often confusing to outside observers. An individual may adhere to Buddhism while also following Confucian or Taoist tenets. More than one fourth follow the traditions of a folk religion called *Shamanism*. Important to *Shamanism* are geomancy, divination, avoiding bad luck and omens, warding off evil spirits, and honoring the dead.

The family is the foundation of society and is bound together by a strong sense of obligation and loyalty among its members. The father is the head of the family. He and the oldest son are given great respect. In the extended family, the oldest members are given the most respect. When a person reaches his sixtieth birthday, the family members give him a grand celebration, called *hwan'gap*, because of the symbolism of the 60 year cycle obtained by combining the 12 "Heavenly Stems" and the 10 "Earthly Branches." This computing system was invented by the Chinese in the second millennium BC. Basically it is the day one has lived through the complete cycle of the zodiac. They may have saved for years just to pay for this celebration, because in the past it was rare that someone reached this age. A similar celebration is given when a child reaches his first birthday. Due to their long standing Confucian tradition, Koreans value education very highly. Education is considered the key to success, respect, and power. Education is compulsory for ages six to twelve. Secondary schools demand long hours and high performance. In order to enter a university one must pass an extremely difficulty entrance exam. Students study intensively for months in order to pass it. In fact, once they have passed it and entered the university, they do very little studying for the next year because of "burn out." The educational and cultural level of Koreans is first among all nationalities in China and second only to North America and Europe. Koreans like sour and spicy dishes. Rice, millet, and *kimch'i* (a spicy, pickled cabbage) are eaten at almost every meal. Various soups are also served at every meal. One of my favorites is *pulkogi,* strips of marinated and barbecued beef. They also eat lots of fish and rice cakes. Fruit, especially watermelon, are eaten as desserts. Barley tea is served with most meals unless one is drinking beer or wine.

Customs and Courtesies

Koreans are very warm and courteous. They are particular about tidiness and cleanliness. When entering someone's home, everyone removes their shoes at the door. In a traditional Korean home, guests are seated on cushions on the floor. Men sit cross-legged and women tuck their legs to one side behind them. Guests are given the warmest and best position. Refreshments are usually served and refusing them is considered rude. When celebrating at home, all the family members sing and dance, making for very lively entertainment. When they go out to a restaurant they love Karaoke and drinking. The more they drink, the more they love to sing.

Lunar New Year, also known as *Sol lal,* is Korea's most important holiday and is celebrated for three days. In downtown Seoul at midnight a bell tolls 33 times to welcome in the new year. By tradition, one must stay awake all night. Children are told if they fall asleep, their eyebrows will turn gray. All dress in traditional clothing. Tradition also dictates that food be set in front of the photographs of one's ancestors and that younger family members bow deeply before their grandparents, parents, and elder siblings. Families enjoy a feast of holiday foods including *ttokkuk* (rice cake soup) and *su-jong-gwa* (punch made of honey and persimmons). They also play traditional games, fly kites, and socialize with friends and relatives. One of the main traditions is to expel evil spirits at the end of the old year. Another is to settle all financial debt and begin a new year debt free. *Ch'usok,* Harvest Moon Festival, is Korea's version of our Thanksgiving. Families congregate from all over the country to visit their ancestral tomb to offer food in honor of the dead. *Ch'usok* calls for a staggering variety of foods boldly spiced with red pepper, garlic, onions, leeks, sesame seeds, sesame oil and soy sauce. These are accompanied by *song p'yon,* half-moon-shaped rice cakes filled with either chestnut, sesame seeds and sugar or beans and a heady rice wine (which can be very potent). Other public holidays are Independence Movement Day on March 1, Children's Day on May 5, Buddha's Birthday (sometime in May according to the lunar calendar), Memorial Day on June 6, Constitution Day on July 17, Independence Day on August 15, National Foundation Day on October 3, and Christmas on December 25. Other days marked by various celebrations which are not official are Arbor Day on April 5, Armed Forces Day on October 1, and Korean Language Day on October 9.

Divination, the art of foreseeing future events, has been an integral part of Korean culture since at least 37 BC. Geomancers are engineers of psychic influences. They align doors, desks, beds, etc. according to the configuration of the earth and the temperament of its elements. Many Koreans consult a *feng shui* (wind and water) man before buying a car, building a house, opening a business or anything that warrants a major personal or professional decision. The number four is considered unlucky so they use the letter "F" instead of the number. Gifts with odd numbers of items are given. Never give a set of four to a South Korean even though many items are packaged that way in the U.S. Red is not worn as it is an indication of aggression. Koreans love to sing and dance. They make it a point of honor to master their traditional dances. They dance on every happy occasion. For example, a Korean wedding begins with feasting and ends hours later with prolonged dancing.

Spain

The Landscape

The Kingdom of Spain, one of the largest countries in Western Europe, is located in the extreme southwest of Europe. It occupies about 85 percent of the Iberian Peninsula which it shares with Portugal to its west. In the northeast it borders France, from which it is separated by the tiny principality of Andorra and the great Pyrenees Mountains. Spain's only other land border is Gibraltar, now a British colony. Elsewhere the country is bounded by water. To the east and southeast is the Mediterranean Sea and to the north, northwest and southwest is the Atlantic Ocean. The Bay of Biscay, an inlet of the Atlantic Ocean, lies to the northwest. Spain's territory also includes the Canary Islands, a famous resort in the Atlantic Ocean just off the northwestern African mainland, and the Balearic Islands in the Mediterranean. Cueta and Melilla are two small enclaves in northern Morocco that Spain has ruled for centuries. Most of Spain consists of a large, high plain in the center of the country called the Meseta Central which is almost completely surrounded by mountains. Along the Mediterranean Seaboard there are coastal plains, some with lagoons. The capital is Madrid. The climate varies by region. In general, the country has cool winters and hot summers. The temperature is usually milder along the coasts.

The Economy

In 1959 the country was on the verge of an economic collapse. The government then established the Economic Stabilization Plan. This plan allowed a less restrained market economy which resulted in a fuller integration of Spain into the international capitalist economy. From 1960 until 1974 Spain experienced a rapid economic growth period known as the Spanish economic miracle. The economy grew an average of 6.6 percent per year. Three factors were responsible for this "miracle." The first was foreign investment in Spain by the United States and West Germany. The second factor was tourism which became the country's largest industry. Spain, with its many beaches, warm climate, and bargain prices, became an attractive destination, especially for Americans and Europeans. The third factor was emigrant remittances. From 1959 until 1974 more than three million Spaniards left the country in search for work. These emigrants sent large sums of money back to Spain, more than $1 billion in 1973 alone. Since then the overall pace of economic growth has been slow in Spain compared to other western European countries although conditions have improved substantially since the country joined the European Union in 1986.

The service industry (including tourism) is by far the largest sector of the economy, employing about 60 percent of the population. Manufacturing industry employs about 21 percent and agriculture employs about 11 percent of the workforce. Important heavy industries are automobiles and mopeds, metals and metal manufacturing, iron and steel bars, chemicals, and shipbuilding. Textiles and apparel including footwear are also important industries. Agriculture products include fresh fruits, vegetables, nuts, grains, and wine grapes. Spain is a world leader in the production of wine. Fishing has long been an important industry as well. The government has taken steps to assure that traditional crafts or *artesania*, survive against competition from mechanized industry. It is known for its leather goods. It is also famous for its handmade musical instruments, especially guitars.

The People

The population of Spain is about 39.5 million. The Spanish are a composite of Mediterranean and Nordic ancestry but are considered a homogeneous ethnic group. However, one important difference in Spain from the rest of western Europe was the invasion of Arabic-speaking Muslims from the Middle East and North Africans in AD 711 which dominated much of the country for 800 years. Spain gained access to many scientific advances made by the Muslims. Spain's cultural mix became even richer during the Middle Ages because of the presence of a large and influential Jewish population. Medieval Spain witnessed one of the periods of greatest cultural achievement in Jewish history. Spain has also been strongly identified with the Roman Catholic Church, but since 1978 Spain has had no official religion and the Spaniards have enjoyed complete freedom of religion. More than three fourths of the population lives in urban areas. Madrid, the capital, has the largest population with about four million. Barcelona is the next largest with about three million people. Spain has four official languages. Castilian Spanish is the main language of business and government. The other official languages are Catalan, Galician, and Basque. Spanish is the language of instruction except in Catalonia where Catalan is used. English is the most common second language, followed by French.

Spaniards place a high value on what others think of them. Peer and family pressure are strong in addressing personal behavior. Personal pride and appearance are very important. People seek to project an appearance of affluence and social status. Regional pride is quite apparent. The Spanish are quite talkative and enjoy giving advice even when not requested. They consider it their duty to correct "errors" they see in others (just like the Russians). They have a relaxed attitude toward rules and punctuality. This gregarious people have no problem speaking to complete strangers. Visits are prearranged; arriving unannounced is impolite. However, an invitation to one's home may be just a polite courtesy. Ignoring such invitations is acceptable and sometimes even expected. Lunch, which is the main meal of the day, eaten between 2 and 3p.m. is followed by the famous "siesta,"a two to three hour break in the day. Business, shopping, and school hours reflect this pattern. Virtually everything except bars and restaurants is closed. The workday resumes in the late afternoon, between 4:30 and 5 p.m., and continues until 8 p.m. Dinner is the lighter meal usually taken between 9 and 10PM.

The bars, which are open all day, generally serve food as well as drink. It is a widespread custom to go for a snack, *tapa*, before meals. Typical *tapas* are mushrooms in garlic sauce, marinated seafood, Spanish omelettes, lamb brochettes, and octopus in paprika sauce. Spanish cooking varies widely according to region. Considered the most elaborate and prestigious are the Catalan and Basque cuisines. The most widely eaten meat is pork, but in much of the country lamb is eaten on special occasions, a Catholic tradition. The Spanish have long consumed large amounts of fish and seafood. Fresh vegetables, especially lentils and chick-peas, and fruits also form an important part of the Mediterranean diet. Fried foods are cooked in olive oil. Spaniards eat in the continental style with the fork in the left hand and the knife in the right. Upon finishing the meal, one places the knife and fork side by side on the plate; leaving them crossed or on opposite side of the plate indicates one wishes to eat more.

The family is important in Spain. With the heavy influence of the Roman Catholic Church, divorce is relatively low. The father is the head of the home while the mother's duties are caring for the house and the children. Children live with their parents until they marry, regardless of age. Education is compulsory between the ages of six and sixteen. However, most students attend school until they are 18. Many schools are operated by the Roman Catholic Church or by private organizations. Middle and upper income families spend a good share of their income on private education. Spain has 31 state-run universities and an increasing number of private ones.

Customs and Courtesies

Spain is famous for its holidays and fiestas. National holidays are Christmas, New Year's Day, the Day of the Three Kings, or Epiphany, (January 6) when Christmas gifts are opened, Holy (Maudy) Thursday, Good Friday. Easter, and Easter Monday, Corpus Christi, the Feast of Saint James on July 25th, All Saint's day on November 1st, Constitution Day on December 6th, and the Feast of the Immaculate Conception on December 8.

The Christmas Season has recently taken on much more importance than even Easter. Since the Virgin Mary is Spain's patron saint, the holiday season begins with the Feast of the Immaculate Conception on December 8 is celebrated by dancing *los Seisos*. This dance of six is performed by young boys in lavish costumes in front of Seville's Gothic cathedral. As the holiday approaches, towns and cities hold parades featuring *gigantes*, or grotesques, which are towering papier-mache and wood creatures depicting mythological or historical figures. Manned by hidden stilt-walkers, they frolic and dance through the streets. Another tradition is for friends to give each other *cestas de Navidad*, willow baskets over-flowing with hams, bottles of wine, sugared almonds, marzipan, and *turron* (an almond candy.) Companies also present these baskets to their employees. Christmas Eve, called *Noche Buena*, is a time for family reunions and family feasts. The feast may include a whole fish baked in white wine, garlic, and tomato, cold almond soup, leg of lamb or suck-ling pig. Afterwards, everyone goes to church for a special midnight mass known as *Misa del Gallo* (Mass of the Rooster), so called because it ends just before dawn when roosters crow.

Each city and region celebrate their own special fiesta, often honoring their patron saint. People love these fiestas, planning them well in advance with great enthusiasm. Activities include fireworks, bullfights, soccer matches, amusements, and dancing and parading in brightly colored regional costumes. Upward of 15 hundred fiestas are held across Spain in one year. One of the most celebrated of these fiestas is *Fiesta de San Fermin* (the Running of the Bulls) in the town of Pamplona held in July. The fiesta's most anticipated event is the *encierro*, the early morning running of six bulls through narrow cobblestone streets to the bullring. The fiesta takes all day and has three stages– first the matador tests the bull with his cape in order to get to know how the animal fights, second the picadores and banderilleros weaken the bull with their lances and darts, and third is the life-death confrontation of the bull and the matador. By the end of the day six bulls have been killed by three matadors.

In Spain, gift giving is an important facet of both socialization and busi-ness. Spaniards receive gifts from family and friends on both their birthday and their patron saint's day. In business, a gift is given <u>after</u> a relation-ship has been formed, never in the beginning as this may look like a bribe. Gifts should always be beautifully wrapped. On occasion a Spanish host will present a gift to a guest. This gift should be opened immedi-ately to show courtesy and gratitude. Be very careful about admiring someone's possessions such as a scarf or pen because the owner may feel obliged to give it as a gift. When invited to dinner at a Spaniard's house, it is appropriate to bring wine, flowers or candy. Avoid chrysan-themums and dahlias as they are associated with death and arrangements with 13 flowers are considered bad luck.

Taiwan

The Landscape

Taiwan's official name is the Republic of China. This country is small but important. It is an independent country, though it is claimed by China who, since 1949 has considered it a province of mainland China. However, Taiwan's government has the power to rule the island. Its capital is Taipei. Taiwan lies in the Pacific Ocean approximately 100 miles off the southeast coast of mainland China in East Asia. It is separated from mainland China by the Taiwan Strait. The islands of Japan are separated from Taiwan by the East China Sea. The Philippine Sea lies to the southeast. The Bashi Channel, to the south, separates Taiwan from the Philippines. The South China Sea lies to the southwest. Taiwan has two distinct regions. The eastern two thirds of the country is composed almost entirely of mountains and hills, running north to south which forms the backbone of the island. The western plains contain the country's best farmland which is where most of the Taiwanese live. The two important rivers are the Yellow River and the Yangzi River. The people settled around the basins of these rivers. Three major city areas have developed. The largest is Taipei and its port of Chi-lung in the north. Next in size are Kao-hsiung, in the southwest, and Tai-chung in the northwest.

The Economy

During the second half of the 20th century, Taiwan developed into one of Asia's leading economies. This growth was achieved through a three phase strategy. The first was the modernization of agriculture and the development of extractive industries. The second was the development of modern secondary manufacturing industries in the form of many small cottage industries. Since the system was flexible, it could easily adapt to changing global economic trends. The third, begun in 1965, was the modernization of service industries. Taiwan is in the top 20 percent of trading countries. One quarter of Taiwan's total area is arable, and all available land is fully cultivated, including sloping areas, dry riverbeds, and reclaimed tidal lands. Rice is the single most important crop. Other important crops are sugarcane, citrus fruits, corn, pineapple, sweet potatoes, and bananas. Fishing and fish farms are also important. Agriculture however, today contributes only about two percent of Taiwan's income. Manufacturing accounts for almost 40 percent of Taiwan's gross domestic product and service industries account for 60 percent. Most industries are privately run. By the late 20th century manufactured goods accounted for more than 95 percent of all exports. Major exports are appliances, computers, electronics and electrical products, machinery, clothing, textiles, toys, and communications equipment. Taiwan trades mainly with the United States, Japan, Europe, and China through Hong Kong. Taiwan's foreign reserves are among the largest in the world. It is a major international investor especially in Asia and mainland China. Taiwan's wealth allowed it to engage in a $300 billion modernization program that has significantly improved everything from schools to sewer systems and roads. Its labor force is highly skilled. Unemployment and inflation are low. The annual gross national product per capita is around $13,500. The currency is the *New Taiwan dollar* (NT$).

The People

Taiwan has a population of about 22.5 million people. The Han, or ethnic Chinese, make up about 98 percent of this population, which is divided into two groups. Early immigrants to the island from the mainland of China came mostly from the Fujian province, on the southeast coast. The Fujianese are often called the Taiwanese. The version of Chinese they speak is called the Taiwanese dialect. The Taiwanese make up most of the Han population on Taiwan, approximately 84 percent. A much smaller group of the Han population is made up of the descendants of the Chinese Nationalists who fled mainland China in 1949. These "mainlanders" as they are called, comprise about 14 percent of the population and have historically controlled much of the political power in Taiwan. They see Taiwan as a province of China, not an independent country, and themselves as the true rulers of Mainland China. The official language is Mandarin Chinese. However, most people speak Taiwanese. The remaining two percent are the original inhabitants of Taiwan known as the Malayo-Polynesian aborigines, who mostly live in the mountains today. About 75 percent of the population now live in cities and towns, which has resulted in overcrowding.

The people of Taiwan are reserved, quiet, refined, generous, and friendly. They have the same values as other Chinese. They abide by the Confucian philosophy of ancestor veneration, respect for elders, and living in harmony. It is totally unacceptable to cause anyone to "loose face". This reflects not only on the person, but also the entire family. Ninety-three percent of the people practice a religion which is a combination of Buddhism, Confucianism, and Taoism. Freedom of religion is guaranteed in Taiwan. The family is the core unit and often contains grandparents and relatives of the extended family. Moral standards are very high. Rice is eaten with almost every meal and it is impolite to leave any rice in one's bowl. Each person at the table has a personal bowl of rice. He then serves himself from dishes of vegetables and meat placed in the center of the table. Small amounts are taken as often as necessary and placed in the individual rice bowls. Often soup is also served. Meals are eaten with chopsticks and soup spoons. It never ceases to amaze me how fast my Asian friends can consume their rice with chopsticks. The bowl is held close to the mouth. Bones are placed on the table or on a plate provided for that purpose. Noodles, seafood, chicken, pork, vegetables, and fruits are frequently consumed. Sauces are also an important part of the meal. Soy milk is a common drink for breakfast. Dinner is the main meal of the day. It includes soup, rice, and meat or vegetables dishes. Most everything is stir fried. When finished, the chopsticks are placed side by side on the table. Dumplings, wanton, and spring rolls are typical Han foods.

Customs and Courtesies

Numerology plays a large role in Taiwanese day to day life. Some numbers are considered lucky and some are bad luck. Others derive their meaning simply from the sound. For example, the sound of "four" sounds like the word death in Chinese and is never used. The letter "F" is used instead. Addresses are chosen on the basis of numbers, as are phone numbers and license plates. Company names, wedding dates, and meeting dates and times are chosen on the basis of numerology. That is why it is necessary to have the Chinese person decide on a date and time for a business meeting. If the numbers are unlucky, the meeting will not go well. Even a child's name may be chosen according to the strokes a fortuneteller say the Chinese characters should contain. Here are some of the significant numbers to remember. Gifts are **never** given in groups of four (*Si*) as it is considered a particularly bad omen. Six (*Lin*) represents the six Chinese elements of nature (wind, mountain, river, lightning, moon, and sun) and is a very lucky number. Eight (*Ba*) sounds like the Chinese word for "prosperity" and is favored as part of a business address. Thirteen (*Shi san*) is considered unlucky just as it is in Western cultures.

The Lunar New Year is the country's biggest holiday. Technically it falls on the first moon of the first month. Very little gets done during the weeks before and after this three-day event. Visitors can forget making hotel and airline reservations if they have not made them a year in advance because this is the time many Taiwanese living abroad choose to reunite with friends and family. Rates can also double or triple during this season. New clothes are worn, debts are paid off, ancestors remembered, and relatives paid visits. Lots of family games are played, gifts are distributed and many companies pay double wages or large yearly bonuses. Small red envelopes, filled with paper money in even denominations, are given to children and service personnel. Holiday banquets usually feature fish because fish (*yu*) sounds like surplus (*yu*) or prosperity. It is a great honor to be invited to one of these banquets. Other official holidays include Founding Day on January 1, Youth Day on March 29, Chiang Kai-shek's death on April 5, the Birth of Confucius and Teacher's Day on September 28, Double Ten National Day on October 10, Sun Yat-sen's Birthday on November 12, and Constitution Day on December 25. The summer Dragon Boat Festival and the Mid-summer Festival are two other important annual celebrations.

Giving a gift is a way of showing appreciation for a job well done, reinforcing a friendship, or expressing a desire for a prosperous future to the receiver. The Taiwanese love to give gifts in accordance with their religious and philosophical approach to life that requires a charitable and ungreedy approach to material goods. Gifts should always be given and received with both hands. Gifts are never opened in front of the person. This saves one from looking disappointed in front of the other person. The value of the gifts given and received should be comparable. Gifts should never be wrapped in black or white. These colors are reserved for funerals. They should be wrapped in red, gold, pink, or yellow as these are auspicious colors. Red is used for wedding invitations, implying a promise of success. If you are fortunate enough to receive this invitation, do not even consider declining it. It is virtually a cultural subpoena. And even if you cannot attend, you are still required to send a wedding present of cash only. A standard gift might be $38 per person, but do not round it off to $40 or any amount with a 4 in it as this is considered to be a very unlucky number. Funeral invitations come in a white envelope and a gift of money should be sent in a white envelope even if you are unable to attend. Again, a gift of $38 is standard. If attending a funeral one should wear black because only close relatives wear white. It is important to note that weddings and funerals can only be performed on days with lunar or numerological significance which means a funeral could be delayed weeks or even months after someone's death.

Thailand

The Landscape

Officially the Kingdom of Thailand, a constitutional monarchy, Thailand lies in the heart of Southeast Asia and extends down the Malaysian Peninsula. It is bordered by Myanmar on the west and northwest, Laos on the north and east, Cambodia on the southeast, and the Gulf of Thailand and Malaysia on the south. The central region contains much fertile agricultural land as well as Bangkok, the capital and largest city. Bangkok is a key point on round-the-world air routes. It is also the political, commercial, cultural, and transportation center of the country. The north is mountainous with thick forests containing primarily teak. Overcutting has decreased these forest reserves. Rice paddies are cultivated along river banks and in the central part of the country. The southward extension into the Malay Peninsula gives Thailand long coastlines on the Gulf of Thailand and on the Andaman Sea. The Peninsular Thailand in the south is mountainous and covered with jungles. This is the principal source of rubber and tin, making Thailand a major world producer of both. Chief towns of the peninsula are Hat Yai and Songkhla, (the second largest port in the country), and the port of Bangkok (the largest on the

Chao Phraya River). Thailand's inland waterways are a complex, inter-connected system of rivers, streams, and canals. Even today barges and boats carry over half of the cargo moved in the central plain. Thailand has a tropical and monsoonal climate.

The Economy

The economy is heavily agricultural, employing about 70 percent of the work force. Rice is by far the leading crop. In fact Thailand is the world's leading exporter of rice. Industry is growing and employs about 11 percent of the work force as well as producing the bulk of Thailand's export earnings. Other commercial crops are rubber, sugarcane, corn, tapioca, kenaf, cotton, jute, and fish. Fish provides most of the protein in the diet. Marine and fresh water fisheries are important as are deep-sea catches including mackerel, shark, shrimp, and crab which are main export items. Thailand is also a major exporter of farmed shrimp. Iron ore, gold, and precious and semiprecious stones (especially sapphires and rubies) are mined on a smaller scale. Industry is chiefly centered on the processing of agricultural products such as rice milling and sugar refining. Tourism is a leading source of foreign exchange and handicraft produc-tion has a ready market in the tourist trade. Thailand also has a substantial hydroelectric potential which is being developed. Projects have been constructed on the Ping, Melong, Phong, and Songkhram rivers. During the 1980s and 1990s, electronics became an important product causing a substantial rise in the per capita GDP. Electric appliances and integrated circuits are part of the country's manufacturing base. Thailand's real gross domestic product per capita is $7,104 which has dramatically increased in the last decade. However, poverty affects about one third of the rural population, though it is declining in the urban areas. The currency is the *baht* (B).

The People

Thailand has a population of 61.2 million. Less than one fourth of the population lives in cities. Bangkok's population varies from five to nine million depending on the time of year. The great flux in numbers is caused by the constant movement of migrant workers. Thailand is an ethnically heterogeneous nation, in spite of Thais constituting 85 percent of the population. The ethnic groups can be divided into three categories: Thais, Hill Peoples of the north, and Chinese and minorities in the south. The Chinese minority is large, accounting for almost 15 percent of the population. Local trade is chiefly in the hands of the Chinese and as a consequence there is considerable tension between the Thais and Chinese. The Central Thai comprise about 32 percent of the population. Because a Central Thai identity is prestigious, Central Thai retain their identity whether they live in the central regions or elsewhere in the country. The second largest Thai group is the Hill peoples of the north who comprise about 30 percent of the population. They are also known as the Northeast Thai or Thai Lao indicating their similarity to the Lao across the border. They live mainly in the poor northeast region where they subsist by growing rice and other crops and tending cattle and water buffalo. Other minorities are Muslim Malays found in the southern peninsula, Cambodians found in the southeast and on the Cambodian border, and the Vietnamese (chiefly recent refugees who live along the Mekong River). Thai is the official language and the Central Thai dialect the major form taught in schools and used in all official affairs, although minorities generally speak their own languages. English predominates among the Western languages.

Thailand means "Land of the Free." Thailand is the only country in Southeast Asia that was never colonized by European powers. Thailand also means "The Land of Smiles". The Thai are a people of laughter with a pleasant, smiling attitude that life is to be enjoyed and that problems and setbacks should not be taken too seriously. They have a deep respect for their King and Queen who should never be maligned, even with humor. One does not conduct oneself in a loud or boisterous way in public or disrupt a sense of harmony by criticism. Education has been a priority of the government. Western style education was introduced in the early twentieth century. Therefore, education is free and compulsory through the sixth grade. The educational process is extremely competitive, even in elementary grades in Bangkok. It is similar to Japan's system in that one's quality of life depends on one's quality of education. Even to enter grade one, many private schools set up their own exams for children who are often prepared by enterprising enthusiastic upper and middle class parents. Other than exams, the most notorious way to enter many famous private schools comes from "donations" or money under the table. Although the literacy rate is 94 percent, school attendance drops about 50 percent in secondary education. Entrance exams for government universities are brutal with only ten percent of applicants actually being accepted. Therefore, many go to private colleges and universities or attend a number of vocational schools around the country. It is very fashionable for students from upper and middle classes to study abroad, especially in America.

Thai cuisine, known for its great variety and tastiness, is one of the best in the world. It is a mixture of Mon, Lao, Chinese, and Indian cooking. An important part of Thai cuisine is the chilies and spices used that give its unique taste. Also many delicious tropical fruits are part of this cuisine. Authentic preparation and cooking of many dishes can be very complicated and time consuming. Rice is usually the main course with side dishes of meat and vegetables. Glutinous or sticky rice is generally eaten with the fingers, while noodles are eaten with chopsticks, and general food is eaten with a spoon and fork. Although the norm is three meals a day, the Thai love to eat whenever they like and have perfected the art of snacking. In urban areas one can find something to eat 24 hours a day. *Yum,* a category of hot and sour salads, can take up as much as a page on a restaurant's menu. *Yumwunsen,* vermicelli salad, is usually cooked with minced meats or fish and mixed together with a fish sauce, lime juice, sugar and fresh chilies. The real taste of the it comes from adding fresh celery, mint, and basil leaves. Many other *Yum* can be created with different meats and vegetables.

Customs and Courtesies

More than 95 percent of Thais are Buddhists and regional people adhere to their own religious traditions. About four percent of the population are Muslims, most in the south. A mixture of Theravada Buddhism, Hinduism, and animism is the core of Thai beliefs, cosmology, and cultures. Many Chinese Thais follow Mahayana Buddhism, Confucianism, and ancestor worship. Animism is pervasive in which spirits are believed to inhabit almost everything such as living trees, houses, earth, etc.; all these forms of life can help or harm humans. Many Thai wear small, good luck Buddhist amulets that have been blessed by monks to keep away evil spirits. Never ask to touch someone's amulet. Tattoos are also thought to have similar powers. Tribe members who convert to Buddhism believe that tattoos will free them from their ancestor spirits. Spirit houses can be seen everywhere including in houses, neighborhood communities, office buildings, shopping malls, and hotels. Numerous cults have emerged, especially among the urban middle class, to meet the spiritual needs of the people. Some Buddhist sects and temples (*wats*) have become large, politically involved, business-like organizations.

Most holidays are of a religious or royal nature. *Songkran,* the Thai New Year, is held April 13 through 15. It is derived from Hindu astrology and is the longest holiday of the year. Traditionally, it is a time for cleaning Buddha images, returning home to visit relatives and the graves of ancestors, presenting small gifts, and blessing friends and relatives by sprinkling a little white powder and then a little perfumed water on them. Today, the celebration has become a mass water fight leaving everyone soaked. Westerners are a prime target for buckets of cold water or high-powered water pistols, sometimes with clay added to the mixture. It is clearly the messiest holiday in Thailand. *Loy Krathong* is an animistic holiday which takes place on a full moon in October or November when the rivers are at their height. This festival is celebrated to appease the water spirits to give them plenty of water and prevent floods throughout the year. Lit candles, coins, and flowers are set afloat in banana-leaf boats (*krathong*), creating magical scenes throughout the country. The Chinese New Year in mid-February is not an official holiday, but it is a big festival among those who have Chinese ancestors, which includes much of

Bangkok. This holiday and *Songkran* are two times of the year when very little gets accomplished in Bangkok. Other holidays are the birth-days of the King (December 5 and Queen (August 12, Chulalongkorn Day (October 23 honoring the "beloved monarch" who abolished slavery and introduced many reforms, Royal Ploughing Ceremony (May 11, and Coronation Day (May 5. Gift-giving is a integral part of Thai life. Refusing a gift is an extreme insult. Western rules against being "corrupted" by gifts from business contacts are considered rude and uncouth. Thai life is still communitarian, with the workplace being an extension of village life. This separation of business from pleasure and of business relation-ships from friendships strikes Thais as unnatural. Thais love beauty so gifts should be wrapped exquisitely in vibrant colors. Gifts should have good quality, but not be overly expensive. They should be given in person, not sent. When invited to someone's home bring something for the whole family such as nice chocolates or a souvenir from your country, or nice fruit. Roses and tulips are also fine, but carnations and marigolds are for funerals and lotus flowers are for temple offerings.

Vietnam

The Landscape

The Socialist Republic of Vietnam consists of the former Democratic Republic of Vietnam, or North Vietnam, and the former Republic of Vietnam, or South Vietnam, which were reunited in 1976. It is located in the eastern part of the Indochinese Peninsula in Southeast Asia and has a coastline of almost 1,440 miles, much of which faces the South China Sea. It is bordered by China on the north, Cambodia and Laos on the west, the Gulf of Tonkin on the east, and the South China Sea on the south. The country has six island groups and 14 separate mountain ranges. Northern Vietnam is quite mountainous. The population is concentrated in the two main river deltas, the Red River in the north and the Mekong River in the south. South of the Red River delta are the Central Lowlands, a narrow coastal strip where short, often torrential rivers, flowing from west to east, form fertile deltas. Along the Western edge of the country are hills and densely forested highlands. The south-ernmost part of the country is dominated by another lowland that is much more extensive than the one in the north created by the Mekong River. This area with its warm climate and rich alluvial soil is ideal for wet rice cultivation. Some of these areas support two rice crops per year.

The Economy

Once war-torn and ruled by a rigid central government, Vietnam has made progress over the past ten years in moving from a planned economy to a market economy, opening up to foreign investment, maintaining consistent rapid growth, and now targeting entry into the World Trade Organization by 2005. Growth in GDP has been in excess of five percent for the last three years. However, it has a long way to go before catching up with its neighboring Southeastern Asian countries. A long-awaited bilateral agreement normalizing trade relations with the United States was signed in 2000 and became fully effective in 2002. Vietnam's exports to the United States have begun to expand rapidly under the new agreement. Imports are also rising rapidly driven by foreign investment and rising consumer spending.

Agriculture is the mainstay of the economy, employing two thirds of the workforce. The main products are rice and fish. The deltas of the Red and Mekong rivers, as well as other lowlands, are the prime rice growing regions. Other crops include corn, sweet potatoes, and cassavas. The fishing industry has considerable potential in the rich offshore fishing grounds. A variety of fish species are caught in addition to prawns, lobsters, and crayfish. The heavy industrial base is concentrated in the north. Vietnam's primary export industry is mining. Large amounts of coal and sizable deposits of phosphates, manganese, bauxite, chromate, and other metal ores are produced. Machine tools, iron, steel, and fertilizer operations also contribute to this sector. Light manufacturing and processed agriculture products are focused in the south such as textiles and apparel.

Vietnam is developing a young, well-educated, energetic workforce in urban areas, many of whom desire to be traders or business entrepreneurs, so many small shops are opening throughout the country. Entrepreneurs have turned Ho Chi Minh City (formerly Saigon) into a bustling commercial center. Even Hanoi is becoming more cosmopolitan and business oriented. These young people do not want to work for the government, which desperately needs talented people to improve Vietnam's education, health, and bureaucracy. The PPP gross national income per capita in 2002 was $2,240. The currency is the *dong* (D).

The People

Vietnam had a population of 81 million in 2002. Eighty-eight percent of the population is ethnic *Kinh,* or Vietnamese. About two percent of the population is Chinese living mostly in urban areas, who form an important merchant class. There is a significant population of Cambodians near the Cambodian border and at the mouth of the Mekong River. There are also about 50 minority groups who live in the highlands, each with its own language and culture. Vietnamese is the official language, but many minorities speak their own language at home. The language has been influence by classical Chinese more than any other language, although it contains traces of Mon-Khmer (Cambodian), Thai, and other Southeast Asian dialects. To the Vietnamese their language has the sound of poetry and much of their literature is indeed poetry. More than 35 percent of the population is younger than age 15. The majority live in rural regions with about five million living in Ho Chi Minh City (formerly Saigon) and three million in Hanoi. There are a large number of immigrant and refugee communities in the United States and elsewhere.

The Vietnamese lived under Chinese domination for a thousand years. Vietnam's legacy from China continues to today and includes ideas about government, philosophy, script, education, religion, crafts and literature. They have a deep sense of national pride and independence. They have a great respect for hierarchy and take care to demonstrate respect to all they consider their superiors and demand respect from those they consider their inferiors. Children respect their teachers and elders. The Vietnamese have very high morals. They value marital fidelity, civility, generosity, gentleness, reserve, modesty, and hard work. The lazy, selfish, and disloyal are despised. Neighbors help each other, families support each other, and there is a tremendous hope for a future of wealth and security. Because they have struggled and been at war for so many years, today they believe in forgetting about the past and focusing on the present and the future.

The Vietnamese see their family as the most important element of their lives. Families are patriarchal with the mother being in charge of the care of the children and working beside her husband in the fields. One of the major problems in the country is the high growth rate in the population. Many families have four or five children, sometimes even many more. Children are seen as a valuable assets who can help in the fields, do chores around the home, and help care for the elderly. Many have extended families that include grandparents, aunts and uncles. The youngest son inherits the parental home and is obliged to care for his elderly parents. Individuals are identified primarily by their patrilineal ties and larger kin groups are defined through the men. Thus are considered either the mother of a male child or the wife of a husband. While womanhood is idealized, romanticized, and serenaded, men still have more rights and opportunities. Children begin school at age five and most complete their elementary schooling in five years. The government offers twelve years of free schooling, but for many parents the cost of school books and the loss of earning power when a child is in the classroom is too large a burden for a child to attend a secondary school for four additional years. If the child can pass an examination, he can then go on to high school. High school graduates are considered fortunate because they can receive better jobs with higher pay and more respect. University education is free to qualified students, but there is stiff competition for very limited space. The government has begun allowing students who can afford tuition, and do not qualify for a government subsidy, to enter a university as a paying student. There are three private universities. Most students who receive higher degrees live in urban areas.

Vietnamese cuisine has a reputation throughout the world for being one of the greatest cuisines in the world. Combining French and Chinese traditions, this cuisine in upper-class homes has a rich sophistication that rivals Chinese and Thai cooking. It is known for its delicacy of taste. Food is purchased on a daily basis and many vegetables and fruits are home grown. Vegetables include bamboo shoots, soybeans, sweet potatoes, corn, greens of various kinds, onions and other root crops. Fruits include bananas, coconuts, mangos, mangosteens, and pineapple. Noodle dishes are also popular. Rice is eaten at virtually every meal including breakfast. Rice is also eaten with leafy green vegetables or in soup. Fresh fish is readily available. Fish is almost as important as rice and very plentiful from the sea, rivers with their numerous tributaries, streams, and channels. There are plentiful varieties of fish which are often fresh or dried. Many dishes are prepared with a traditional liquid sauce made from fermented fish called *nuoc mam*. A distinctive Vietnamese dish is *pho*, a hot soup containing any variety of noodles in sauce with vegetables, onions, and meat or fish. Another favorite dish is *cha gio*, thin rice paper rolls filled with noodles, pork, crab, eggs, mushrooms, and onions. These tightly packed rolls are then deep fried. Fowl such as chicken, ducks, and geese add protein to the diet. Pork and beef are only consumed by the wealthy and on special occasions. The Vietnamese love to charcoal-broil filleted fish. They drink tea with their meals and throughout the day and evening. When entertaining, they will serve their guests rice wine, beer, soft drinks or coffee.

The Vietnamese eat three times a day using chopsticks and rice bowls. Each member of the family sits on a mat or a table, each holding a bowl of rice. It is considered lazy to eat from a rice bowl on the table. In the middle are several bowls of vegetables in sauce and or a plate of fried vegetables or meat. Using chopsticks, each member takes a bit from the communal dish, alternating with bites from his or her own bowl of rice. Soups are eaten with large spoons. One never leaves food in one's rice bowl, but no one takes the last bit from the communal bowls. Westerners may be horrified at their table manners. Vietnamese eat loudly, slurping, sucking, chomping which is considered evidence that people are enjoying their food.

Customs and Courtesies

About 55 percent of Vietnamese practice Buddhism, while twelve percent are Taoist and approximately 7 percent are Roman Catholic. Many practice a combination of various religions. The *Cao Daism* religion combines elements of belief and practice from Buddhism, Christianity, and Taoism. Revered saints include Jesus Christ, Buddha, Joan of Arc, Charlie Chaplin, Victor Hugo, and Napoleon Bonaparte. Those who believe in Cao Daism believe they are combining the best of all the world's religions. However, the philosophy Confucianism has enormous influence throughout the country. Confucianism emphasizes good behavior, education, and respect for hierarchy. Taoism emphasizes beliefs in the spirit world and ancestor worship. It also includes belief in geomancy, which focuses on the importance of aligning human objects and activities with the landscape. A father's grave must face the proper direction or his son will suffer. The Vietnamese Buddhists believe in reincarnation and karmic destiny, which is the belief that human reap what they sow. Different Buddhist sects exist in the country, including a group call the *Hoa Hao*, each emphasizing a different aspect of the religion. Most homes have an altar to their ancestors which holds a small vase of flowers, some incense, a plate of food, and candles. On the first and middle days of each lunar month these objects will be placed on the altar and incense and prayers will be offered up to the ancestors for support in overcoming misfortunes and obtaining good luck.

There are eleven major lunar holidays in Vietnam, but the major one is the Lunar New Year (*Tet Nguyen Dan*) which occurs on the first full moon of the new year in late January or early February. Most Vietnamese save their money all year for this national equinox festival. The festival will last anywhere from three days to two weeks. It is estimated that as many as 40,000 return to their ancestral home each year to celebrate. Offices, farm production, government, and businesses all grind to a halt for the celebration. Old debts are settled, houses are cleaned, and new clothes bought. People ask for forgiveness from one another, gifts are exchanged, children receive "lucky money" in red envelopes, and banquets are lavish. Every household buys a pair of watermelons; the redder the fruit, the luckier the family will be in the coming year. Be prepared to dine endlessly and richly as the Vietnamese like to show their generosity and culture to foreigners. Items such as tea, kumquat trees, candied ginger or coconut, and flowering peach or apricot branches, are all believed to bring good fortune. *Banh chung* (rice cakes filled with pork and mung beans) are a particular treat. *Tet trund nguyen* is another significant holiday celebrated on the full moon of the seventh lunar month. It is a day to pardon the sins of the dead by reading the *Vu Lan* (Buddhist prayer book).Other holidays include International New Year's Day on January 1, Labor Day on May 1 and September 2, the day Ho Chi Minh declared independence.

Vietnamese Americans

Before 1970 only about 3,788 Vietnamese had immigrated to the US. The first real wave of Vietnamese immigration began on April 30, 1975. By the end of that year some 130,000 Vietnamese refugees had entered the United States. These early refugees tended to be well educated and wealthy and were high ranking military and government officials. Because of the US's involvement in the Vietnam War, the government felt responsible for South Vietnam refugees. Congress passed the Indochina

Refugee Act in 1975 allowing up to 200,000 Southeast Asians to enter the country. It also allocated $405 million in resettlement aid to help them start a new life in America. The situation in Vietnam worsened and some 85,000 refugees climbed into boats in 1978 to cross the sea to safety. These folks became known as the "boat people." In 1980 Congress passed the Refugee Act allowing more Vietnamese refugees to enter the country. This second wave, comprised of 95,000 in 1980 and 86,000 in 1981, was allowed to enter the United States. The Orderly Departure Program was put into effect in 1982 to reduce the number of people risking their lives in boats to escape Vietnam. Between 1983 and 1991 another 66,000 Vietnamese entered the US. In 1987 Congress passed the Amerasian Homecoming Act to help Amerasian teenagers (the children of Viet-namese women and American military men) and their families immigrate to the US. By 1991 the total estimated Vietnamese Americans was 850,000 of which about 250,000 were American born. (Worldmark P 442).

The government attempted to spread these refugees throughout the country by providing a sponsor for each one. The sponsor was respon-sible for helping them learn English and adapt to a new way of life. However, family and kinship groups are very important to traditional Vietnamese, so they began a secondary migration with the US to rejoin their families. A large number of them have settled in "Little Saigons" south of Los Angeles, California and south of Houston, Texas. Although there are not many Catholics in Vietnam, about 40 percent of Vietnamese-Americans are Roman Catholic. This is due both to the high percentage of Roman Catholics among the first wave of refugees and the involve-ment of the Roman Catholic organizations in refugee resettlements. There are now about 100 Vietnamese-American Catholic communities, with 22 official parishes, and over 800 Vietnamese American priests and nuns in the US. However, most Vietnamese-Americans are Buddhist of the "Northern School," also known as Mahayana Buddhism. Their biggest holiday is *Tet*, the Vietnamese New Year. Since every Vietnamese has two birthdays, their personal birthday and *Tet*. *Tet* has become a community-wide birthday party.

One of the biggest issues with Vietnamese-Americans is child abuse. Corporal punishment is an accepted and expected mode of discipline in traditional Vietnamese families. Current American culture regards physical beatings as child abuse. Therefore, cross-cultural conflicts occurs regularly between Vietnamese-American parents and non-Vietnamese teachers, social workers, neighbors, and others. Now these children are beginning to ask for help from teachers and police. It is important to understand one of the Vietnamese healing methods. It is that of rubbing tiger balm into the skin with the rough edge of a coin which leaves marks that are sometimes misinterpreted by other Americans as signs of child abuse. It is also important that Americans understand that Vietnamese cuisine contains large amount of garlic and hot peppers, so much so that

Vietnamese-American exude the garlic odor. This can be very offensive to the American nose. The Vietnamese American have had to learn to reduce their garlic intake in the interest of wider community relations.

Vietnamese-Americans describe themselves as *tran can cu,* which expresses a combination of hard work, persistence, ambition, and patience. They have been very successful in family-run businesses including restaurants, specialty grocery stores, laundries, tailor shops, convenience stores, beauty salons, car repair garages, and real estate offices. The US Census Bureau counted a total of 25,671 Vietnamese-American businesses throughout the United States in 1987, with combined receipts equaling $1.36 billion.

Wales

The Landscape

Wales is a region of great scenic beauty. It has retained a character of its own, despite its union with England since 1536, due in large part to the Celtic culture of its people and its landscape of hills and small mountains,. Wales is bordered on the north by the Irish Sea, on the west by St. George's Channel, on the south by the Bristol Channel, and on the east by a number of English counties. It stretches 136 miles from north to south but varies in width. The north extends about 90 miles in width, the middle extends around 40 miles, and the south extends more than 100 miles from east to west. The main mountain range is the Cambrian Mountains that extends from north to south and contains the highest mountain in Wales known as, Mt. Snowdon. The Brecon Beacons is the dominant range in the south. Along the English border are smaller ranges including the Berwin Mountains, Beacon Hill, Radnor Forest, and the Black Mountains. Its wide expanse of coastline on the west varies from rugged rock scenery to stretches of golden sand. The valleys of the west coast are sheltered from the cold east winds so they have an extremely mild climate. Seaside resorts have sprung up to become the playgrounds for the tourist trade. Wales has farmland, mountains, valleys, and rivers of such scenic beauty that one fifth of the country has been designated as parkland. The Severn and Wye are two of Britain's longest rivers. They provide hydroelectric power and drinking water for the English Midlands as well as Wales. The largest lake is Bala in northern Wales. To the east of Bala is Pistyll Rhaeadr, the highest waterfall in England and Wales. The climate is mild and wet. Cardiff is the capital in the south.

The Economy

The Welsh economy had relied heavily on its coal fields until it became uneconomical to mine them. The typical deep mines could not compete with open cast mines. This long history of mining in Wales with terrible unemployment, accidents, struggles with mine owners, is a major Welsh folk memory especially in the South. During the 1980s the economy was transformed from heavy industries into light industries based around new physical infrastructure development and the attraction of investment from overseas. For much of the 1980s and early 1990, Wales was one of the most successful regions in the European Union in attracting foreign capital. Multinationals from the United States, Europe, and Japan formed alliances with companies in Wales to produce light industries in the areas of electronics, automotive parts, and chemicals. The services sector has also come to dominate local economies by attracting financial and business services companies in call center investments. The industrial wealth of Wales is concentrated in the southern counties bordering the Bristol Channel. This area has large steelworks in Port Talbot, oil refineries in Milford Haven, tinplate and copper foundries. With the migration of workers from the north to the southern industrial areas, the economy has become increasingly reliant on consumer electronics, automotive parts, chemicals, tourism, information technology, and other service-related industries. This has left North Wales sparsely populated where most of the agriculture is located. Sheep graze in large numbers on the sprawling moorlands and hill slopes. Cows are found in the lowland areas. Milk and cattle are sent to the English market. Of the small amount of farmland used to grow crops, most is used to grow barley, wheat, potatoes, and oats. Farms are generally small and many are subsidized by the government. Tourism has become one of the main industries. According to the Wales Tourism Alliance its members represent 7000 businesses of which over 95 percent are micro/small operations. Tourism accounts for 7 percent of the GDP with 10.9 million tourism trips, with a value of 2.6 billion sterling poounds. Real gross domestic product per capital in the UK is $18,620 which has more than doubled in a generation. There is an ongoing effort to close the gap between the wealthy and the poor. The currency is the *sterling pound (£)*.

The People

The population of Wales is about 2.9 million people. About half of the population lives in the industrial urban areas of the south, mainly in Cardiff, Newport, Swansea, and in the valleys to the north of these cities. The rest live in small towns and villages throughout the country. The Welsh are proud of their culture and heritage of Celtic origin. They regard themselves as a nation separate from England. The nationalist party Plaid Cymru, founded in the 1920s, had its first member elected to Parliament in 1966. At the same time the Welsh Language Society was founded which advocated the increased use and official recognition of the Welsh language and organized support for other nationalist issues. About 25 percent of the people speak Welsh and everyone speaks English which is also an official language. In 1997 the Welsh people voted to form a Welsh assembly that would give them a say in governing the country. The assembly was formed in 1999.

The Welsh are known for their warmth and hospitality. They are also emotional, inquisitive, quick-tempered, and individualistic. Local pride is well developed; every Welsh person feels a strong attachment to a particular place. Family and kinship are extremely important in Wales. In fact, Welsh loyalty is first and foremost to the family and they dote on their children. People are friendly with their neighbors and acquaintances always stop to chat, however briefly, when they encounter each other. Invitations to tea are readily extended and accepted. The Welsh wear western style clothing except during festivals. Their food in unpretentious, down-to-earth farmhouse cooking using everyday ingredients such as national vegetables and leeks. The well known Welsh Rarebit is actually a genuine Welsh dish. Of course it has nothing to do with rabbit. It consists of toast coated with a mixture of milk, eggs, cheese, and Worcestershire sauce. The cheese is a very sharp cheese. Soups and stews usually contain leeks. The Welsh are known for the excellent quality of their lamb, fish, and seafood. They are also known for their variety of hearty desserts including *bara brith* a popular bread made with raisins and currents that have been soaked in tea overnight. In Wales, lunch is called dinner and dinner is called supper. Tea can be a substantial meal in itself. The most important meal of the week is the Sunday dinner which may include a chicken or a rolled cut of meat called a "joint of beef." The Welsh eat with the knife in the right hand and the fork in the left in the continental style. People do not use fingers to pick up food. The napkin is placed on the lap; elbows are not placed on the table. Pubs are popular for socializing.

Education is important to the Welsh and follows the same pattern as that in England. Schooling is compulsory from the age of 5 until 16. Students take an exam at age 11, after which they attend either middle schools that prepare them for admission to college, comprehensive schools that provide general education, or technical schools which offer vocational training. For such a small country, Wales has an extensive university system. The University of Wales has campuses at Cardiff, Swansea, Lampeter, Bangor, and Aberystwyth and also includes the Welsh School of Medicine and the Institute of Science and Technology. The University of Glamorgan is found in Pont-y-Pridd. The national sport is Rugby also known as rugby football. Football and cricket are also popular.

The Welsh live in a modern, industrialized, Christian country. Housing differs in rural and urban areas. The Welsh usually live in houses instead of *flats* which is the English word for apartments. However in the bigger cities *flats* are common. Rural dwellers have traditionally lived in white-washed stone cottages and farmhouses. Many cottages consisted of one or two rooms with a sleeping loft accessible by a ladder from the kitchen or an outside stairway. Another type of traditional house was the long-house, a single story structure housing the family at one end and the animals at the other end. Many families have renovated their older houses by adding rooms, porches, and modern conveniences. Semi-detached, similar to the duplex in America, are also common. The coal mine areas look a little different. Because of the topography of the area, the mining towns took the form of long narrow strips along the valley beds, with houses built in terraces on the hillsides. Today, many picturesque old cottages have been turned into vacation homes.

Customs and Courtesies

John Wesley had a strong influence on the Welsh beginning in the 18th century so many Welsh are Methodists. There are also a large number of people, about 120,000, who adhere to the Anglican Church. The Presbyterian Church has some 75,000 members with 180 ministries. There is one Catholic province. The Welsh generally observe religious practices quite strictly and few people work on Sunday. Wales has the same holi-days as England. Legal holidays include New Year's Day, St. David's Day on March 1st for the patron saint of Wales, Good Friday, Easter, Easter Monday, a Spring Bank holiday (the last Monday in May or the first Monday in June), a Summer Bank Holiday (the last Monday in August or the first Monday in September), Christmas, and Boxing Day on December 26th. On St. David's Day daffodils are sold everywhere. People wear them on the lapel or decorate their homes with them in celebration of the patron saint's day. Every January, the Festival of St. Dwyhwon, is cele-brated as the patron saint of lovers. This is slowly being replaced by St. Valentine's Day.

The Welsh are a very musical people, world renowned for their Celtic music. The Welsh choral tradition includes celebrated male choirs, soloists such as Margaret Price, Geraint Evans, Bryan Terfel as well as pop vocal-ists like Tom Jones, Shirley Bassey, and Bonnie Tyler. Important cultural institutions are the Welsh Arts Council, the Welsh National Opera Company, and the National Museum of Wales. Dylan Thomas is a famous poet, and well known actors are the late Richard Burton and Sir Anthony Hopkins.

In Conclusion – Now That You Have Walked in Their Shoes

I think Dorothy Day summed up this book perfectly in her statement "The courteous gesture increases one's respect to others. To act lovingly is to begin to feel loving and certainly to act joyfully brings joy to others which in turn makes one feel joyful."(Maggio p. 19). This book is about showing respect to our visitors from other countries. In order to do this we must understand their countries and their cultures, their ways of thinking and believing, their customs and courtesies.

It occurred to me that there was a need for American librarians to better understand these other cultures. In fact that was the resounding message I received from the librarians I surveyed. I chose twenty seven developed and newly industrialized countries because people from these countries are coming to our shores on a more regular basis, some for a temporary stay, but many others on a permanent basis. As they settle in our communities, we need to accept them and help them keep their cultures alive. This really is not a new concept. We see it in the many festivals around our country: The Irish Festival, The Greek Festival, The Latino Festival, Octoberfest, Ethnic Expo, etc. The purpose of the book is to get librarians to become more pro-active with their customers. One cannot really do that unless one has a better understanding of the various cultures.

The book begins by stating the challenges we face in the library world today. One can set up an Information Booth with a person sitting there, but for the most part people will not come up to it. Many people are afraid to show their ignorance. Many are afraid they will be embarrassed if they ask the wrong question. Wal-mart has done a great job in the pro-active greeting. They really get in your face. We need to do more of that in our libraries, but not in an offensive way. Chapter One discusses how we can do this better. It talks about how we as "Roving librarians" can better interact with our clientele. We take away the barrier of the Reference Desk and try to see ourselves and our facility from the perspective of the client. This is not an easy feat. We become very vulnerable or at least have that feeling. We do not want our cozy little world shaken up by these foreigners. Well, tante pis (too bad). That is what is happening in our world.

Chapter Two discusses how we can better make our customers feel welcome. How one is greeted makes all the difference in the world in their library experience. When a person greets you with a bow, *please*, bow back! It may feel uncomfortable at first, but you will quickly adapt. If you send the signal that you are too busy or too important or not approachable, then you are and you will not be approached. In most of the countries discussed, time is not of the essence. Relationships are more important and they are built over time. If we could just take the time to learn to say "Buenos Dias" to our Latino customers, who are ever growing in numbers, it would show that you care enough to take that first step. This chapter also discusses the various gestures in the different cultures and their meanings. The two major gestures that should be avoided at all costs when dealing with people from other countries is the pointing of the index finger and the "OK" sign. Both are considered quite rude, even vulgar in some countries. It is better to point with the entire hand. The United States is no longer an isolated country. We learned this on September 11, 2001.

Chapter Three addresses the issue of respect for each other. The courteous gesture conveys respect for another human being. However, what one thinks is a courteous gesture in this country, may not be in another country. Asians do not touch; Latinos touch often. Americans think of direct eye contact as conveying respect; Asians do not. Prolonged direct eye contact with an Asian is considered rude. I have also found the age of a person is very important in certain cultures. One day there was an Asian at the circulation desk. He seemed to be having a problem with the student behind the desk. I intervened. He explained the problem to me. At that time nothing was resolved, but because I took an interest in the situation, he seemed greatly relieved to have been approached by an older person with authority.

The cultural misunderstanding between the Asian and the black student is real. It frequently happens. Many people have approached me with, as my mother would say "with a chip on their shoulder." That "chip" totally disappears as soon as they sense they are being treated with respect and care. Patience is one of the most lacking attributes in American society. One must develop a more patient attitude.

Chapter Four discusses the art of conversation. The most important issue is one of being understood. Slow down your speech. If you speak distinctly, you must slow down your speech. Give the person with whom you are speaking, time for them to comprehend what is being said. Explain your thought process. Explain what you are doing and why. Don't just walk away from a person in your search for the answer. Ask them to come with you in your search to help them. Take the time to explain the not-so-evident problem that one might encounter in your institution. Ask for a name and telephone number so that you may check to see if that book really is on the shelf and get back to them. The computer may say the book is available when in fact it is not. Take time to thoroughly analyze the situation.

International visitors have their own pre-conceived notions about who we are. Our fast-paced way of life, they see as arrogant. They see our movies and television shows and think everyone is like those people from Hollywood. They often think we are too busy to bother with them or that we sit around and read the newspaper all day long. We must change these misconceptions. We must be good-will ambassadors for our country. We can do this by successfully translating a request into the correct answer for our satisfied customers. This may mean breaking the request into segments, especially if the question is broad in nature. As someone once said, and I really do not know who it was, "You eat an elephant one bite at a time." Many people miscalculate the time required to do research or find an answer. If it is really important, they will spend the time believe me. As librarians, we can save them lots of time because we know our collections and where to find what they need. One way to better teach international students is to show them how the information is organized. A guide like the *Reader's Guide to Periodical Literature Index* can not only show them this, but can help them see other possibilities for the retrieval of the information. The same is true for us. If we are using words or phrases that are obviously not sinking in, use other terminology, similar phrases they may better understand. Instead of using "ascertain", a word I love, use "determine".

The second most important aspect of Chapter Four is to realize the customer is not an expert in using the facility in which you are the expert. We must approach our customers as if they were stepping into our facility for the very first time. You would not expect them to be familiar with your home, if they had never visited it. Do not assume they understand any part of the library or its contents. The difficulty here lies in determining where they need clarification. You do not want to insult their intelligence or their knowledge. If you start explaining something they already know, they usually will let you know straight away. So then you can move on.

Chapter Five is about communication. In fact the whole book is about communication and cultures. Previous chapters have discussed subsets of the overall subject of communication. This chapter analyzes other ways we communicate either conscientiously or unconsciously. I was raised by the good nuns who taught us that every one is special, a unique creation of God and I see everyone that way. Because I grew up in an individualistic society, I see each person as their own being. I frequent a special restaurant here in town. What makes it so special? Everyone knows everyone. Guests are greeted with a hug by the waitress and when asked how they are doing, the guests tell them how they are doing. This is genuine caring, not just lip service.

Nothing turns a person off faster than another person's inability to listen actively. How many times have I been talking to someone, and I can just see they are not listening to a word I am saying, but waiting for me to take a breath so they can interrupt me. You know there are thousands of things going through their mind and not one is about the subject at hand. We have all experienced it. The fastest way to detect it is by asking the question, "How many times have I heard the "I" word in the space of a minute? Active listening means really hearing what the other person is saying. It is also respecting the other person.

People do not always say what they mean or mean what they say. In conversing with people from many other cultures, it is not polite to simply say, "No." There are various ways to say the same thing with different nuances. By understanding the culture, one can better understand their verbal communication. For months I have called my friend at work just to confirm a meeting place. She works in an office comprised entirely of Chinese professors and students. One student in particular was having trouble speaking over the telephone. At first it was, "No, Leslie not here." Hang up. It progressed to "May I take a message?" This took a while, then hang up. Most recently it was, "She is here somewhere, not here right now. May I take a message? I will tell her you called. Have a nice day." This is quite a feat for this student.

Avoid jokes. They do not translate well and you take great risk of insulting the other person. It is best to limit the conversation to what is pleasant for the visitor to discuss. Sports are always a safe bet. Encourage you visitors to speak out. Only by doing this over and over will they become more proficient at our language and they will gradually build their self confidence. Americans simply do not understand the concept of "Saving Face" yet it is the most important skill to learn when dealing with Asians. If this is the only thing you take away from this book, I have fulfilled my purpose. It means avoiding any kind of embarrassment, no matter how little. We, who are a country of jokes and comedy and constantly embarrassing people, just do not understand that this is not acceptable in some cultures. Exercising patience is another huge issue. One must slow down when interacting with people from other countries.

Understanding the significance of proper eye contact can not only be helpful, it can save you from a fight as in the case of the Asian student and the black student. Americans often tower over Asians in stature. Keeping your distance allows an Asian to feel actually taller than he is. Touching is seldom done in a business sitting. In Indonesia, for religious reasons, men and women do not touch in public, not even a hand shake, and one never touches anyone on the head, especially not that of a child. The rest of the chapter provides the dos and don'ts of communication on the various countries taken from the web site

Chapter Six is about etiquette. Many a business deal has fallen apart because there was a lack of knowledge of proper etiquette. It is defined as the forms prescribed by custom or authority to be observed in social, official, or professional life. Learn the customs of the country with which you are dealing. The Asian American Services Committee of the Chicago Public Library has a web page on Asian Etiquette: www.chipublib.org/003cpl/asian_heritage/committee/etiquette.html. Etiquette requires a sensitivity of the situation at hand. Throughout the book I have talked about table manners. If you are invited to dine in another's home or at a ethnic restaurant, observe your host and follow suite. Be as generous with your time as possible. Most importantly, be considerate of others less fortunately placed than you, especially with those in your or others employ. They deserve our respect. Etiquette is not one-upmanship.

Etiquette entails observing your surroundings. It means dressing in professional business attire if that is the setting in which you find yourself. It means being gracious. It means possessing social skills. Jacqueline Kennedy was the very essence of etiquette. When she went to France, she spoke French. She gave elegant dinner parties. She followed diplomatic protocol to the letter. She wore beautiful and very conservative clothes. She taught us the importance of being polite to everyone. She inspired us to strive to become the best we could become. Our hair found new styles, our hats found new homes on our heads, not in the closet. Properly answering the telephone became crucial. We wore hats and gloves to church. We wore evening attire to attend the theater. We partied, but in a socially responsible way. Etiquette is simply knowing the rules of proper civil behavior.

Chapter Seven deals with diplomacy. When one thinks of diplomacy one thinks of international negotiations or the diplomatic core and foreign policies. I am using it in the library setting in the context of tact, negotiations in the reference interview with international visitors. It is a sort of sign language which tells a distinguished person that he is recognized for what he is and what he represents. It means going that extra mile to help those in most need of your help. It often means making exceptions, bending the rules, reaching out that hand of understanding. I discuss the power of observation as opposed to just seeing. This allows one freedom from judgement. It gives us the ability to step back so we can see the full truth.

The spirit of application means doing the task at hand right now, not five or ten minutes from now. It means actually applying oneself to the task at hand, to be fully engaged. The negotiator must possess that penetration which enables him to discover the thoughts of men and to know by the least movement of their countenances what passions are stirring within. This means understanding when a student is on the verge of tears or when someone is truly frustrated beyond the point of accepting any help. These can be difficult times when a patron has to be educated about the system or informational structure. With diplomacy we smooth away difficulties, we apologize, we try to make things right. With diplomacy we maintain a tranquil and patient nature. We remain open to suggestions, complaints, all comments whether they make us feel good or bad. Robert Frost once said, "Education is the ability to listen to almost anything without loosing your temper or your self-confidence." That's diplomacy.

Chapter Eight is about the latest and most important trend coming down the track for librarians. We now need to assess, like faculty, our students' learning, not our teaching ability. This new way of doing things is part of the core of this book. If students are not learning from the lecture mode, then try another way. Many international students have been taught by the rote method. They simply repeat what they have been taught to memorize. They are taught not to question their teachers. In this country, students are taught critical thinking. However, if they have not learned the material, how can they think critically about its validity? Students are given the assignment to find an article on an industry, not companies in the industry. Demonstrating on the screen the difference in the articles helps them comprehend the differences in the information. Walking someone through the process of how a resource works cuts the learning time in half.

Another important aspect in working with international visitors is to repeat what you have said in several different ways. If they do not understand what is being said in one way, they may well understand it in another way. "Hi Jack!" and "Hijack!" have two very different meanings. Become pro-active, yes even to the point of pushy. In my example I did not leave the patron alone until I knew he knew how to manipulate the database. I take the time to make sure the patron knows what he is doing regardless of the resource. This takes time, but the student waiting for your help knows that if you are taking that much time with this student, you will also take that kind of time with him. He then becomes patient. If you are impatient, he will also sense that. I end the chapter on being user friendly: When you arrive at work, greet others with "hello" or "good morning." Check to make sure you are actually doing this, you may think you are when in actuality you are not. Use the 10 to 5 feet rule. Acknowledge someone 10 feet from you, greet someone 5 feet from you. And finally, do say "goodbye" at the end of the day, even if you have to acknowledge you are leaving a little early.

Chapters Nine and Ten are about the cultures of the 27 countries covered: Argentina, Brazil, Canada, China, England, France, Germany, Hong Kong, India, Indonesia, Ireland, Israel, Italy, Japan, Mexico, Philippines, Poland, Russia, Scotland, Singapore, South Africa, South Korea, Taiwan, Thailand, United States, Vietnam, and Wales. It describes their homeland, their economy, the people, their family life, their educational structure, their religions, holidays, and superstitions, and their customs and courtesies. There is a short history of each ethnicity, different tribes and languages spoken. Included also are the folklore, beliefs, and magical practices of the various countries. I have mentioned major festivals and their significance to the country's life. Also described are the various ways of dressing, the reasons for that attire, and costumes of a region. Colors, numbers and flowers have tremendous significance in different countries. We should know about these beliefs and abide by them. For instance, never give a gift packaged in fours to an Asian. The word for four in Chinese sounds like death. Many buildings will have a 3A or 3B floor instead of a fourth floor. Such traditions are sacrosanct.

This book is intended to be a simple primer on the different cultures. It is also meant to be used as a quick reference when you know you will be meeting with someone from another country. We must understand the values of others. Just because someone comes from a Communistic country, this does not necessarily make them an atheist. When I began this book there was very little information on the cultures of some of these countries and there still is very little written information on some of the cultures. It is my hope that this book will lead to a better understanding of those with whom we come in contact here in the United States. There does seem to be some repetition, and this is intentional. Say it once and I may hear it, say it twice and I may really hear it, say it thrice and it begins to sink in. Happy reading.

Bibliography

Abalahin, A. J. "Filipinos." *Worldmark Encyclopedia of Cultures and Daily Life.* Ed. Timothy L. Gall. Detroit: Gale, 1998. 203–212.

Abdoulaye, Kaba. "State of Library and Information Science Education in Malaysia." *Journal of Education for Library and Information Science.* 45 (1) (Winter 2004): 1–14.

Al-Amoudi Hussein. Interview. Student worker, Business Library. The Ohio State University, Columbus, Ohio, November 2004.

"Americans." *Worldmark Encyclopedia of Cultures and Daily Life.* Ed. Timothy L. Gall. Detroit: Gale, 1998. 32–39.

"Argentina." *The Columbia Encyclopedia*, 6th ed. New York: Columbia University Press, 2003. www.bartleby.com/65/. 7/21/2003.

"Argentina." *Culturgrams: the nations around us.* Chicago: Ferguson, 1997.

"Atlantic Provinces of Canada." *Culturgrams: the nations around us.* Chicago: Ferguson, 1997.

Barr, Robert B. and John Tagg. "From Teaching to Learning – A New Paradigm for Undergraduate Education." *Change.* 27 (N/D '95): 12–25.

Bell, Arthur, Ph.D. and Gary G. Williams, Ph.D. *Intercultural Business.* Barron's Educational Series, 1999.

Bilal, Danai M. "International Students' Acquisition of Library Research Skills: Relationship with Their English Language Proficiency." *The Reference Librarian* 24 (1989) : 129–145.

"Blarney Stone." *The Encyclopedia Americana: International Edition.* Danbury, CT: Grolier, 1998.

"Brazil." *The Columbia Encyclopedia*, 6th ed. New York: Columbia University Press, 2003. www.bartleby.com/65/. 7/23/2003.

"Brazil." *Culturgrams: the nations around us.* Chicago: Ferguson, 1997.

Bucher, Richard D. *Diversity Consciousness: Opening Our Minds to People, Cultures, and Opportunities.* Second Edition. New Jersey: Prentice Hall, 2004

Bundy, Alan. "Changing Lives, Making the Difference: The 21st Century Public Library." *Australasian Public Libraries and Information Services* 16(1) (Mar.2003): 38–49.

"Canada." *Britannica Elementary Encyclopedia.* 2003. Encyclopaedia Britannica Online. 10 July, 2003 http://search.eb.com/ebk/article?eu= 370941.

Carlzon, Jan. *Moments of Truth.* New York: HarperCollins Publishers, 1987.

Castaneda, S. Garcia. "Spainards." *Worldmark Encyclopedia of Cultures and Daily Life.* Ed. Timothy L. Gall. Detroit: Gale, 1998. 365–368

Cole, Gregory. *Passport Indonesia.* San Rafael, CA: World Trade Press, 1997.

"Communication." *Britannica Student Encyclopedia* from Encyclopaedia Britannica Online. 21 Oct, 2003 http://search.eb.com/ebi/article?eu= 295578.

"Communication." *Encyclopaedia Britannica.* 2003. Encyclopaedia Britannica Online. 21 Oct. 2003 http:// search.eb.com/eb/article?eu= 25393.

Curry, Jeffrey and "Jim" Chinh Nguyen. *Passport Vietnam.* San Rafael, CA: World Trade Press, 1997.

Daeg de Mott, D. K. "African Americans." *Worldmark Encyclopedia of Cultures and Daily Life.* Detroit: Gale, 1998. 11–14.

Daeg de Mott, D. K. "American Immigrants." *Worldmark Encyclopedia of Cultures and Daily Life.* Detroit: Gale, 1998. 24–31.

Daeg de Mott, D. K. "Chinese Americans." *Worldmark Encyclopedia of Cultures and Daily Life.* Detroit: Gale, 1998. 107–110.

Daeg de Mott, D. K., "Vietnamese Americans." *Worldmark Encyclopedia of Cultures and Daily Life.* Detroit: Gale, 1998. 442–444.

David M. Kennedy Center for International Studies, Brigham Young University. *Culturgrams: the nations around us.* Chicago: Ferguson, 1997.

De Callieres, Monsieur. *On The Manner of Negotiating With Princes.* Notre Dame, IN: University of Notre Dame Press, 1963.

"Diplomacy." *The Encyclopedia Americana*. International Edition. Danbury, CT.: Grolier Incorporated, 1998: 141–150.

Dougherty, Richard M. "Getting a Grip on Change." *American Libraries* 28 (August 1997) : 40–42.

Duvall, Lynn. *Respecting Our Differences: a guide to getting along in a changing world*. Minneapolis, Mn: Free Spirit, 1994.

Engel, Dean & Ken Murakami. *Passport Japan*. San Rafael, CA: World Trade Press, 1996.

Engel, Dean William. *Passport USA*. San Rafael, CA: World Trade Press, 1997.

"England." *Culturgrams: the nations around us*. Chicago: Ferguson, 1997.

Ferraro, Gary. Fourth Edition. *The Cultural Dimension of International Business*. New Jersey: Prentice Hall, 2002.

Ferraro, Gary. *Global Brains: Knowledge and Competencies for the 21st Century*. Charlotte, NC: International Associates Inc., 2002.

Flamini, Roland. *Passport Germany*. San Rafael, CA: World Trade Press, 1997.

Foster, Dean. *The Global Etiquette Guide to Mexico and Latin America: Everything You Need to Know for Business and Travel Success*. New York: John Wiley & Sons, Inc., 2002.

"France." *Culturgrams: the nations around us*. Chicago: Ferguson, 1997.

"France." *The Columbia Encyclopedia*, 6th ed. New York: Columbia University Press, 2003. www.bartleby.com/65/. 7/13/2003.

"France."*Encyclopaedia Britannica*. 2003. Encyclopaedia Britannica Online. 13 Jul, 2003. http:// search.eb.com/eb/article?eu=370970.

Francia, Luis. *Passport Philippines*. San Rafael, CA: World Trade Press, 1997.

Gall, Timothy L., ed. "Canadians." *Worldmark Encyclopedia of Cultures and Daily Life*. Detroit: Gale, 1998. 97–101.

Garcia Marco, Javier and Maria del Carmen Agustin Lacruz. "Educating the informational professional of the 21st century: A ten-point proposal based on the Spanish context." *Education for Information* 18(2/3) (Oct. 2000): 141–53.

Gendzier, S. "French." *Worldmark Encyclopedia of Cultures and Daily Life*. Detroit: Gale, 1998.

Gioseffi, Claudia. *Passport Italy*. San Rafael, CA: World Trade Press, 1997.

Griego, Adan and Carlos R. Delgado. "Argentina puts the library at the center of the global village." *American Libraries* 29 (6) (June/July '98): 40.

Grzeskowiak, Andrew. *Passport Hong Kong.* San Rafael, CA: World Trade Press, 1996.

Harte, L. "English." *Worldmark Encyclopedia of Cultures and Daily Life.* Detroit: Gale, 1998.

Harte, L. "Welsh." *Worldmark Encyclopedia of Cultures and Daily Life.* Detroit: Gale, 1998.

Harvey, Ross and Susan Higgins. "Defining fundamentals and meeting expectations: Trends in LIS education in Australia." *Education for Information.* 21 (2/3) (September 2003): 149–157.

Hayden, Carla D. "Library Issues are Global." *American Libraries* 34(9) (October 2003): 5.

Helms, Cynthia Mae. "Reaching Out to the International Students Through Bibliographic Instruction." *The Reference Librarian* 51/52 (1995) : 295–307.

Herrington, Elizabeth. *Passport Brazil.* San Rafael, CA: World Trade Press, 1998.

Hess, Melissa Brayer and Patricia Linderman. *The Expert Expatriate: Your Guide to Successful Relocation Abroad.* Maine: Intercultural Press, Inc., 2002.

Hodge, Sheida. *Global Smarts: The Art of Communicating and Deal Making Anywhere in the World.* New York: John Wiley & Sons, Inc., 2000.

Hofstede, Geert. *Culture's Consequences: International Differences in Work-Related Values.* London: Sage Publications, 1984.

Http://www.cyborlink.com/besite

"Indonesia." *Indonesian Business Etiquette.* Nov. 16, 2003 http:www.cyborlink.com/besite/indonesia.htm

"Ireland." *Britannica Elementary Encyclopedia.* 2003. Encyclopaedia Britannica Online. 25 Sep, 2003. http://search.eb.com/ebk/article?eu= 370991.

"Ireland." *The Columbia Encyclopedia,* 6th ed. New York: Columbia University Press, 2003. www.bartleby.com/65/. 7/13/2003.

"Ireland." *Culturgrams: the nations around us.* Chicago: Ferguson, 1997.

"Irish." *Worldmark Encyclopedia of Cultures and Daily Life.* Detroit: Gale, 1998.

James, David L. *The Executive Guide to Asia-Pacific Communications*. New York: Kodansha International, 1995.

Jablon, Judy, Amy Laura Dombro, and Margo L. Dichtelmiller. *The Power of Onservation*. Washington, D.C.: Teaching Strategies, 1999.

Jackson, Miles M., Ed. *International Handbook of Contemporary Developments in Librarianship*. Westport, CT.: Greenwood Press, 1981.

Joseph, Nadine. *Passport France*. San Rafael, CA: World Trade Press, 1997.

Joshi, Manoj. *Passport India*. San Rafael, CA: World Trade Press, 1997.

Keating, Kevin. *Passport Korea*. San Rafael, CA: World Trade Press, 1998.

Kett, Alexandra. *Passport Singapore."* San Rafael, CA: World Trade Press, 1998.

Kissel, Natalie. *Passport Poland*. Novato, CA: World Trade Press, 2000.

Kramer, Melinda G. *Business Communication in Context: Principles and Practice*. New Jersey: Prentice Hall, 2001.

Krupnik, I., Rev. "Russians." *Worldmark Encyclopedia of Cultures and Daily Life*. Detroit: Gale, 1998. 332–339.

Le Blanc, C. "China and Her National Minorities." *Worldmark Encyclopedia of Cultures and Daily Life*. Detroit: Gale, 1998. 168–175.

LeBlanc, C. "Han." *Worldmark Encyclopedia of Cultures and Daily Life*. Detroit: Gale, 1998, 243–246.

Levinson, David. *Ethnic Groups Worldwide: A Ready Reference Handbook*. Phoenix, AZ: Oryx Press, 1998.

Li, Jenny. *Passport China*. San Rafael, CA: World Trade Press, 1996.

Liu, Mengxiong. "Library Services for Ethnolinguistic Students." *Journal of Educational Media & Library Sciences* 32 (3) (1995) : 239–246.

Lott, James E. *Practical Protocol: A Guide to International Courtesies*. Houston, TX: Gulf Publishing Company, 1973.

Lurssen, N. "Colored People of South Africa." *Worldmark Encyclopedia of Cultures and Daily Life*. Detroit: Gale, 1998. 103–106.

Lurssen, N. "The English in South Africa." *Worldmark Encyclopedia of Cultures and Daily Life*. Detroit: Gale, 1998. 149–152.

Maggio, Rosalie, ed., *Women on Life: A Book of Quotations*. New York: MJF Books, 1997.

"Making Judgements and Greeting."http://www.allaboutrespect.net

Malat, Randy. *Passport Mexico*. San Rafael, CA: World Trade Press, 1996.

Mandel-Campbell, Andrea. *Passport Argentina.* Novato, CA: World Trade Press, 2000.

"Maquiladoras." *The Columbia Encyclopedia,* 6th ed. New York: Columbia University Press, 2003. www.bartleby.com/65/. 9/23/2003.

Martino, Jean-Marie. *Diversity: An Imperative for Business Success.* New York: The Conference Board, 1999.

McCook, Kathleen de la Pena, Barbara J. Ford, and Kate Lippincott. *Libraries: Globla Reach – Local Touch.* Chicago: American Library Association, 1998.

Meek, Michael. "The Peacekeepers: Students use mediation skills to resolve disputes." *Teaching Tolerance,* Fall 1992, pp. 46–52.

Micossi, Anita. "Bite the Wax Tadpole." *Corporate Legal Times.* 10 (108) (November 2000):BWB6.

Milord, Susan. *Hands Around the World: 365 Creative Ways to Build Cultural Awareness & Global Respect.* Charlotte, VT: Williamson Publishing, 1992.

Mitchell, Charles. "Passport Russia." San Rafael, CA: World Trade Press, 1998.

Mitchell, Charles. *Passport South Africa.* San Rafael, CA: World Trade Press, 1998.

Mortland, C. A. "Vietnamese." *Worldmark Encyclopedia of Cultures and Daily Life.* Detroit: Gale, 1998. 806–812.

Nicolson, Harold. *Diplomacy.* London: Oxford University Press, 1963.

Ormondroyd, Joan. "The International Student and Course-Integrated Instruction: The Librarian's Perspective." *Research Strategies* 7 (4) (Fall 1989) : 148–158.

Pachter, Barbara and Marjorie Brody. *Complete Business Etiquette Handbook.* New Jersey: Prentice Hall, 1995.

Pachter, Barbara with Susan Magee. *When the Little Things Count . . . And They Always Count.* New York: Marlowe & Company, 2001.

"People's Republic of China." *Culturgram.* Provo, UT: David M. Kennedy Center for International Studies, Brigham Young University, 1997.

"Philippines." *Britannica Student Encyclopedia.* 2003. Encyclopaedia Britannica Online. 25 Sep, 2003. http://search.eb.com/ebi/print?eu= 298457.

"Philippines." *The Columbia Encyclopedia,* 6th ed. New York: Columbia University Press, 2003. www.bartleby.com/65/. 11/24/2003.

"Philippines." *Culturgrams: the nations around us.* Chicago: Ferguson, 1997.

"Poland." The Columbia Encyclopedia, 6th ed. New York: Columbia University Press, 2003.

"Poland." Culturgrams: the nations around us. Chicago: Ferguson, 1997.

"Poland." *Britannica Student Encyclopedia.* 2003. Encyclopaedia Britannica Online. 25 Sep, 2003. http://search.eb.com/ebi/print?eu= 298556

"Poles." Worldmark Encyclopedia of Cultures and Daily Life. Detroit: Gale, 1998. 308–311.

Pitchon, P. "Argentines." *Worldmark Encyclopedia of Cultures and DailyLlife.* Detroit: gale, 1998.54–58.

Pitchon, P. "Brazilians." *Worldmark Encyclopedia of Cultures and Daily Life.* Detroit: gale, 1998.54–58.

"The Power of Observation." *Perspectives in Behavioral Performance Improvement.* (September 2002): 19.

Poytner, Don and Mindy Bingham. Fourth Edition. *Is There a book inside you?* Santa Barbara, CA: Para Publishing, 1996.

Rajanala, Dr. Venkata Satyanarayana Rao, Visiting Scholar. Interview. Senior Scientist. National Academy of Agricultural Research Management, Hyderabad, Andhra Pradesh, India 500 030. (Indian Council Agricultural Research) November 9, 2004.

Ratzek, Wolfgang. "Core Competencies of Front-Line Employees: The German Contribution to a New Service Culture." *The Reference Librarian* 75/76 (2002): 277–84.

Rhee, Siyon, Janet Chang, and Jessica Rhee. "Acculturation, Communication Patterns, and Self-Esteem Among Asian and Caucasian American Adolescents." *Adolescence* 38 (152) (Winter 2003): 2.

Riedinger, Edward A. Interview. Head of the Latin American Library Collection, The Ohio State University, Columbus, Ohio. November 2004.riedinger.4@osu.edu.

Rosenthal, Donna. *Passport Israel.* San Rafael: World Trade Press, 1997.

Rothwell, J. Dan. *In Mixed Company.* Australia: Thomson Wadsworth, 2004

"Russia." *Culturgrams: the nations around us.* Chicago: Ferguson, 1997.

"Russia." *Britannica Student Encyclopedia.* 2003. Encyclopaedia Britannica Online. 11 Dec, 2003. http://search.eb.com/ebi/print?eu=298924.

"Russia, Country Profile." *Economist Intelligence Unit Limited.* 2004. Http://db.eiu.com/reports.asp?title=Country+Profile+Russia&valname= CPRUD501&doc_i . . .

"Russian Americans." *Worldmark Encyclopedia of Cultures and Daily Life.* Detroit: Gale, 1998. 384–386

Sandy, John H. "By Any Other Name, They're Still Our Customers." *American Libraries* 28 (August 1997) : 43–45.

Schauber, Ann C. *Working With Differences in Communities.* Corvallis, OR: Oregon State University Extension Service, 2002.

"Scotland." *Britannica Elementary Encyclopedia.* 2003. Encyclopaedia Britannica Online. 25 Sep, 2003. http://search.eb.com/ebk/article?eu= 371488

"Scotland." *Britannica Student Encyclopedia.* 2003. Encyclopaedia Britannica Online. 11 Dec, 2003. http://search.eb.com/ebi/print?eu=299063.

"Scotland." *The Columbia Encyclopedia,* 6th ed. New York: Columbia University Press, 2003. www.bartleby.com/65/sc/Scotland.html. 9/25/2003.

"Scotland." *Culturgrams: the nations around us.* Chicago: Ferguson, 1997.

Shaley, C. "African Brazilians." *Worldmark Encyclopedia of Cultures and Daily Life.* Detroit: gale, 1998. 14–17.

"Singapore." *Britannica Elementary Encyclopedia.* 2003. Encyclopaedia Britannica Online. 16 Dec, 2003. http://search.eb.com/ebk/article?eu= 371107.

"Singapore." *Britannica Elementary Encyclopedia.* 2003. Encyclopaedia Britannica Online. 16 Dec, 2003. http://search.eb.com/ebk/article?eu= 371307.

"Singapore."*Britannica Student Encyclopedia.* 2003. Encyclopaedia Britannica Online. 16 Dec, 2003. http://search.eb.com/ebi/print?eu= 299196.

"Singapore." *Culturgrams: the nations around us.* Chicago: Ferguson, 1997.

Sonnenschein, William. *The Practical Executive and Workforce Diversity.* Illinois: NTC Publishing Group, 1997.

"South Africa." *Britannica Elementary Encyclopedia.* 2003. Encyclopaedia Britannica Online. 16 Dec, 2003. http://search.eb.com/ebk/article?eu= 371067.

"South Africa." *Britannica Student Encyclopedia.* 2003. Encyclopaedia Britannica Online. 16 Dec, 2003. http://search.eb.com/ebi/print?eu= 299274.

"South Africa." *Culturgrams: the nations around us*. Chicago: Ferguson, 1997.

"Spain." "Spain." *Britannica Elementary Encyclopedia*. 2003. Encyclopaedia Britannica Online. 2 Feb. 2004 http://search.eb.com/ebk/article?eu=371068.

"Spain." *Culturgrams: the nations around us*. Chicago: Ferguson, 1997.

"Spain." *Encyclopaedia Britannica*. 2004. Encyclopaedia Britannica Online. 2 Feb. 2004 http:// search.eb.com/eb/article?eu=115197.

"Spain." *Encyclopaedia Britannica*. 2004. Encyclopaedia Britannica Online. 2 Feb. 2004 http:// search.eb.com/eb/article?eu=115198.

"Spain." *Encyclopaedia Britannica*. 2004. Encyclopaedia Britannica Online. 2 Feb. 2004 http:// search.eb.com/eb/article?eu=115201.

"Spain." *Encyclopaedia Britannica*. 2004. Encyclopaedia Britannica Online. 2 Feb. 2004 http:// search.eb.com/eb/article?eu=115201.

Storti, Craig. *Cross-Cultural Dialogues: 74 Brief Encounters with Cultural Difference*. Yarmount, Maine: Intercultural Press, 1994.

"Taiwan." *The Columbia Encyclopedia,* 6th ed. New York: Columbia University Press, 2003 www.bartleby.com/65/sc/Scotland.html. 2/19/2004.

"Taiwan." *Culturgrams: the nations around us*. Chicago: Ferguson, 1997.

"Taiwan." *Encyclopaedia Britannica*. 2004. Encyclopaedia Britannica Online. 19 Feb. 2004 http:// search.eb.com/eb/article?eu=115303.

"Taiwan." *Encyclopaedia Britannica*. 2004. Encyclopaedia Britannica Online. 19 Feb. 2004 http:// search.eb.com/eb/article?eu=115304

"Taiwan." *Encyclopaedia Britannica*. 2004. Encyclopaedia Britannica Online. 19 Feb. 2004 http:// search.eb.com/eb/article?eu=371077.

"Thailand." *The Columbia Encyclopedia,* 6th ed. New York: Columbia University Press, 2003 www.bartleby.com/65/sc/Scotland.html. 2/19/2004.

"Thailand, Kingdom of." *Culturgram*. Provo, UT: David M. Kennedy Center for International Studies, Brigham Young University, 1997.

"Thailand." *Encyclopaedia Britannica*. 2004. Encyclopaedia Britannica Online. 19 Feb. 2004 http:// search.eb.com/eb/article?eu=120920

"Thailand." *Encyclopaedia Britannica*. 2004. Encyclopaedia Britannica Online. 19 Feb. 2004 http:// search.eb.com/eb/article?eu=120921.

"Thailand." *Encyclopaedia Britannica*. 2004. Encyclopaedia Britannica Online. 19 Feb. 2004 http:// search.eb.com/eb/article?eu=371080.

"United Kingdom: Economic Overview." *Countrywatch.* http://www. country.com 7/2/2003

"United States of America." *Culturgram.* Provo, UT: David M. Kennedy Center for International Studies, Brigham Young University, 1997.

U.S. Bureau of the Census. (2002). The Asian Population 2000: Census 2000 brief Retrieved February, 2003, from http://www.census.gov/ prod/2002pubs/c2kbr01–16.pdf.

U.S. Department of Commerce. *Statistical Abstract of the United States: 20003.* (123rd Edition). Washington, D. C., 2003.

Urquhart, G., Rev. "Scots." *Worldmark Encyclopedia of Cultures and Daily Life.* Detroit: gale, 1998. 351–355.

Van Slyck, Abigail A. "The Librarian and the Library: Why Place Matters." *Libraries & Culture.* 36 (4) (Fall 2001) : 518–523.

"Vietnam." *Britannica Student Encyclopedia.* 2004. Encyclopaedia Britannica Online. 11 Mar. 2004. http://search.eb.com/ebi/print?eu= 299765.

"Vietnam." *The Columbia Encyclopedia,* 6th ed. New York: Columbia Uni-versity Press, 2003 www.bartleby.com/65/vi/Vietnam.html. 3/11/ 2004.

"Vietnam." *Culturgram.* Provo, UT: David M. Kennedy Center for Inter-national Studies, Brigham Young University, 1997.

"Vietnam: Economic Overview." *Countrywatch.com.* 2003. Http://www. countrywatch.com/cw_print.asp?vCOUNTRY=187&SECTION=SUB&T OPI. . .15 Mar. 2004.

"Wales." *Britannica Student Encyclopedia.* 2003. Encyclopaedia Britannica Online. 11 Mar. 2004. http://search.eb.com/ebi/print?eu=299809.

"Wales." *The Columbia Encyclopedia,* 6th ed. New York: Columbia Uni-versity Press, 2003 www.bartleby.com/65/wa/Wales.html. 3/11/2004.

"Wales." *Culturgram.* Provo, UT: David M. Kennedy Center for Inter-national Studies, Brigham Young University, 1997.

"Wales." *Encyclopaedia Britannica.* 200. Encyclopaedia Britannica Online. 25 Sept. 2003 http:// search.eb.com/ebk/print?eu=379202

"The Welsh Economy." Cardiff Business School. http://www.weru.org.uk/ economy.html.

Winfeld, Liz. *Training Tough Topics.* New York: AMACOM Books, 2001.

Wise, Naomi. *Passport Thailand.* San Rafael: World Trade Press, 1997.

Wongthes, Mukhom and Dolina Millar. "Thai." *Worldmark Encyclopedia of Cultures and Daily Life.* Detroit: gale, 1998. 758–763.

World Development Report 2004: Making Services Work for Poor People. Washington, D. C.: Oxford University Press and The World Bank, 2003.

Zemke, Ron. Third Edition. *Delivering Knock Your Socks Off Service.* New York: Performance Research Associates, 1998.

Index